The Buchanan Book.

A.W Patrick Buchanan

Copyright © BiblioLife, LLC

This book represents a historical reproduction of a work originally published before 1923 that is part of a unique project which provides opportunities for readers, educators and researchers by bringing hard-to-find original publications back into print at reasonable prices. Because this and other works are culturally important, we have made them available as part of our commitment to protecting, preserving and promoting the world's literature. These books are in the "public domain" and were digitized and made available in cooperation with libraries, archives, and open source initiatives around the world dedicated to this important mission.

We believe that when we undertake the difficult task of re-creating these works as attractive, readable and affordable books, we further the goal of sharing these works with a global audience, and preserving a vanishing wealth of human knowledge.

Many historical books were originally published in small fonts, which can make them very difficult to read. Accordingly, in order to improve the reading experience of these books, we have created "enlarged print" versions of our books. Because of font size variation in the original books, some of these may not technically qualify as "large print" books, as that term is generally defined; however, we believe these versions provide an overall improved reading experience for many.

THE BUCHANAN BOOK

THE LIFE OF

ALEXANDER BUCHANAN, Q.C.,

OF MONTREAL,

FOLLOWED BY AN ACCOUNT OF THE

FAMILY OF BUCHANAN,

BY

A. W. PATRICK BUCHANAN, K.C

Printed for Private Circulation.

MONTREAL,
1911

ADDENDA ET CORRIGENDA.

Page 22: Line 14 read " proctor " for " procter "
" 123: Delete the note at foot of page. Owing to want of space it has been found necessary to omit an account of Chief Justice Sir Francis Godschall Johnson by the writer, which appeared in a Montreal newspaper at the time of his death, and which was to have formed part of the Appendix.
" 137: Line 17 read " controverted " for " cultivated."
" 189: See Appendix for notes 1 and 2.
" 191: Gertrude, widow of George Buchanan, of Keston Towers, Kent, died 29th June, 1911, aged 74 years.
" " Jane Elizabeth, daughter of John Buchanan, of Lisnamallard, died 3rd December, 1910, at Lisnamallard, Omagh, Tyrone, aged 88 years.
" 192: Anna Sophia, widow of Alexander Carlisle Buchanan, of Riverdale, Omagh, died 2nd January, 1910, at Morden, Manitoba, aged 68 years.
" 194: Line 10 read " Ethel Elizabeth " for " Ellen Elizabeth."
" " Mina, wife of Col. Lewis Mansergh Buchanan, C.B., died 1st April, 1908, at Edenfel, Omagh, Tyrone.
" " Col. Lewis Mansergh Buchanan, C.B., died 23rd April, 1908, at Edenfel, Omagh, Tyrone.
" " Ethel Elizabeth, daughter of Colonel Lewis Mansergh Buchanan, C.B., and wife of William Pike Grubb, died 1st November, 1910, at Claremont, Osborne Park, Belfast, aged 46 years.
" " Major L. E. Buchanan has issue a daughter, Phyllis, born 9th October, 1909.
" 238: Capt. James Buchanan Whitla died 1st May, 1911, at Barnes, Surrey, aged 76 years.
" 240: Ada Dorothea, daughter of the late Col. Theo. Higginson, C.B., married 3rd August, 1910, E. H. Greg of Beechfield, Swinton, Lancashire, son of E. H. Greg, of Quarry Bank, Cheshire.
" 247: William F. Forbes has issue a daughter, Margaret McKenzie, born 4th September, 1910.
" " Eveline Ellen, daughter of Capt. J. B. Clay, married 11th May, 1911, Frederick E. Archibald.
" " Harold Bonham Clay, son of Capt. J. B. Clay, married 15th December, 1911, Helen Catherine, daughter of T. Ridley Davies.
" 248: Olive Bancroft, daughter of Reginald H. Buchanan, married 15th November, 1911, Osmond William Dettmers.
" 444: Mary Meade, only daughter of the Honble. Mr. Justice Buchanan and Lady Buchanan, of Clareinch, Claremont, S. Africa, married 11th April, 1912, Major Edward Leigh, Hampshire Regiment, son of late Francis A. Leigh (formerly 10th Hussars), of Rosegarland, Co. Wexford.

To
B. L. Q. B.

THIS BOOK

IS

AFFECTIONATELY DEDICATED.

This Edition is limited to three hundred signed copies, of which this copy is

No. 97

CONTENTS.

	Page
Life of Alexander Buchanan, Q.C., of Montreal	1
The Buchanans of that Ilk	161
The Buchanans of Blairlusk	187
James Buchanan, H.B.M. Consul at New York	197
The Buchanans of Carbeth	251
The Buchanans of Ardoch	259
The Gray-Buchanans of Scotstown	265
The Buchanans of Auchmar	271
The Buchanans of Hales Hall	281
The Buchanans of Spittal	287
The Buchanans of Blairvockie	299
The Buchanans of Montreal	303
Family of Dr. George Buchanan of Fintona, co. Tyrone	313
The Buchanans of Arnpryor	325
The Buchanans of Lenny	333
The Buchanans of Auchineden	339
The Buchanans of Arnpryor (second family)	345
The Buchanans of Powis	349
The Buchanans of Gartacharne	355
The Carrick Buchanans of Drumpellier	363
The Buchanans of Auchintorlie	373
The Buchanans in Campsie and Baldernock	383
The Buchanans of Drummikill	389
The Buchanans of Drumhead	395
The Buchanans of Finnick-Drummond	401
The Leith-Buchanans of Ross Priory	407
The Buchannans late of Miltoun	411
A Genealogical Note	417
The Quatercentenary of George Buchanan	423
Some Distinguished Buchanans	431
Some Buchanans in the United States of America	451
Appendix	477

ILLUSTRATIONS.

Alexander Buchanan, Q.C., from the original painting in the possession of A. W. P. Buchanan, K.C.......	Frontispiece	
Doctor John Buchanan, 49th Regiment of Foot, from a miniature........	Opposite page	4
Doctor John Buchanan, from a pastel.	" "	16
The Place of Buchanan, from a drawing by J. P. Neale, engraved by M. J. Barenger, 1787, and reproduced by kind permission of James Maclehose & Sons, Glasgow......	" "	59
Mary Ann Buchanan, wife of Alexander Buchanan, Q.C.	" "	84
House of Alexander Buchanan, Q.C. ..	" "	148
Hon. G. C. V. Buchanan	" "	150
Wentworth James Buchanan	" "	154
Alexander Brock Buchanan	" "	156
Mrs. A. Brock Buchanan	" "	158
Col. Lewis Mansergh Buchanan, C.B., of Edenfel.....................	" "	192
James Buchanan, H.B.M. Consul at New York	" "	197
Elizabeth Clarke, wife of James Buchanan	" "	207

INTRODUCTION.

As the name indicates this book contains the life of Alexander Buchanan, Q.C., of Montreal, Canada. It gives a brief account of his father, Doctor John Buchanan, of the Forty-Ninth Regiment of Foot and some time Surgeon on the Hospital Staff of the Army in Canada. It is also an attempt to bring down to the present day in concise form the history of the Family of Buchanan and of its various branches. According to tradition the family was originally Irish, the first of the clan in Scotland being Anselan Buey Okyan. Some years ago the following article, which the writer considers worth reproducing, appeared in an American newspaper:

"The Scottish Highlanders connect the ancient Irish with modern civilization—the era of the round towers and the Danish invasion, with the age of the scientific method; the days of the ancient Feans, whence the appellation of Fenian, with this Nineteenth Century, in which, by commerce and utilitarianism at large, the romance of humanity has been quite evaporated, or metamorphosed into life-painting of a life less large and heroic in pageantry, if covered with a greater number of layers of civilization.

"The first glimpse that authentic history affords of the stem of this family is offered in connection with the battle of Limerick—a sort of Celtic St. Bartholomew, with a nobler and more patriotic purpose. After six centuries of struggle,

Ireland had succumbed to the rule of the Danish hordes, which, from the fourth century to the eleventh, had indulged in almost annual invasions of England, Scotland, and Ireland. The order of Feans—giants—was first instituted in Ireland to repel these irruptions; and their general was termed King of the Feans, still the native Irish term for general. The less ancient order of Dalgheass was, upon the destruction of the order of Feans in the fifth century, instituted as a sort of national guard, notwithstanding the vigilance of which the Danes succeeded in bringing the Irish under subjection, with Sueno, the father of Canute, as King of Denmark, England and Ireland, both held by Scandinavian usurpation.

"The Limerick slaughter is generally referred to this year, and was executed by one of those witty stratagems by which the insolence of an enemy is sometimes turned to his destruction. Sueno, in honor of his birthday, ordered a general *fete* and celebration throughout the kingdom; and the Danish Governor of Ireland distributed orders to all the department commanders to repair to Limerick to assist at the festival, ordering the Irish nobility, his vassals, to send in a couple of thousand of the most beautiful of their daughters to amuse the Danish officers. The nobility, apparently submitting, thus introduced into the city a couple of thousands of Irish youth, yet beardless, dressed as women, and concealing long Irish skeins or daggers in their skirts, with orders to assassinate the Danish officials in their tipsiness, and possess themselves of the guard-house. Successful in this, the conquerors gave the signal to an Irish band concealed in the adjoining woods; and a massacre, only paralleled in contemporary annals by that instigated by Ethelred in England, was the consequence.

"One of the Irish boys who on that fatal night entered Limerick as liberators, was Anselan Buey Okyan, pronounced Buey O'Kane, and corrupted into Buchanan. These Okyans are reputed to belong to the Milesian stem of the Irish nobility.

"This somewhat traditional massacre must have occurred at the opening of the eleventh century —for in 1016 Anselan Buey Okyan (or Anselan O'Kane the Fair) emigrated to Scotland, where he was introduced by a nobleman, probably one of the ancient earls of Lennox, to King Malcolm II., who employed him in service against the Danes, then under the famous Canute, to whom tradition attributes the story of Canute and the sea. Having won honorable distinction in several battles with the Danes, the young adventurer was granted estates in the North of Scotland, inclusive probably of Pitwhondy and Strathyre, and a coat of arms, which is substantially the present blazon, and is described as: Or, a lion rampant sable, armed and langued gules, holding in his dexter paw a sabre proper.

"Descended from the Ulster Irish princes what insignia belonged to Okyan previous to this grant, annals have left no record; and thus the family dates from the Scottish stem of Anselan the Fair, with estates in the north about the year 1125—possibly a trifle later, possibly a trifle earlier.

"It was first a dependence of the earls of Lennox, but never assumed any of the armorial designations of that ancient Scottish family, though this was the custom in those days, as is evidenced by the fact that most of the surnames of Teviotdale and Douglassdale assume parts of the Douglass arms, and those of Murrayland the arms of the Murrays.

"Tradition records that Anselan Okyan married one Dennistoun, by whom he had a son named

John, in whose favor Alcuin, Earl of Lennox, made a grant of the Wester Main. Third in order comes another Anselan, and is succeeded by Walter as fourth lord, his son Girald (or Bernard) succeeding to the title, to be succeeded by Macbeath, of which Macbeth is a Shakespearian form. Anselan son of Macbeath, and seventh lord, was again the recipient of a grant from the Earl of Lennox, of an island in Lake Lomond. The grant, dated 1225, identifies the island as Clareinch, a dissyllable that afterward became the war-cry or slogan of the Okyans, the passing of which from mouth to mouth was the signal for all the effective forces of Okyans to rendezvous on the shore in sight of the island-seat of the family. This slogan was superseded by the fire-cross signal, which consisted of a faggot crossed at the end, with a bar marked at the extremities by fire. Gilbert, son of the last-named, and first to assume the surname of Buchanan, was succeeded by Sir Maurice, who had three sons—Maurice, his successor; Allan, who married the heiress of Lenny; and John the reputed ancestor of a third ramification of this antique family.

"The second Sir Maurice was contemporary with Robert Bruce and the famous Sir William Wallace; and the annals record that the former, after his defeat at Dalree, by Macdougal of Lorn and his adherents, wandered alone and on foot to Lake Lomond, where he was secreted by Sir Maurice, after lying over night at King's Cave, near that sheet, with which is associated the legend of the spider; and finally conveyed to a place of safety. Then comes another Walter, a second John, and then the famous Sir Alexander, through whose valor the battle of Bauge was won to the Scots and the dauphin of France in the year 1420. He engaged the English general, the Duke of

Clarence, in single combat, and, slaying him, turned the tide of victory. For this service the dauphin rewarded him with the following addition to the family arms:—A second tressure round the field, flowered and counterflowered, with *fleurs de lis* of the second, and in a crest a hand *coupée* holding a duke's coronet, with two laurel branches wreathed round the same; which addition was retained by the Buchanans ever after. Alexander fell at the battle of Vernoil in 1424, and was succeeded by Sir Walter, his brother, to whom Lennox granted the estate of Ledlewan, who married Isabel, daughter of the Duke of Albany.

" From the third son of this Sir Walter comes the Carbeth limb of the family tree, whence its known American representatives are descended.

" The family has, since the days of the historian of Scotland, born in 1506, held the position of one of the most illustrious literary families of Scotland, having been identified from George, the author of "De Sphæra," "De Jure Regni apud Scotos," to the present day, with Scottish historical writing and the poetry of the North. In the time of the Reformation George Buchanan was, next to John Knox, its ablest advocate.

" The Carbeth *stirps*, one of the six descended from the famous Anselan, dates from Sir Thomas of Gartincaber, who acquired Carbeth about the year 1476, and had two sons, Thomas and John, and was succeeded by the former. Three Thomases of Carbeth follow, then three Johns and one William, which brings the record within the limits of the present century.

" From the third cadet of the Carbeth stem came John of Blairluisk, whose first son, George, relinquishing his Scottish honors, emigrated to Ireland, and settled in Tyrone county. Of his four sons, John and William erected families in the county of Tyrone, George in Munster, and Thomas in Donegal. William was succeeded by his son Patrick, who in his turn was succeeded by Robert, the ancestor of the Pennsylvania stock centred in Meadville. Robert had two sons—Thomas, late a military celebrity in Cumberland county, Penn., and Alexander.

"A second American stock, representative of the Carbeth lords, descends from George of Munster, is located at Louisville, Ky., and was, in 1857, represented by two brothers, George and Andrew; while from Thomas of Donegal was descended the late President of the United States, James Buchanan; a namesake, James Buchanan, recently British Consul at the port of New York, was descended from John of Tyrone. Belonging to this branch also are the Buchanans of Northern New York; Thomas, who married a kinswoman, a Livingstone; their son George, who was the father of the well-known authoress, Mrs. Gildersleeve Longstreet, of New York city.

"Thomas of Cumberland county had four daughters, who were all living in 1857, but without issue. Alexander, of the same county, was the father of five sons and two daughters, to wit, Robert, James, Mary, Alexander, Thomas, Sarah, and John, of whom Robert, the eldest, removed to Cincinnati, carrying the stock West; four died early, and, John excepted, without issue, and two, Alexander and Mary, settled at Meadville. Robert of Cincinnati left one son, Charles M., married about the year 1856; Alexander, the third son, had five sons and four daughters; John left one daughter; Mary, who married a Mr. Compton, had three sons and four daughters; and Sarah, whose husband was Dr. Ellis, of Meadville, left a daughter.

"To return to the direct line, Sir Walter was succeeded by his eldest son, Patrick, who in turn resigned the lordship to his son Walter, the fourth of the name, in 1474. The next in the succession was Patrick, the second of the name, whose wife was daughter of the Earl of Argyle. After George, the seventeenth laird, came John, who married a daughter of Lord Livingstone. The succession was continued regularly to the twenty-second laird, who was John, the third of the name, and who married for first wife Mary, daughter of Lord Henry Cardross, and died in 1682, leaving two daughters. With him the lairdship, after continuing in the name six hundred and sixty-five years without interruption, expired, the estates having been put out of entail by his immediate predecessors, and now became entirely alienated, and the title, " Buchanan of that Ilk," extinct. The estates passed into the hands of the Duke of Montrose.

" At the present time many of the name of Buchanan hold possessions within the bounds of the old clan and the vicinity, and the descendants of the cadets of the old lairds keep the estates which have remained in the families for hundreds of years. Among the latter are Arnpryor, Lennie, Carbeth, Auchmar and others.

" Buchanan of Lennie claims to be the present chief.

" The clan plaid or tartan of the Buchanans is green, red, and yellow, with chequers of medium size. The badge worn in the bonnet is a sprig of the large bilberry.

" The paternal arms have descended with trifling alteration for eight and a-half centuries, reckoning to the present date. The blazon, as seen in the engraving, is described as follows:—

" Or, a lion rampant sable, armed and langued gules, within a double tressure, flowered and counterflowered with *fleur de lis* of the second.

"Crest: a hand couped holding up a ducal

coronet proper, with a laurel wreath inclosing it, disposed orleways proper.

"Supporters: two falcons garnished or.

"Ancient motto above the crest: '*Audaces Juvo.*' *I favor the daring.*

"Modern motto in compartment: '*Clarior Hinc Honos.*' *From this a brighter honor.*"

As the above article shows, certain branches of the family migrated to Ireland, the most notable of which were the cadets of Carbeth and Spittal. It is difficult to fix the exact date of these migrations which took place towards the latter part of the seventeenth century, but they were probably the result of the Plantation of Ulster begun by King James I, in 1611. "The success of the "plantation," says Charles George Walpole in his Short History of the Kingdom of Ireland (1882), "became apparent in a few years, when commis-"sioners were sent down to inspect the progress "which was being made. The English and Scotch "gentry who had taken up the land, were *bona* "*fide* occupying it with their wives and families. "The Londoners had fortified Derry—London "Derry, as thenceforth it was called—with ram-"parts twelve feet thick, drawbridges, and battle-"mented gates. Fair castles, handsome mansions, "and substantial farm-buildings were springing up "in every part of the country; 'fulling mills' and "'corn mills' were utilizing the ample water-"power; windmills were spinning on the rising "ground; lime kilns were smoking, in preparation

INTRODUCTION xiii

" for more extensive building operations. There
" were smiling gardens and orchards and fields
" in 'good tillage after the English manner.'
" Market towns and villages were rising, with
" paved streets and well-built houses and churches;
" schools and bridges were in course of construc-
" tion."

The County of Tyrone appears to have been the chief place of settlement of the Buchanans, and there were several distinct families of that name living about Fintona and Omagh. In 1691 a George Buchanan was High Sheriff of County Fermanagh, and he is apparently the same George Buchanan whose name appears on the list of those attainted by King James II, in his Parliament held in Dublin in 1689, belonging to the counties of Fermanagh and Tyrone, as given by Dr. William King, Dean of St. Patrick's, in the Appendix to his work on the State of the Protestants in Ireland, where it is given as " George Bochanon of Enniskilling, Esq."

The writer wishes to offer his grateful thanks to those members of the family who so kindly answered his enquiries and gave him information regarding their different branches.

1st OCTOBER, 1911.

LIFE

OF

Alexander Buchanan, Q.C.

CHAPTER I.

Alexander Buchanan, the subject of this Sketch, was descended from the old Scotch family of Buchanan of Blairvocky.[1] The estate of Blairvocky was situated at the foot of Ben Uird, or Blairvocky Hill, in the neighbourhood of Loch Lomond, in the Trossachs. The last representative of this family, William Buchanan, last Laird of Blairvocky, towards the close of the sixteenth century, sold his estate and went to Ireland, where he settled in the vicinity of Omagh, in the County of Tyrone.

Alexander Buchanan was the eldest son of Doctor John Buchanan, of His Majesty's 49th Regiment of Foot, who was born in the year 1769, at Eccles Green, near Fintona, in the County of

---

[1] The name "Blairvocky" or "Blairvockie" means bushy plain—plain full of cottages—or the place where the roebuck feeds.

Tyrone, where his father, Alexander Buchanan, lived. This Alexander Buchanan, who was descended in a direct line from the above William Buchanan, last Laird of Blairvocky, is called of Ednasop or Milltown, having obtained a lease of the premises of Milltown in the year 1783. Milltown is the old name of Ednasop, a townland adjoining Fintona, and now forming part of the town. He had previously lived at Eccles Green in the townland of Donacavey, distant about one mile from Fintona.

Samuel Burdy, who has been called "an Irish Boswell," writing, in 1792, in his "Life of the late Revd. Philip Skelton," Rector of Fintona from 1766 to 1780, thus describes Fintona as it appeared at that time:—

"Fintona is a market-town in the County of Tyrone, five miles distant from Omagh. The proper name of the parish is Donacavey, but as Fintona is the market-town, the parish by custom assumes that name. It is six miles square, and though of a coarse soil was even then tolerably well cultivated. It also has two hundred acres of glebe, seventy of which lie near the town, but the rest is mountainous, and consequently of little value. A third part of the parish is tithe-free, which made the living, though so large, and with such a glebe, worth scarce five hundred a year . . . . There is a market in Fintona every Friday, and also some stated fairs in the year, when they usually have violent quarrels. The twenty-second of June is a remarkably quarreling fair. But they were then even more furious quarrellers than at present, as the private stills were more numerous, and of course the people more disorderly."

In the town of Fintona, Burdy says, the people were almost all Presbyterians, but in a short time Skelton brought over nearly the whole of these to the Established church.

A recent description says:—

"The town of Fintona is situate in the southern portion of the County Tyrone. It stands on the property of the late John S. Eccles, Esq., D.L. Its ancient castle, of probably Elizabethan times, is now in utter ruin; but its situation was admirably adapted to overawe and command the entire town."

Alexander Buchanan of Ednasop died in 1810, at the advanced age of 94 years. His death is said to have been caused by breaking his leg. His wife, Jane, died in 1790, aged 51 years. Besides their son John, they had Beavor, William, George and Mary. Beavor and William lived at Fintona, and George at Omagh. The daughter Mary married Mr. Gerrard Irvine and lived at Lisnagore, Irvine's Town, near Omagh.[1]

John Buchanan, the father of Alexander Buchanan, the subject of this Sketch, having studied for the medical profession, for which he appears

---

[1] William Buchanan of Fintona died in 1834, aged 70 years.

Beavor Buchanan of Fintona died unmarried in 1836, aged 69 years.

George Buchanan, of Omagh, died unmarried in 1843, aged 73 years.

Mrs. Irvine died in 1841, aged 72 years.

William Buchanan of Fintona left four sons: (1) Alexander Buchanan of Ednasop, who died unmarried in 1850, aged 47 years; (2) John Buchanan, of Ednasop, who died unmarried in 1853, aged 43 years; (3) Beavor Buchanan, of Tullybroom, who died unmarried in 1856, aged 44 years, and (4) George Buchanan, of Ednasop and Tullybroom, who died unmarried in 1890.

to have been eminently qualified, entered the army and became in due course Surgeon of the 49th Regiment of Foot. It is not known now where he studied medicine and surgery. In those days, in order to qualify for the post of army surgeon, it was necessary to pass the College of Surgeons: its Court of Examiners had to examine all army and navy surgeons, their assistants and mates, and also to inspect their instruments.

He was present with his Regiment, commanded by Lieut.-Colonel Isaac Brock, afterward Sir Isaac Brock, at the celebrated attack of Copenhagen, by Lord Nelson, on the 2nd of April, 1801. Of this battle Tupper, in his Life of Sir Isaac Brock, says:—

"On the 27th February of that year (1801) the 49th regiment, then about 760 rank and file, embarked at Portsmouth on board Nelson's squadron there, which got under weigh at daylight the next morning, and proceeded to the Downs. The squadron next sailed for Yarmouth roads, where his lordship placed himself under Sir Hyde Parker, the commander-in-chief of the fleet destined for the Baltic. Nelson was anxious to proceed with the utmost dispatch, and with such ships as were in readiness, to the Danish capital, so as to anticipate by the rapidity of his movements the formidable preparations for defence which the Danes had scarcely thought of at that early season; but to his annoyance, the fleet, which consisted of about fifty sail, of which forty-one pendants, including sixteen of the line, did not leave Yarmouth roads until the 12th of March. The land forces were equally distributed on board of the line of battleships. On the 15th the fleet was in some measure scattered by a heavy gale of wind, which prevented its reaching the Naze until the 18th. The next

DOCTOR JOHN BUCHANAN,
49th Regiment of Foot.

day the fleet appears to have been purposely detained off the Scaw, and did not reach Elsinore until the 24th. Here a few days were lost in deliberation, and it was not until the 30th of March that the fleet proceeded through the Sound with a top-sail breeze from N.W. The semi-circular form of the land of Elsinore, which was thickly studded with batteries, caused the ships to pass in a form truly picturesque and nearly similar, but the forbearance of the Swedes, who did not fire a gun, happily enabled them to incline towards the Swedish shore, so as to avoid the Danish shot, which fell in showers, but at least a cable's length from the ships. The whole fleet came to an anchor about mid-day between the island of Huen and Copenhagen, and it was soon perceived that the various delays had enabled the Danes to line the shoals near the Crown batteries, and the front of the harbour with a formidable flotilla. When the preparations for the attack were completed, Lieut.-Colonel Brock was appointed to lead the 49th in storming the principal Treckroner or Crown battery, in conjunction with five hundred seamen under Captain Fremantle, as soon as its fire of nearly seventy guns should be silenced; but the protracted and heroic defence of the Danes rendering the attempt impracticable, Colonel Brock, during the hard-fought battle, remained on board the "Ganges" of 74 guns, commanded by Captain Fremantle, with the light Company and the band; and at its close he accompanied Captain Fremantle to the "Elephant" 74, Nelson's flag ship, where he saw the hero write his celebrated letter to the Crown Prince of Denmark."

In the spring of 1802, John Buchanan came to Canada with the 49th on the staff of Lieut.-Colonel Brock. The regiment was stationed at different times at Montreal, York, Fort George and Quebec.[1] In 1803, being ordered to move

---

[1] The facings of the 49th Regiment were full green, white lace with two red and one green stripe. After thirteen years service in Canada the Regiment was embarked for England on the 25th May, 1815.

with his regiment to Fort George, he was compelled to leave his wife, who was in bad health, at Three Rivers, where her illness soon after proved fatal. He was very intimate with Brock, who had a high opinion of him. They were of the same age.

Under date 26th February, 1803, Brock writes as follows from Montreal to Major Green, the Military Secretary:—

"Hospital Mate Buchanan will accompany the detachment going to Fort George. The uncommon healthy state of the garrison has enabled me to comply with that gentleman's desire of going for a few weeks to Three Rivers where he is likely to be of great utility and service in his profession. I cannot speak too highly of his attentions and merit, and as he has a wife and three small children to maintain, I presume in his behalf to entreat the Lieutenant-General to sanction his receiving the different allowances, to which he would have been entitled, had he remained stationed here, and if it were possible to permit his returning with the detachment of the 41st Regiment, it would be conferring an additional and great obligation on himself and family."

Brock writes on the 19th February, 1804, from Fort George to Major Green,—

"Thinking that Doctor Walsh would certainly be here, Doctor Buchanan made the necessary arrangements to begin his journey on this day, I have not therefore thought it necessary to disappoint him, there being few in hospital and Doctor Kerr having offered to give his attendance as long as it was required.

The very great attention which Doctor Buchanan has given to his duty since he has been attached to the 49th Regiment, and the superior professional abilities which he unquestionably has, on different occasions, evinced, require that his merit should be made known to General Hunter, which I request you to do accordingly."

In a postscript which reveals Brock's kindly disposition, he says:—

"If you possibly can prevail on some good natured soul, to assist Mr. Buchanan with a seat to Kingston, you will confer a great obligation on a very worthy man. This I insert without his knowledge."

William Foster Coffin, in his "War of 1812," writes of Brock:—

"Like the white horse in a battlepiece by Wouvermans, in every delineation of this war, Isaac Brock stands forth from the canvas, the central figure and commanding feature of the scene. It will not be uninteresting, therefore, to offer, at the outset, a brief sketch of his earlier career. He was born in the Island of Guernsey, in 1769, the year which gave birth to Napoleon and Wellington. He was descended from an old and respected family. He obtained his first commission in 1785, served in the West Indies, was promoted rapidly, thanks to the havoc of the climate; and, by the force of a vigorous constitution, survived to command the 49th Foot as senior Colonel in the expedition to Holland in 1799, where he made his mark under adverse circumstances. In 1801 he was selected with his regiment to serve under Lord Nelson, in his memorable attack on Copenhagen. In 1802, Brock accompanied his regiment to Canada, and was, for the next ten years of his life, identified with the existence of a country which he ultimately governed wisely, defended nobly, and which points to his grave as the monument of his glory. He was a man of natural capacity, self-cultivated, resolute and endowed remarkably with the qualities of forethought and foresight. His correspondence, imperfectly preserved, makes us regret that so much should have been lost. These memorials of an honest, modest and truly brave nature, have furnished the greater part of these details. In person he was tall and athletic, with a commanding bearing and gentle manner. In private life he was irreproachable, universally respected by those who did not know him, and loved by those who did. His public life speaks for itself."

In the year 1805 Doctor Buchanan was ordered to York (now Toronto), having been selected by His Excellency, Lt.-General Hunter, Commander-in-Chief of His Majesty's Forces in the provinces of Upper and Lower Canada, to be his medical adviser. But apparently he was later ordered to St. Johns, as on the 18th July of that year he memorializes General Hunter asking not to be sent to St. Johns and stating, "my pride was flattered on being ordered to York. "There I had every prospect of gaining something "from my professional labours, and besides, the "ultimate advantage, which must attend the per-"son whom your Excellency selects to wait on "your person." His wish was evidently gratified and he seems to have remained at Quebec. The death of General Hunter which took place suddenly at 4 o'clock in the forenoon of the 21st of August, 1805, during one of his official visits to Quebec as Commander-in-Chief may have had some effect on Doctor Buchanan not proceeding to St. Johns. He permanently settled in Quebec, where he soon acquired a large and lucrative practice. He was one of the Surgeons appointed to examine those who applied to be Licensed as Physicians and Surgeons, or as it is now called

Board of Examiners, which appointment he held at the time of his death. In 1815, the other members at Quebec, were James Fisher, M.D., James Macaulay, William Holmes and Thomas Lloyd.

His practice was not confined to the city but extended to the country. In the inventory of the succession of Jacques Nicolas Perrault, Seigneur of River Ouelle, who died on August 5th, 1812, his account for professional services rendered amounted to £42. 7. 2. He was distinguished for his professional ability. It is said that on one occasion he was summoned from Quebec to attend the Governor at Niagara, in those days of slow locomotion an arduous undertaking. De Gaspé, in his Memoires, in narrating the circumstances of the death of the Honourable Charles Tarrieu de Lanaudière, which took place at Quebec in the autumn of the year 1811, mentions Doctor Buchanan:—

"Being seventy years old at the time of his tragic death, Mr. de Lanaudière was yet full of vigor and still rode on horseback with as much ease as a young man. Being invited to dine at Notre Dame de Foi at the house of a Mr. Ritchie, he offered a seat in his gig to his friend, George Brown, whose son, a Colonel in the English Army, has since played a certain role in the trial of Queen Caroline, the wife of George IV. A young groom on horseback followed the carriage.

"Doctor Buchanan, a friend of Mr. de Lanaudière, observed to him during the dinner that he was eating fish that was half cooked, which was very indigestible.

" 'Bah!' said he, 'I am very hungry. I have never had indigestion in my life, and I shall certainly not begin to have it now at my age.'

"As they were leaving towards midnight, Mr. de Lanaudière gave orders to his servant to drive Mr. Brown home, while he would return on horseback. 'It is such a fine night, said he, 'that it will be a pleasant ride for me.' The young groom on his return to the house, unharnessed the horse, and went into the house to await his master, but unfortunately fell asleep.

"Between five and six o'clock in the morning a servant of Bishop Mountain's going to a farm belonging to his master, perceived a horse, which was calmly feeding near the inanimate body of a man covered with hoar frost. For by a cruel fatality, although it was only in the beginning of September, there had been a hard frost during the night Great was the surprise of this man in recognizing in this spot and at this hour Mr. de Lanaudière.

"Nevertheless, it was he who lay inanimate on that same battle field where half a century before he had fought; on the very spot, perhaps, from which his bleeding body had been carried to the General Hospital.

"Seeing that he was still alive, this man hastened to loosen his cravat; and Mr. de Lanaudière recovered consciousness. He survived this accident three weeks, but spoke very little. The physicians were of the opinion that he would have recovered his health had it not been for the intense cold to which he had been exposed for almost six hours."

During the latter part of his life, Doctor Buchanan lived at No. 17 Parloir Street, at Quebec, which he had bought on the 2nd February, 1811. On the site of this house now stands the Archbishopric of Quebec. Here he had for neighbour the Honourable Francois Baby. This house was sold on the 9th May, 1815, for fourteen thousand dollars. In the Quebec Mercury of Tuesday the 16th May, 1815, appeared the following notice which gives some idea of his style of living:—

"On Wednesday next the 17th instant at the house No. 17 Rue du Parloir, next door to the Honourable Frans. Baby, at one o'clock, the valuable household furniture of Doctor Buchanan, consisting of mahogany bedsteads, Chests of Drawers, Sideboard, Dining, Card and Breakfast tables, Sofas, Chairs, Carpets, Feather Beds, Matrasses, Silver Spoons, Plated Candlesticks, Knives and Forks, Decanters, Glasses, a blue China Table Sett, a Glass Dessert Ditto, a handsome Grate, Stoves, Kitchen Utensils, etc., also,—

Port, Madeira, Sherry, Claret and Albaflor, Wines of a Superior quality;

A few medical books and book case;
A considerable quantity of drugs;
A cow and calf;
Cariole, harnesses, saddles and bridles;
Carts and a great variety of other articles."

In "Maple Leaves," Sir James Lemoine writes:—

"The Abbé (Casgrain) thus describes Parloir Street—a narrow thoroughfare which skirts the very wall of the Ursuline Chapel, where the gallant rival of Wolfe has slumbered for 133 years in the grave scooped out by an English shell: "Little Parloir Street was one of the chief centres where (in 1758-59) the *beau monde* of Quebec assembled; two *salons* were in special request; that of Madame de la Naudière and that of Madame de Beaubassin; both ladies were famed for their wit and beauty. Montcalm was so taken up with these *salons* that in his correspondence he went to the trouble of locating the exact spot which each house occupied; one, says he, stood at the corner of the street facing the Ursuline Convent, the other, at the corner of Parloir and St. Louis Street. Madame de la Naudière, *née* Geneviève de Boishebert, was a daughter of the Seigneur of River Ouelle, and Madame Hertel de Beaubassin, *née* Catherine Janet de Verchères, was a daughter of the Seigneur of Verchères. Their husbands held commissions as officers in the Canadian Militia. It was also in Parloir street that Madame Péan, often referred to in Montcalm's letters, held her brilliant court."

Doctor Buchanan married, first, Lucy Richardson, who was born in England, and came with him to Canada, and died at Three Rivers on the 25th November, 1803. At the time of his wife's death he was Assistant-Surgeon to the 49th and Hospital Mate on the Staff of Canada, and on duty at Fort George. The certificate of her burial pathetically records that no relations were present.[1]

The personality of Lucy Richardson seems to have passed away into oblivion. It is not known where she was born, who were

---

([1]) The Revd. R. Q. Short officiated at her burial and Louis Gugy and Alex. Clifford signed the Register as witnesses.

The Hon. Louis Gugy was the son of Col. Barthelomew Gugy, an officer in the French Service who came to Canada. His uncle, the Hon. Conrad Gugy became an officer in the English Service in Canada, and at one time owned the St. Maurice Forges at Three Rivers, and was Seigneur of the Fiefs of DuMontier, Grand Pré and Gros Bois. He was also a member of the Executive and Legislative Councils. He died at Montreal on the 10th April, 1786. Louis Gugy was appointed Sheriff of Three Rivers on the 13th August, 1805, and on the breaking out of the war in 1812 he resigned his office to command the Militia. After the war he was elected a member of the House of Assembly and on the 3rd March, 1827, he was appointed Sheriff of Montreal, which he held until 1837. He died in July, 1840. He was the father of the Hon. Bartholemi Conrad Augustus Gugy.

her people, the circumstances of her betrothal, or the date and place of her marriage. Her very features have as it were mysteriously disappeared. A miniature of Lucy Richardson was in the possession of the family until the 16th of December, 1827, when "the house adjoining the shipyard of Messrs. Hart Logan & Co. (at Montreal) formerly used as St. Mary's Foundry," and then occupied by Alexander Buchanan, the subject of this Memoir, " was broken into by some robbers," and the "miniature was carried off." A reward of five pounds "was offered to be paid on the apprehension and conviction of the depredators," but apparently without success.

By this marriage there were three children:—

1. Alexander Buchanan, the subject of this Sketch.
2. John Buchanan, born at Ipswich, in England, in the year 1800. He was educated at Quebec, and on the 25th January, 1815, received from Sir George Prevost, a commission as Lieutenant in the Canadian Voltigeurs under Lieut.-Colonel de Salaberry. On the 25th July, 1815, he retired on half pay, and about 1820, he engaged in the lumber business on the Ottawa in partnership with William Coffin. He married at L'Orignal, U.C., on the 20th August, 1829, Catherine Grant, daughter of Hon. Alexander Grant. of Duldregan House, near L'Orignal, in Upper Canada, and died at Niagara Falls, Upper Canada, in December, 1837, He had issue.—

   (1) Lucy, who died young, in 1847.;
   (2) Jane Louise Buchanan, unmarried, of L'Orignal;
   (3) Alexander Grant Buchanan, of Brooklyn, N.Y., born at Clarence, U.C., on 1st November, 1833; married, in 1878, Anna Field, but has no issue.

3. Jane Mary, born on the 25th December, 1801, at Chelsea, in England, and baptized on the 17th January, 1802, in the Parish Church of St. Luke, Chelsea. On the death of her father's second wife she made her home with the Perraults, with whom she lived until her marriage on the 3rd November, 1820, at Quebec, to Captain William Hall, widower. She died on the 30th March, 1872, at Hamilton, Ont., They had issue:—

> (1) Georgiana, born 14th September, 1823, at Quebec; married at Hamilton, U.C., on 12th September, 1851, to Daniel Stuart Busteed, merchant, at that time of Montreal and later of Cross Point, Que. She died on September 26th, 1895, at Restigouche, P.Q., leaving issue:—
>
> (1) Agnes Mary; (2) Emma Jane.
> (2) James, born in 1824 at Quebec, and died the same year.
> (3) Agnes Margaret, born 8th January, 1826, in Greenock, Scotland, married on June 24th, 1846, to John Clark, of Ross-shire, Scotland, and later of Cleveland, Ohio, and died there on June, 1901, leaving issue:—1. Agnes Dyherr, died in 1851;(2) John Buchanan, born 9th November, 1849, at Hamilton, U.C., (3) Jane Margaret McLeod, died January, 24th 1895; (4) Catharine Lucy Leigh, died in 1857; (5) Georgiana; (6) Mary Alexandrina; (7) Florence, died in 1863; (8) William Hall, died in 1864.
> (4) William, born in 1834, at Sorel, and died in 1854, at Bahia, South America.

Doctor Buchanan married secondly, on the 14th February, 1809, at Quebec, Ursule Perrault, daughter of the Hon. Joseph Francois Perrault, for many years Prothonotary of the Court of King's Bench for the District of Quebec. At this time he was forty years of age. They were married by the Revd. Salter Jehosaphat Mountain, officiating Anglican Minister at Quebec, in the presence of Joseph Francois Perrault, father; Joseph Perrault, Junior, brother, Hon. Francois Baby, uncle, and the Hon. Oliver Perrault, Louis Perrault, Jean Baptiste D'Estimauville, Grand Voyer of the District of Quebec, Hon. Jean Baptiste Le Comte Dupré, Seigneur of St. Francis and D'Argenteuil and Charles Voyer, cousins of the bride. She was born on the 4th August, 1785, and died of consumption the same year as she was married, and was buried on the 28th December, 1809, in the Catholic Church at Quebec.

Doctor Buchanan had also a son named George, born at Quebec in August, 1805. This George was, by his father's will, left the sum of five hundred pounds, which was to be put out at interest and secured on good landed property, the interest to be applied to his support and education, until he was twenty-one years old, when he was to receive the principal. After his father's death, he went to live with Mr. Joseph Francois Perrault. He was educated at Dr. Wilkie's school at Quebec, and on the 31st July, 1821, was indentured by his brother, Alexander Buchanan, Advocate, then of Montreal, to Mr. Perrault, as law student and clerk, Mr. Perrault agreeing to teach him the law and the practice of advocate, solicitor and counsel, besides "lodging, heating and nourishing him," and allowing him to keep for his own maintenance the thirty pounds of annual revenue which he had. He appears to have given up the law and studied medicine, but abandoning this also, he studied navigation, and in 1822 left Canada on a sea voyage. He returned in 1828 and left again in 1830. He died at Liverpool on the 25th October, 1870, aged 65 years, leaving a son, George Buchanan, now living at Liscard, near Liverpool, in England, from whom the following account of his father has been received:—

"My father should have been a doctor, but unfortunately he was placed with an undesirable man in Quebec, whose name I forget, and being left very much to himself, and coming into contact with sea-going men, he left his occupation and ran away to sea. Some years after he returned to Canada and joined his brother John, who was then lumbering in the backwoods, and remained with him until John married. My father again took a roving commission, following the sea until 1846, when he married my mother, a native of Milford Haven. He took one more voyage to sea, and in the following year settled down in Liverpool, where he resided until his death in 1870, at the age of 65. Whilst following the sea, he spent a considerable time in the British Navy."

The Doctor died at the residence of Mr. Perrault, at Quebec, on the 16th October, 1815. By his Will, five hundred pounds was left to his son George, and the rest of his estate to "Alexander, "John and Jane Mary Buchanan, his three chil- "dren, issue of his lawful marriage with the late "Lucy Richardson, his late wife, deceased,—to "be divided between them equally, share and

DOCTOR JOHN BUCHANAN.

"share alike." He appointed "Joseph Fran-
"cois Perrault, Esquire, one of the Prothono-
"taries of His Majesty's Court of King's Bench,
"and Andrew Stuart, Esq., Advocate, his friends"
to be the executors of his will. Mr. Andrew
Stuart was appointed tutor to Alexander and
John, and Mr. J. F. Perrault to Jane and George,
and Mr. Claude Denechau was appointed sub-
tutor to the four children.

The following notice appeared in the Quebec
"Gazette" of Thursday, 19th October, 1815:—

"Died. On Monday night last, John Buchanan,
Esq., late Surgeon on the Hospital Staff of the
Army in Canada, and during several years one of
the most respectable and extensive Medical Prac-
titioners in this City."

In appearance, Doctor Buchanan was tall.
As he grew older, he stooped slightly. While a
young man he had a high colour, and, as was the
custom of the day, wore his hair in a queue. His
features were rather small and regular, with firm
lips. In later life his hair was white, his forehead high and well developed. His face, which
inclined to the lengthy oval, had a gentle and
somewhat sad expression.

CHAPTER II.

1798-1819.

ALEXANDER BUCHANAN'S BIRTH AND EDUCATION — HIS FELLOW STUDENTS AT WILKIE'S SCHOOL— HE STUDIES LAW AND IS ADMITTED TO THE BAR—HIS GREAT DILIGENCE.

Alexander Buchanan was born at Gosport, in England, on the 23rd April, 1798, and came with his parents to Canada in 1802. It is to be regretted that very little is known of his early life. All that can now be learned is that he went to the celebrated school of Dr. Daniel Wilkie, familiarly known as "Bon homme Wilkie,"in Quebec.[1] At this school he had as classmates many

---

[1] Of Dr. Wilkie, Sir James Lemoine writes in "The Scot in New France " :—

"There are indeed many Scotch names associated with our press. Space precludes us from enlarging more of this subject. We cannot, however, close this portion of our enquiry without naming Daniel Wilkie, LL D., the editor of the 'Quebec Star,'—a literary gazette founded in 1818—still better remembered as the esteemed instructor of Quebec youth for forty years.

Dr. Wilkie was born at Tollcross, in Scotland, in 1777, one year later than John Neilson; he settled in Quebec in 1803, and died here on the 10th May, 1851.

Among those present this evening, I see some of his former pupils. Alas! the frost of years has silvered their locks! Dr. Wilkie ' broke the bread of science' to several youths, who subsequently won honor among their fellow men. Among the illustrious dead, might be recalled (in the days when the able member for Birmingham, England, John Arthur Roebuck was indentured, at Quebec, in 1818, as law student, to Thos. Gugy, Esq., Barrister, brother of Col. B. C. A. Gugy, late of Darnoc, Beauport), a favorite pupil of the Doctor, the late Hon. Judge Hy. Black, as well as the eminent jurist and scholar, Alex. Buchanan, Q.C., late of Montreal;

who later became distinguished. Among them was Henry Black, afterwards an eminent Queen's Counsel, and for many years Judge of the Vice-Admiralty Court in Quebec, whose judgments are remarkable for their learning. Chief Justice Duval and Judge John Samuel McCord, father of Mr. David Ross McCord, K.C., of Temple Grove, Montreal, were also among his school fellows. His brothers, John and George, were also educated at this school.

Here it was that Alexander Buchanan laid the foundation of his knowledge as a classical scholar, which even at that early day showed itself. In 1810, he won the First Prize for Greek. This was a Greek version of the New Testament, in which was written the following inscription:—

> "Alexandrum Buchananum ob insigne in discenda Linguæ Graecae diligentiam et progressum superiorem hoc præmio donavit."
>
> D. WILKIE.

Quebec,
IX d. Cal. Jany., 1810.

Hon. Mr. Justice T. C. Aylwin, Judge Chas. Gates Holt. Among those still moving in our midst, one likes to point to Chief Justice Duval, Judges Andrew Stuart, George Okill Stuart, and Hon. J. Chapais, Hon. David A. Ross, Messrs. Francis and Henry Austin, Daniel McPherson, N.P., R. H. Russel, M.D., and John Russel of Toronto, M.D.

Dr. Wilkie's pupils had the following truthful words inscribed on the monument they erected to their patron in Mount Hermon Cemetery :—

> ' He was a learned scholar
> An indefatigable student of philosophy and letters
> An able and successful instructor of youth
> Of genuine uprightness and guileless simplicity
> A devout, benevolent and public spirited man.'

This volume was published in 1794, in London, and on the cover is printed the following:—

A. B.
1810.
Olim Meminisse Juvabit.

He was very fond of reading the ancient authors in the original. His aptitude in the study of languages was remarkable, and he became a fine linguist, being, of course thoroughly conversant with French, which he spoke with great purity. He also knew German and Italian, and had a knowledge of Dutch, Spanish and Portuguese.

On leaving school, to use Burke's well-known words, "he was bred to the law, which is, in my "opinion, one of the first and noblest of human "sciences—a science which does more to quicken "and invigorate the understanding than all the "other kinds of learning put together; but it is "not apt except in persons very happily born, "to open and to liberalize the mind exactly in "the same proportion."

He entered on its study on the 27th April, 1814, at Quebec, when he was indentured to the distinguished Andrew Stuart, who was Solicitor General of Lower Canada from 1838 to 1840.[1]

---

[1] He was born in 1786 and was the brother of the Hon. James Stuart. He was admitted to the Bar on the 5th November, 1807, appointed Solicitor General on the 25th October, 1838, and died on the 21st February, 1840.

Doctor Buchanan, who was a party to his son's Articles of Clerkship, which he signed "John Buchanan, M.D.," paid one hundred pounds to Andrew Stuart, who agreed to take and accept of the said Alexander Buchanan as his clerk during the said term of five years, and during the said term in the best manner that he can inform and instruct him in the profession, practice and business of an advocate, attorney and procter. He further agreed that at the end of the five years, at the request and costs of the said Alexander Buchanan, to use his best endeavours to procure him to be admitted and commissioned as an advocate, attorney and procter in His Majesty's Courts in the Province.

He was admitted to the Bar on the 13th of May, 1819, receiving his commission of advocate of Lower Canada from the Duke of Richmond, then Governor in Chief.

About this time he formed the valuable habit of keeping common place books, remarkable proofs of his diligent and acquiring mind. With a view of forming his style, he made "translations of various passages in the ancient authors but chiefly of the speeches in the writings of the ancient historians," as he himself entitles his transcript of them. Among these were the speech of Camillus to the Roman People on their intended emigration to Veii after the departure of the Gauls under Brennus, who had almost totally destroyed the City of Rome; Plato's defence of

Socrates; from Livy, the trial of Demetrius upon a charge of parricide preferred against him by his brother Perseus; the First Oration of Demosthenes against Philip with introduction; the battle of the Ticini between Scipio and Hannibal, Scipio's Harangue and Hannibal's address; the speech of M. V. Corvus to the seditious soldiers; on the Shortness of Human Life translated with another extract from the Greek of Mimernus, and the Falcon translated from Boccaccio's Decameron.

CHAPTER III.

1819-1820.

HE LEAVES FOR EUROPE—VISITS ST. PAUL'S CHURCH AND SEES SIR ISAAC BROCK'S MONUMENT — HIS DESCRIPTION OF THE POETS' CORNER IN WESTMINSTER ABBEY—AT THE BRITISH MUSEUM AND EAST INDIA HOUSE — HE GOES TO OXFORD AND ROOMS IN WORCESTER COLLEGE — HE DESCRIBES THE BODLEIAN LIBRARY, THE ASHMOLEIAN MUSEUM WITH ITS CURIOSITIES, AND THE DIFFERENT CHURCHES AND COLLEGES — HIS SECOND VISIT TO OXFORD AND ITS VICINITY — HE GOES TO GODSTOW TO SEE FAIR ROSAMOND'S TOMB — HE BREAKFASTS AT WOODSTOCK AND OBTAINS ADMISSION TO BLENHEIM—HE SEES SHAKESPEARE'S BIRTHPLACE.

After being called to the Bar, and receiving his share of his father's estate, he decided to spend a year in travel, and, "On Sunday the third day of October, 1819," he writes in the very valuable Journal which he kept during his travels, and has left, "at about five o'clock in the afternoon, I sailed from Quebec on board the ship 'Pusey Hall,' Capt. Forster, bound for London."

On the 11th of November, five pounds of biscuits were, he says, served out as an allowance to each man for a week, and on the 18th of that month, he says, "being short of provision we were this day put upon the allowance of one biscuit and a short allowance of meat."

The voyage, which was otherwise uneventful, lasted seven weeks, and on Monday, the 22nd November, he landed at Dover and dined at Steriken's New London Tavern. At 5 p.m. he started in a mail coach from Dover, took tea at 7.30 p.m. at Clement's Inn in Canterbury, and at about midnight arrived at Rochester, where they slept. Next day he made a tour on foot through Rochester, Chatham and Brompton, and says:—

"Rochester Cathedral is a large and beautiful specimen of Gothic architecture ; here it was that I first saw painted glass in the three windows on the left hand in entering the Cathedral. There is a small church opposite to the cathedral which appears by a Latin inscription over the door to have been rebuilt in 1624. There are at Chatham three different sets of elegant barracks, which I visited—the Marine barracks, the Artillery barracks, and the Chatham barracks for the line. There are the ruins of an ancient castle opposite the Cathedral at Rochester. Over the River Medway at this place is a stone bridge which has fallen down in the centre."

At 1.30 p.m. he left Rochester, and passed through Stroud, Gravesend, Deptford, etc., to London over Westminster Bridge, and arrived at the Golden Cross, Charing Cross, at about 7 p.m. on the 23rd November, 1819, and for a short time took up his quarters at the Golden Cross. Afterwards he took lodgings at No. 13 Essex street.

While in London he visited everything worthy of interest. Of St. Paul's Church he writes:—

"I went into the church alone and visited the vaults where are deposited, among others, the remains of the great Nelson and of Admiral Collingwood. In the body of the church and in the different aisles, monuments have of late been erected; the principal are those erected to the memory of Howard the philanthropist, Dr. Johnson, Sir Wm. Jones, Sir Joshua Reynolds, Lord Rodney, Earl Howe, Abercrombie, Moore, Collingwood, Cornwallis, Nelson and Brock. The monument to Brock is a military one on which are placed a sword and a helmet. His corse reclines in the arms of a British soldier, whilst an Indian pays a tribute of regret for his fall."

He says of his visit to Westminster Abbey that he examined with the greatest attention the monuments and tombs in the Poet's Corner, of which he has left this description:—

"The first on the door and at the left hand is the monument of Johnson, with the simple inscription:—'O Rare Ben Johnson' (*sic*.)

"Next to him is the monument of Spenser with the following inscription:—

'Hare lyes (expecting the second comminge of our Saviour Christ Jesus) the body of Edmond Spencer the Prince of Poets in his tyme, whose divine spirrit needs noe other witnesse then the workes which he left behinde him, he was born in London in the year 1553 and died in the yeare 1598.'

Underneath are the following words:—

'Restored by private subscription 1778.'

"Next to Spenser is the monument of Milton raised by Benson, under him is that of Gray with an inscription by Pope, and in the same corner, Mason, Prior and Draiton. Near Draiton's monument and on the same side is Cowley's erected by George, Duke of Buckingham. Dryden's monument is near the same spot with this inscription:—

'John Dryden natus 1632. Mortuus Maii i, 1700. Joannes Sheffield Dux Buckinghamensis posuit 1720.'

"In another corner the first monument on the left hand is that of the immortal Shakespeare with the following inscription above his statue:—

'Gulielmo Shakespeare anno post mortem CXXIV.
Amor publicus posuit.'

His statue reclines on a pedestal and points to a scroll which is lying on it containing the following words from his own sublime works:—

'The cloud cap't towr's
The gorgeous palaces
The solemn temples
The great globe itself
Yea all which it inherit
    Shall dissolve
And like the baseless fabric of a vision
Leave not a wreck behind'

"On the left side of Shakespeare's monument is Thomson's, inscribed as follows:—

'James Thomson Aetatis 48, obiit 27 Aug., 1748.'

'Tutored by thee Sweet Poetry exalts
With music, image, sentiment and thought
Her voice to ages and informs the page
Never to die.'

This monument was erected MDCCLXII.'

"Next follow the monuments of Rowe and of Gay. Above a door near the latter monuments is one erected to Goldsmith:—

'Olivarii Goldsmith
Poeta, Physici, Historici
Qui nullum fere scribendi genus
    Non tetigit,
Nullum quod tetigit non ornavit,

Sive risus essent movendi,
  Sive lacrimæ,
Affectuum potens at lenis dominator,
Ingenii sublimis, vividus, versatilis,
Oratione grandis, nitidus, venustus,
Hoc monumento memoriam coluit
  Sodalium amor,
  Amicorum fides,
  Lectorum veneratio;
Natus Hibernia, Forneiæ Lonfordiensis
  in loco cui nomen Pallas,
  Nov. XXIX. MDCCXXXI.
  Eblanæ literis institutus
    obiit Londini
  Ap. IV. MDCCLXXIV.'

"Here also is a monument to Addison with a long Latin inscription and next Dr. Barrow's.

"Opposite to Shakespeare's monument and at his feet lie the remains of Samuel Johnson with a stone slab inscribed:—

'Samueli Johnson, L.L.D.
obiit XIII. die Decembris anno Domini
MDCCLXXXIV ætatis suæ LXXV.'

"Near Johnson's remains are deposited those of Richard Brinsley Sheridan who died 7 July, 1816. Alongside of each other are the monuments of Isaac Casaubon, the critic, and of William Camden; and above Camden's is that of David Garrick."

His visit to the Gallery of Antiquities of the British Museum is equally interesting and is thus recorded:—

"I went early this morning (Friday 17th December, 1819) with Goodman to the British Museum and remained till four o'clock P.M. amusing myself in the Gallery of

Antiquities with the superb collection of marbles and terra cotta works.

There was a head of Pericles which struck me as a piece of workmanship of singular beauty; it is inscribed simply, PERICLES. There is a fine bust of Augustus, and many busts of the Antonines, Hadrian and the later Emperors. I was much pleased with the discobulus. The Elgin collection is truly magnificent; here are considerable portions of the Parthenon, consisting of metopes, bas reliefs, friezes, &c., parts of columns and some colossal statues. I saw also a fragment of a trophy from the field of Marathon, and two or three altars and other marbles from the plains of Troy. I saw also the celebrated Sigean inscription written in the very ancient Greek characters and in the boustrophedon manner. The famous Rosetta stone with three inscriptions, the first in hieroglyphics, the second in the vernacular language of Egypt, and the third in Greek, all commemorative of the actions of one of the Ptolmies. It would be endless to recount all the sculptural beauties which I had hardly time to examine in the whole course of this day. But there is one statue of small dimensions, very remarkable for its beauties—it is the statue of a fisherman with a basket in his hand—the anatomical beauties of this figure are surprising and I was assisted in developing them by the observations of my friend Goodman who accompanied me."

He speaks of the East India House, where he saw—

"among other Oriental curiosities the dreams of Tippoo Saib in his own handwriting, and his copy of the Koran most elegantly written on parchment gilt—the tiger's head of solid gold which adorned the foot of his throne and which is said in its present state to weigh sixty pounds—the celebrated inscribed stone and some bricks from the supposed site of ancient Babylon."

He went on two occasions to Oxford to see his friend Shortt and while there he occupied rooms in Worcester College belonging to a student absent during vacation. He writes of Oxford and its many colleges as they were in the year 1820:—

" 'Worcester College Library,' he says, 'contains thirty thousand volumes of valuable and curious books. In the Quadrangle of the schools, so called from its containing the places of examination and for lectures on different subjects, I first visited the famous Bodleian library and the picture gallery. The room which contains the celebrated Arundelian marbles is rich in other remnants of antiquity consisting altogether of inscriptions.

Among the Pompei statues a full length statue of Cicero appeared to me to possess eminent beauties. The Ashmoleian Museum contains many curiosities, among the more remarkable are the skull of Oliver Cromwell with the well-known scar on the frontal bone. The sword sent by Leo X. to Henry VIII. with the title 'Defensor fidei'—the handle forms with the blade a cross, and in the head of the hilt, which is of crystal is a small painting with the motto 'vigilate.' The helmet which Henry the Fifth wore at Azincour and the sword with which he killed the Duke of Alençon in the same battle. The Duke of Alençon's battle axe which he used at Azincour.

The iron mace of Walworth the Mayor with which he slew Wat Tyler. A lantern of Alfred the Great and an amulet of gold containing a figure of St. Cuthbert which he wore to protect him from the effect of incantation. The sides of this amulet are formed into these letters—'Alfredus jussit me fabricare,'—also his golden tinder box—all found in the Isle of Sheppey and presented to the Museum. A gold watch of Queen Elizabeth inlaid with beautiful opals —the chain of gold is engraved with memoranda—on one of the links the two engraved letters 'E. E.' are supposed to mean the Earl of Essex. The golden tankard which she used every morning at her breakfast. The gauntlet of the Earl of Warwick called the Kingmaker. A boot of Queen Elizabeth, the smallness of which conveys some idea of the beauty of her feet. Also a boot of the unfortunate Duke of York, brother of Edward V. The much mutilated hat of leather worn by Bradshaw in Parliament when sentence was passed on Charles I A pair of spurs of Oliver Cromwell and specimens of spurs of the ancient Britons.

St. Mary's Church is a very beautiful Gothic building. St. Peter's Church is a very old piece of Saxon architecture and was built between the tenth century and the Norman invasion New College has small but beautiful gardens surrounded by part of the ancient walls of the City of Oxford which were repaired in the parliamentary wars and are now very perfect. Magdalen College has some very elegant new buildings and surpasses all the other colleges in the beauty of its walks and park. The favorite haunt of Addison is still called 'Addison's Walk.' Christ Church is the largest of all the colleges and has about four hundred students, but its walks though very extensive are not so delightful as those of Magdalen. The River Isis is a very small stream—as it was frozen over, we went on it to see the skaters.

There is an ancient tower or castle here, but additions have been made to it and it is used as a prison. Near it is an artificial mound of earth with caverns raised by Col. Ingoldsby in the parliamentary wars as a depot for provisions.

The observatory of the University is a fine building in the style of the Temple of the Winds at Athens.

The Radcliffe Library is a fine piece of architecture in a circular form. The circular room intended to contain the library is the most beautiful thing of the kind I ever beheld — the dome which is eighty feet from the floor is richly worked and the floor is formed of alternate brown and white marble slabs. A splendid entertainment was given in this room by the University to the Emperor of Russia and other crowned heads. The Library is not yet filled up and the number of books not very considerable."

On his second visit to Oxford, which took place on the 2nd May, 1820, he mentions that on his progress towards Worcester College, he met his old schoolfellow Tom Davie in High Street. That evening he dined in Hall at Worcester with Shortt and his friend Yolland.

Regarding Ifley on the Isis, about two miles distant from Oxford, he says,—

"This place is remarkable only for a very old Church built in the Saxon style. From a manuscript of Anthony Wood, the antiquity of Ifley Church may be in some measure ascertained. It appears that it was given with its appurtenances by Jeffrey de Clinton to the Canons of Kenilworth in Warwickshire; and this Jeffrey lived in the reign of William the Conqueror. In the Church yard stands a very ancient cross, but its ornamental sculpture has been entirely destroyed by time. Near this cross is a yew tree, whose trunk is of great circumference, supposed to be cœval with the Church."

He attended on the 3rd May, 1820, the examination for degrees at the schools. The following day he walked with his friend Shortt to Godstow, to visit the site of the tomb of the fair Rosamond, mistress of Henry II. The bones which had been carried away by antiquaries some time before that, were found in the Chapter House, which at the time he (Alexander Buchanan) visited it, had been converted into a cow house, and of which he writes:—

"There was a long inscription painted on the wall over the place of interment, a few words of which are yet legible.

The bones of this unfortunate lady were transported here from the Church, which was situated a short distance, by the command of some bigoted ecclesiastic, lest 'the bones of the whore' should profane the holy place."

He thus completes his description of the Colleges:—

"We began the day (5th May, 1820), by visiting the chapels and halls of some of the Colleges. The Chapel of Magdalen is neat but contains nothing remarkable. New College Chapel is by far the finest I saw; its windows are formed of very fine painted glass representing a variety of human figures in the persons of saints. We took a cursory view of the gallery of painting of the Bodleian—the best painting in the room is the school of philosophers, representing almost all the philosophers of Greece attended by some of their pupils, by Guilio Romano. There is also a very fine fruit piece, but I forget whose production it is.

We visited the gallery of painting in the Library of Christ Church College, which contains some very fine pictures. Among the best I remarked—A St. Christopher—and a David and Goliath—figures foreshortened by Michael Angelo Buonarotti,—The family of the Caracci in a butcher's shop,—An Italian buffoon drinking, by Annibale Caracci,—An Emperor on horseback, by Guilio Romano,—A St. Peter, half length, by Caravaggio.—A St. Sebastian, half length,—A Rebecca at the well,—A St. John the Baptist, and the first Prince of Orange, by Guido.—A Descent from the Cross, by Coreggio.—Four portraits with music before them,—Our Saviour, not half length,—Portrait of a woman, half length,—Portrait of the Duke of Alva, by Titian.

We went to see the Sheldon Theatre, which is the place for recitation of prize poems, &c.

Shortt and I went to breakfast at Woodstock. This place is remarkable as the birthplace of Chaucer, where he lived and died.

After breakfast we proceeded to take a view of Blenheim, the magnificent seat of the Duke of Marlborough.

The grounds are as beautiful as verdure, trees and artificial water, the largest sheet of the kind in the world, can make them. There are gentle undulations all through the park, which increases its beauty, and numerous herds of deer, bounding over the green, tend to add life to the scene. As the castle is never opened to strangers before two o'clock, we walked through the park and Combe Lodge to North Leigh, a distance of about four miles, to visit a Roman villa which was lately discovered here. The foundations of all the walls of the building are still remaining, and there are some entire mosaic pavements. There are two baths, parts of which are in a state of good preservation. From the size of the building, its materials and the conveniences which appear to have ministered to the luxury of its owner, we may conjecture that it was the residence of some person of consequence.

On our return to Blenheim we obtained admission into the house, which contains a superb gallery of paintings of the old masters. There is also a fine library, and a small theatre. Many of the rooms are adorned with the Gobelin tapestry representing the battles of the Duke of Marlborough. The Titian room is so called from the paintings on leather by Titian with which its walls are covered."

Returning from Oxford, he passed through Stratford upon Avon, where " having stopped to change horses he had barely time to view the outside of the house where, as is reputed, the immortal Shakespeare was born, which is now occupied by a butcher."

CHAPTER IV.

1820.

COURSE OF READING IN LONDON — HIS FRIENDS — GOES TO THE THEATRES AND SEES KEAN AND MACREADY — HEARS LECTURES IN LONDON HOSPITALS—ATTENDS WESTMINSTER HALL.

"Tuesday, 11th December, 1820.—Breakfasted with Mr. Johnston at the Golden Cross, with whom I remained until two o'clock preparing a petition on behalf of his son to the Lords of the Treasury."

"Saturday, 18th December, 1819.—I was at home and read the whole day till 4.30 p.m., when I went to dine at Morrin's Hotel, Duke Street, Manchester Square, with Mr. John Geo. McTavish, from whence I returned home at about eleven p.m. Besides myself and Mr. McTavish there were at dinner Mr. Cowie, Mr. Swaine of the Hudson Bay Company, and Mr. Johnston.

He mentions having dined with Messrs. Parent and Blanchet, and having called on Mr. Irvine, of Quebec, at Osborne's Hotel, Adelphi.

He was in London on the 31st January, 1820, when he went to see the ceremony of proclamation of King George IV.

During the time he lived in London he was reading steadily. He appears to have mapped out a course of study to which he carefully adhered. His reading was very extensive and consisted of history, the ancient authors and the law. He chiefly read Hallam's History of the Middle Ages, and in the original Aullus Gellius, Cicero, Homer, Xenophon, Tibullus, Plutarch, and the New Testament in the Greek, and Montaigne, Woodeson's Elements of Jurisprudence and Lord Mansfield and and others on the study of Law and Boote's Suit at Law.

While here he spent most of his time with his friend Goodman, who lodged in Castle Court, Cloak Lane; Mr. G. Young, of Gray's Inn; Mr. Stevenson who had lodgings at No. 30 Portman Place, Edgecombe Road; Mr. Tyrell, 11 Paper Buildings, in the Temple; Mr. R. B. Comyn, of the Temple who lived in Pump Court, and a Mr. Johnston. He also saw a good deal of Mr. Jno. Geo. MacTavish, of 13 New Quebec Street; Mr. Stewart, Mitre Court, Cheapside; Mr. Gilmour, Freeman's Court, Cornhill; Mr. Cowie of the North West Company, and Mr. Swaine of the Hudson's Bay Company; Mr. Nivin of Clement's Inn; Mr. Robert Hayes and his cousin Mr. C. Hayes. It was on the motion of the latter gentleman that he was elected on the evening of the 9th February, 1820, a member of the Eccentric Society in London. He also frequented the society of Mr. French of 7 Dalby Terrace, New City Road, Islington, and of the family of Mr. Reynolds. He mentions having dined with Mr. Armstrong, surgeon, No. 6 Baker Street, Portman Square, and having in the evening gone with Mrs. Armstrong to a ball at Mrs. Phillips', Dorset Square, and a few evenings after going to a party at Mr. Armstrong's.

He used to go to the theatres, notably Covent Garden and Drury Lane. At the latter he saw,—

"the performance of Richard III. by the desire of the "Duke and Duchess of Kent, who were both present. "The principal character, Richard III., was played by Mr. "Kean in a most admirable manner."

He saw Macready as Coriolanus and again Kean, this time as Hamlet and later as King Lear. He went to "half play" at the Adelphi and as he says, "by way of conclusion after this we visited the cider cellars in Maiden Lane." He also saw Liston with whose comic powers he was highly amused.

He heard Fletcher, a popular preacher at a chapel in Little Moor's Fields.

With his friend Goodman, who was studying medicine and walking the hospitals, he visited the different hospitals and there heard lectures by the most eminent surgeons of the day.

At the London Hospital he heard a lecture on bronchotomy, etc., dropsy and tapping from Mr. Headington and was there introduced to Sir William Blizzard.

On a subsequent occasion he heard another lecture from Mr. Headington, this time on the cellular membrane. He heard a lecture from Mr. Millington at Guy's Hospital on hydrostatics. At St. Bartholomew's Hospital he had the good fortune to hear a lecture on mortification by the celebrated Abernethy.

On the 24th January, 1820, after breakfast he went to Westminster, where a number of people were assembled to see the Judges arrive in procession to the Court. In the Court of King's Bench, before Chief Justice Abbott and Judges Bayley, Holroyd and Best he listened to an ex parte argument in the case of Madrazo v. Milles, for a new trial in an action for damages brought by some Spanish slave traders against a captain in the British Navy for the detention of the ship and the liberation of the slaves. The damages had been assessed by the jury at upwards of £16,000. Jervis argued for the rule which the Court dismissed. Among other distinguished counsel engaged in this case whom he saw were Scarlett, afterwards Lord Abinger, Campbell, afterwards Lord Chancellor, Peake and Pullen.

He attended also at the Court of Chancery and heard a cause respecting a right of advowson contested between Marquis Townshend, Lord Charles Townshend and the trustees of the late Marquis's estate.

At Doctors Commons in the Court of Admiralty and the Ecclesiastical Court he was an attentive auditor.

He mentions having gone with Mr. Hayes to the Coal Hole in the Strand, a place "which seems to be frequented by coachmen and economical dandies." Among the coffee houses which he patronized while in London were the New England, near the Royal Exchange, George's, near Temple Bar, Button's in Cheapside, the Salopian in Charing Cross, and the One Tun in Jermyn Street.

CHAPTER V.

1820.

HE GOES TO PARIS — PASSES THROUGH ST. OMER, AIRE, ARRAS AND AMIENS—VISITS THE TUILLERIES, THE LOUVRE, VERSAILLES,. THE LUXEMBOURG, THE CATACOMBS, CEMETERY OF PERE LA CHAISE, CHURCH OF ST. DENIS, MALMAISON AND ST. CLOUD—THEATRES AT PARIS—AT ROUEN—RETURNS TO LONDON.

On Sunday the 26th March, 1820, he set out from London in a mail coach, with his friend Wybault, for Dover, where they arrived on Monday at 7 a.m. At 9.30 a.m. they embarked on board a small sloop of about 30 tons, crowded to excess with about sixty passengers. The passage to Calais was performed in three hours and ten minutes. On landing they visited the Hotel de Depin, celebrated for the residence of Sterne. At 4 p.m. they left Calais for Boulogne in a postchaise, and then on to St. Omer, which latter place he found bleak and uninteresting, occasioned by a deficiency of verdure and a scarcity of trees. Of the town itself he has to say:—

"St. Omer is a regularly fortified town and its situation is rather pleasant. We employed the hour during which we were detained here in visiting the curiosities of the place. There is here a very fine cathedral in the Gothic style which contains an ancient but uncouth monument of St. Elsendob, and the tomb of St. Andomarus or St. Omer.

We went to see the old English school here which is now a military hospital."

They then set out for Aire, from where it was his intention to continue the journey to Arras that same night,

"but the rigor of the commandant who would not accommodate us by opening the town gates frustrated our design. This place is strongly fortified, and contains a cathedral of considerable magnitude."

He passed through Arras,

"an old city well fortified and contains a great number of troops, at this moment. The houses are in the old style, built of stone and very heavy in their appearance. There is a very large square or *place* here which was thronged with persons who seem engaged in trade."

At Amiens he and his fellow-travellers were annoyed by the boisterous behaviour of a number of French dragoon officers and soldiers in endeavouring to bring the fares to their ancient level using the words " Vous étranglez les Anglais et les Francais en souffrent."

Of Amiens, he says:—

"There is a cathedral of some beauty here, but which, notwithstanding all the praise lavished on it is inferior to many buildings of the kind which I have seen in England. It was built during the reign of our Henry VI in France."

He arrived in Paris on the evening of the 30th March, and went to the Hotel des Etats Unis, rue Notre Dame des Victoires, and the next day took lodgings at Madam Target's, No. 26 rue des Moulins.

"Friday, 31st March, 1820.—Walked in the gardens of the Thuilleries and the Champs Elysées, which were crowded with carriages and persons on foot during the Promenade de Longchamps, which takes place in the holy week of every year, and originated in the obsolete custom of going to the Monastery of Longchamps to hear the prayers of the nuns."

"Saturday, 1st April, 1820.—The greater part of this day passed away by my being present at a review of a regiment of Hussars on the Champ de Mars. The duc d'Angouleme and d'Oudinot, the Marshal duc de Reggio and other officers of distinction were on the field.

The next day was Easter Sunday when he went to walk in the garden of the Tuilleries which he says, "were rendered extremely gay by the number of persons who were there *en promenade.*" And he goes on to thus criticise the different buildings.

"To-day (2 April, 1820), I saw these gardens to great advantage, the serenity of the weather, the magnificent pile of the Thuilleries, the beautiful new buildings in the Rue Rivoli, the noble appearance of the Admiralty, the budding trees, the fountains and the statues disposed in various parts of the alleys with the greatest taste, rendered the scene enchanting.

"The much vaunted bridge of Iena, now called de l'Ecole Militaire, fell far short of what I expected, It is very plain and not at all comparable in size, architecture or materials to the superb structure of Waterloo Bridge in London.

"The Corps Législatif, of which I saw but the exterior is a beautiful building. The front is, in my humble opinion, in the purest taste of ancient architecture, and bears close similitude to that of the ancient temples.

"L'Ecole Militaire, situated at the bottom of the Champ de Mars, is also a fine structure. The portico in the centre of the buildings is formed of Corinthian columns. It was founded by Louis XV. in 1751 for the education of young gentlemen of slender fortune."

He lost no time in going to see the Louvre.

"I was occupied the greater part of this day (4 April, 1820), in the gallery of painting in the Louvre, but its immense extent (700 paces covered on both sides with paintings) rendered my forming any idea of its beauties in detail impossible. I had barely time this day to walk through the magnificent collection of marbles."

But not having had time, as he explains, to study the paintings in detail he returned on two occasions which he refers to as follows:—

"Went with Mr. Barron to the Louvre, where I received excessive pleasure from the works of Le Brun, Poussin, Vernet, Drouais, Claude Lorraine and Le Sueur of the French school; those of Dow, Van Dyck, Rembrandt and Rubens of the Dutch school, and those of Caravaggio, Annibale Caracci, Correggio, Domeniquin, Guido Remi, Guilio Romano, Leonardo da Vinci, Paolo Veronese, Raffaello, Salvatore Rosa, Tiziano, &c.

"This (20 April, 1820), being the last day of my residence in Paris I thought that part of it could not be better spent than in taking a parting look at the Louvre. After cursorily viewing the gallery of painting, I descended to the superb deposit for pieces of ancient sculpture, where I spent two hours with great satisfaction. The chef d'œuvre here is the celebrated Hermaphrodite Borghese which is represented lying on a mattress with a pillow under its head, and is the finest piece of sculpture I ever saw. This magnificent collection contains also a fine Diana, many Venuses, the Pallas of Velletri, and a gigantic Melpomene, besides numerous other statues, sarcophagi, cinerary urns, sepulchral inscriptions and other valuable relics of antiquity."

In the Louvre he met Mr. Shaw and Mr. Wm. McGillivray.

The different palaces of Versailles, and the Luxembourg, the Catacombs, the Cemetery of Père La Chaise, the remains of the Baths of the Emperor Julian, the Church of St. Denis, the palaces of Malmaison and St. Cloud, he visited in succession and has left his impressions of them.

"The Church of Notre Dame in the Island of St. Louis is the principal structure in Paris. It is a very fine building of its kind but much inferior to Westminster. It contains two fine altar paintings.

"We arrived (7th April, 1820) at Versailles in a diligence. The superb palace here attracted our attention for a considerable time. It has lately undergone repairs rendered necessary by the injuries it sustained during the Revolution. The interior of the chapel is the most beautiful thing of its kind that I have seen. The ceiling which is painted in good style, is supported by a number of large columns of the Corinthian order. The façade of the Palace towards the gardens is strikingly grand when seen through the principal avenues. The garden, laid out in the French taste, is not very pleasing to an English eye, from the regularity with which the trees are planted, the want of grass, and the manner of clipping the trees into unnatural shapes. The grand Trianon, a small palace sometimes visited by Bonaparte, is pleasantly situated. We saw here a relief in Agate brought from Herculaneum and a font of beautiful green Siberian marble given by the Emperor of Russia to the King. The last work of the celebrated Vernet is in one of the rooms of this Palace. The *petit* Trianon is a small palace furnished for Josephine, but was never inhabited by her in consequence of her divorce, which took place about the time that the palace was ready. The English garden in the rear of the last mentioned palace is the most enchanting I ever saw—here are artificial grottos, lakes, rivers, and hamlets, &c.

"I accompanied two French ladies, a Mrs. Strachan and her sister, and Wybault, to the Luxembourg. We took a walk in the gardens and a view of the exterior of the Palace, and afterwards went to the Gallery of Painting, which contains some beautiful pictures by living French painters. The most remarkable were the Leonidas by David, the Murder of Agamemnon by Clytemnestra and Aegisthus, Aeneas relating his Adventures to Dido, and Death of Zenobia, and many others. I saw in the house of the above mentioned ladies a very fine painting of Hector Andromache and Astyanax, and another of a wounded Theban soldier, both by Mrs. Strachan's sister—for the latter painting she received a gold medal from Buonoparte.

"Thursday, (12 April, 1820), we succeded in descending to the Catacombs. We go down a depth of about fifty feet on stone steps, and the whole length of the passages which extend as far as the Barrière d'Enfer are bounded on each side by piles of bones, skulls, &c. Now and then you see on stone slabs or pedestals appropriate sentences from the scriptures or from the more melancholy writings of ancients. We descended in company with about twenty persons among whom were many English ladies. Returning from the Catacombs we visited the Pantheon or Church of St. Geneviève which is a superb mausoleum for the illustrious dead of France. It has a very fine and lofty dome, and the interior of the building is supported by very large fluted pillars of the Corinthian order. The vaults contain no other learned dust but that of Voltaire and Jean Jacques—the remains of a few secondary military characters are deposited here. The exterior portal is grand and is composed of fluted Corinthian pillars.

"I spent the greater part of a day in the beautiful cemetery of Père Lachaise; the principal tomb here is that of the lovers, Abelard and Heloise, which was transported hither from the monastery of Paraclet and is yet in excellent preservation. There is a long inscription on one side in old French relating the heretical opinions of Abelard, his recantation, &c. The bones of Moliere and of Lafontaine were removed from the original place of their interment to this cemetery, where they are placed alongside of each other and covered with most plain stone monuments. There are fine tombs to St. Jean d'Angely, Massena, Delille the poet, and Ginguéne. We had an excellent view of Paris from the high grounds in this delightful spot.

"We went to see the church of St. Sulpice, which has a fine front decorated with colonnades, and two noble towers. After leaving the latter place we went to No. 63 Rue de la Harpe to a cooper's house to see the remains of the baths which belonged to the Palace of the Emperor Julian, called the palace of the Thermes. With some difficulty and danger from frail ladders and landing places, we gained the roof of these extensive baths about seventy feet from the ground. This roof had been covered with a garden, the earth of which they are now removing and by so doing have discovered various canals for the water and flues, &c. They have also found a fragment of a Latin inscription, but it was so small a part of the original slab that I could not find out its meaning

"We took a trip to the Church of St. Denis, which was and is the grand repository for the Royal Family of France after their decease The workmen are now employed in restoring the ancient Royal monuments from the earliest ages which were formerly deposited here, but were injured or removed from this place to places of greater safety during the Revolution. The place which Bonaparte had allotted for his family is a sepulchre for the present dynasty and contains the remains of the late Duc de Berri. The large brazen doors which Napoleon placed at its entrance have been removed and replaced with large marble slabs. The altar piece which contains the bones of St. Denis, the patron Saint of France, is a fine piece of workmanship and highly ornamented.

"This morning Wybault, myself, Mrs. Strachan, her sister, Mrs. Storey, a Portugese lady and Mrs. Drake, set off in an open carriage to visit some of the Royal Palaces. We made a vain application for admission to the Elysée Bourbon. From this we proceeded to Malmaison where we commenced our operations by surveying the gardens, which are pleasantly situated, and well laid out There is a pretty temple of variegated marble to the Goddess of Love built near the small stream which runs through the gardens. There are also some statues in different parts of the grounds which add to the beauty of the place. Near the entrance from the gardens into this estate are two very beautiful obelisks brought from Egypt, covered with gilt hieroglyphics. The palace is a plain looking house, which circumstance gave rise to the name of Malmaison. It belongs to Eugene Beauharnois, and was a favorite haunt of Napoleon's, and was fitted up for the Empress Josephine. It contains a gallery of paintings and a small theatre. We saw the private study of Bonaparte when he was First Consul, which still contains his chair and one of his tables. From the rooms upstairs we had a fine view of the gardens, which, bounded by the stupendous aqueduct to convey water to Versailles, forms a very pretty landscape.

"After surveying the whole of the place we continued our route to St. Cloud. The situation of this palace is superior to that of Versailles, the view from the eminence on which it is built being very extensive, commanding a prospect of Paris, the Bois de Boulogne, and the Seine which flows along the Park of St. Cloud. The park and gardens are beautifully laid out and show more taste than is exhibited in the gardens of Versailles. The gallery of painting contains some good pictures, and the rooms being well furnished gives them a more finished and elegant appearance than those of Versailles or Malmaison."

At the Café de la Paix in the Palais Royal, which was formerly a theatre, and was then a coffee house where the visitors were entertained with exhibitions of feats on the slack rope, he saw Thomas Moore, the poet, with his wife.

He attended at the Palais de Justice in the Cour Royale and Cour d'Assize at Paris.

During his visit here he went to the Theatre Francais where he saw Talma in the character of Leicester in the Mary Stuart by Pierre Lebrun. The other characters were represented by Desmousseaux, Mdlle. Duchesnois and Mde Paradol. At the Italian Opera he heard Garcia, in his own piece Il Fazzoletto and Mde. Ponzi Debeguis.

" Tuesday, 18th April, 1820.—We were occupied almost the whole of this day in settling the troublesome matter of our passports, which went through the hands of the English Ambassador, of the Ministre de l'Intérieur, Ministre de l'Extérieur, Préfet de Police, etc.

After a stay of not quite three weeks in Paris he left for Rouen *en route* for London on the 20th April, 1820, in the cabriolet of the diligence.

"At Rouen," he says, "we gained admission into the church, a superb Gothic building. Within the Choir we found three slabs of stone in the pavement, which escaped the ravages of the Revolution by which this church suffered to a great degree. On one I read the following inscription:—

Cor
Richardi Regis Angliæ
Normanniæ Ducis
Cor Leonis dicti
Obiit anno
MCXCIX.

From the other I copied the following:—

        Ad
   dextrum altaris latus
       Jacet
 Joannes Dux Betfordiæ
   Normanniæ Prorex
     Obiit anno
    MCCCCXXXV.

"The third contains an inscription to the memory of Henry, brother to Richard I.

"In a small square called Place de la Pucelle, there is a public fountain surmounted by a statue of the Pucelle d'Orleans, erected to mark the spot where she was burnt during the Regency of Bedford. The situation of Rouen is one of the most beautiful It is built in a fertile valley watered by the Seine and exhibiting an appearance of high cultivation. The traveller in approaching Rouen from Paris is delighted when from an eminence down which the road descends, the City of Rouen, the river Seine meandering through a rich country, the cathedral with lofty towers and elegantly light spires, the Bridge of Boats, and the shipping in the harbour burst upon his sight and afford a lively and variegated landscape."

He sailed from Dieppe on the 21st April, landed at Brighton the next morning, and was back in London the same afternoon.

CHAPTER VI.

1820.

CHRIST CHURCH SCHOOL — HOUSE OF COMMONS — SOMERSET HOUSE — HE GOES TO IRELAND — BUCHANANS OF OMAGH AND FINTONA — LONDONDERRY — HE SAILS FOR SCOTLAND.

On his return from Paris he took up his quarters at the Crown in Bow Lane. He went with Mr. Reynolds to hear prayers in the hall of Christ Church School, where he saw 700 blue coat boys sit down to supper after prayers.

He attended the House of Commons and heard Broughham, Tierney, Lord Archibald Hamilton, Colonel Davis and Joseph Hume.

He went to the exhibition at Somerset House, where, among a great many paintings, he found very few worthy of notice. The best was "The Reading of the Will," by Wilkie. There was a fine piece of sculpture by Chauncy, of a child sleeping on a mattress in the style of the Hermaphrodite Borghese.

It was at this time he made his second visit to Oxford. On his return from there he went to Ireland, and on the 12th May, 1820, arrived at Omagh. While at this place he was the guest of his uncle, George Buchanan, who was his father's eldest brother. There were then living of his father's family George Buchanan at Omagh; Beavor Buchanan and William Buchanan at Fintona, and Mary Irvine at "Lisnagore."

He says,—

"About a mile from Fintona is Eccles Green, where my grandfather once lived and my father was born."

"Omagh," he says, "is situated in a valley watered by the River Omreagh. The town may contain about two thousand inhabitants, many of whom are in respectable circumstances, there being a considerable linen market here. Near the town is Rash, the grounds of the Earl of Blessington, consisting of extensive plantations."

He went on horseback with his uncle George to "Lisnagore," the house of Mr. Irvine and his aunt.

"From an eminence not far distant," he writes, "I had a distant view of Loch Erne, and the surrounding mountains, which are very abrupt and grand. The etymology of Lisnagore is Irish; it means 'The Goat's Fort,' there being here a perfect Danish Fort."

During his visit at Omagh, he went to Londonderry to pass a few days with his cousin, William Buchanan.

Of this visit he says:—

"30th May, 1820.—Went to Londonderry in the mail coach, where I was hospitably entertained in the house of my cousin, William Buchanan, and during my stay here till the 10th June was most kindly treated by Mr. and Mrs. Orr and Mr. Robinson. I spent one day at Dr. Caldwell's."

Londonderry is described in these terms:—

"Londonderry is a neatly built and clean town, beautifully situated on a rising ground which gives a grand prospect of the River and Loch Foyle. The distant mountains of Macgilligan at the entrance of the Loch, and of a richly cultivated country on either side of the Loch well wooded and diversified by gentlemen's seats. One of these county seats, that of Sir George Hill, I visited in company of Mrs. Orr, Mrs. John Buchanan, Miss Blacker and others; it is called 'Boom Hall,' being near the spot where a boom was laid across the Loch during the contest for religious liberty in James II.'s reign, to prevent the approach of ships of war.

"Londonderry is surrounded by walls of fortification which are celebrated through all Ireland as a wonder of art. Though weak as a fortress it sustained a siege in William III.'s reign, probably through the unskilfulness of the besiegers. There is a passably good public library. The Court House is an exceedingly pretty building with a chaste portal of free stone and is a great ornament to the town and reflects great credit on the spirit of its inhabitants. The cathedral is a rude, venerable building,"

On the journey from Londonderry to Belfast, en route for Scotland, he went around the base of "Macgilligan along the sea shore to Down "Hill the seat of the late Earl of Bristol, now "the property of Sir Hervey Bruce. The house "contains some pictures and some pretty speci- "mens of statuary. At the edge of the precipice, "which overhangs the sea at a tremendous height, "is built a library or study in the form of an " ancient temple. Round the upper part of the "building are inscribed two lines of the beautiful

"'passage in Lucretius, 'Suave mari magno tur-
"bantibus aequora ventis, &c.' "[1]

(¹) APPROPRIATE INSCRIPTIONS FROM LUCRETIUS.

To the Editor of Notes and Queries.—(Montreal Star)

SIR:—On the northern coast of Ireland, I believe in the County Antrim, there is a rocky promontory overlooking the Atlantic, situated on the estate of one Sir Hervey Bruce, nearly opposite Moville, the place where the Allan steamships stop on their way to and from Liverpool and Glasgow.

On this promontory there was standing in 1859 (and may be still) a sort of dismantled round tower, built of cut stone and having a comparatively modern appearance, with a Latin inscription carved around it about twelve feet from its base. A part of this inscription only I can now recall:

"...Mari magno turbantibus æquora ventis...alterius magnum spectare laborem."

In connection with the above, the following information is respectfully sought:—

    1st. What is the object and use of such a tower in such a place?
    2nd. What is the meaning and appropriateness of the Latin inscription?
    3rd. What is the entire inscription, and from what author is it taken?

If you can conveniently find time to throw a little light on these points you will confer a great favor on several of your readers.

Montreal.   ———   H. RANDALL.

    1. I can only conjecture that the tower was built by some man who had retired from the world soured and discontented, and that he was actuated by the feelings described in the quotation that I am about to cite

    2 & 3. It is taken from the beginning of the second book of a Latin poem, "De Rerum Natura," which was given to the world by Titus Lucretius Carus, B C. 57. It is a philosophical didactic poem, composed in heroic hexameters, divided into six books, and containing upwards of seven thousand four hundred lines. I will quote the Latin of the first four lines of the passage referred to by Mr. Randall:

"Suave, mari magno turbantibus æquora ventis,
E terra magnum alterius spectare laborem;
Non quia vexari quemquam est jucunda voluptas
Sed, quibus ipse maliscareas, quia cernere suaves est."

That is: "It is sweet, when the winds are ruffling the waters on a high sea, to behold from land the great toil of another; not be-

The day he was to leave Belfast for Scotland, he says:—

"At 4.30 p.m. I was put into consternation by the premature sailing of the steamboat 'Rob Roy,' in which I had taken a passage and which contained my baggage, but by the exertions of my boatman I reached her. Machine out of order, put into Larne for seven and a half hours. My fellow passengers were a set of good fellows. A Col. Hastings, whose aristocratic pride prevented his mingling with the company; Col. Stuart of the Buffs, whose blunt simplicity of manner and uncouth old dress led us to consider him an assistant surgeon or a quartermaster; Surgeon Morrison, of the Rifle Brigade, who exhibited a curious trait of borrowing 10 s, giving notice that he was subject to forget these trifles and requesting to be reminded of his debt; when he was put in mind of his obligation he paid with reluctance and without giving thanks. A Dutchman and his servant who lived on a true footing of Republican equality. These persons afforded us great amusement by their complaints under sea-sickness. A Sheffield merchant, Mr. Sowerby, a provision merchant at Liverpool and a young Greenock merchant. There was also on board a Capt. Sanders with whom I became well acquainted—he had been Lieutenant of the 'Leander' at the bombardment of Algiers."

---

cause there is any real pleasure in seeing others in distress, but because man is glad to see misfortunes from which he himself is free." The poet continues:"'Tis pleasant, too, to look with no share of peril on the mighty contests of war; but nothing is sweeter than to reach those calm and well-protected temples raised by the wisdom of philosophers, whence thou mayst look down on poor mistaken mortals, wandering up and down in life's devious ways, some resting their fame on genius, or priding themselves on birth, day and night toiling anxiously to rise to high fortune and sovereign power."

Archippus, an Athenian poet, of the old comedy, whose date is about 415 B.C., has a passage (quoted in Meineke's Frag. Comic. Gracor) which somewhat resembles the beginning of the 2nd Book of Lucretius. Translated it is as follows : " How pleasant it is, O mother, to view the sea from the land, when we are sailing nowhere."

CHAPTER VII.

1820.

ARRIVES AT GLASGOW AND HEARS DR. CHALMERS — TRAVELS BY COACH ALONG THE LEVEN — SMOLLETS' HOUSE — LOCH LOMOND — BUCHANAN HOUSE KILLEARN — BEN LOMOND — BALIRVOCKY — EDINBURGH — HOLYROOD PALACE — COURT OF SESSION — FRANCIS JEFFREY AND SIR WALTER SCOTT — HIS IMPRESSIONS OF SCOTLAND — CASTLE OF THE DUKE OF NORTHUMBERLAND AT ALNWICK — YORK CATHEDRAL.

The Rock of Ailsa was seen by him on the 30th June, 1820. The Firth of Clyde and its scenery struck him as resembling the lower part of the River St. Lawrence. The town of Greenock was reached on the night after leaving Belfast.

At Glasgow, where he arrived on the 1st July, he put up at the Buck's Head on Argyle Street. He remarks on the elegance of the streets as to architecture, regularity and materials.

"The College," he points out, "some part has an ancient appearance with towers resembling those of the old prison in Paris. The museum, which belongs to the College, is a new building. Its specimens of mineralogy and natural history are not many, but its anatomical preparations, which were first collected by Dr. Hunter, are probably unrivalled. Its collection of coins is very valuable. The library contains some fine paintings — St. Catherine by Domenichino, a sweet painting — a Virgin and Child, by

Guido—a Head by Titian. There are some border antiquities, being chiefly votive monuments to Hadrian raised by the different legions after the completion of their apportioned parts of the Roman wall."

At St. John's Church at Glasgow, he heard an eloquent sermon from the great Doctor Chalmers.

From Glasgow he and his fellow traveller, Captain Sanders, pursued their way to Dumbarton. They went by the post boy steamboat, and were landed from a boat at the foot of the rock or promontory on which the Castle of Dumbarton stands. They continued their journey in—

"a coach in company with two other coaches, one of which unfortunately drove over a boy at the village of Renton, which occasioned very great ferment, all the inhabitants being in the street threatening vengeance upon us all. We travelled along the beautiful fertile and classic banks of the Leven, where I with pleasure called to my recollection the pretty ode of Smollett:—

'On Leven's bank while free to rove,
And tune the rural pipe to love,
I envied not the happiest swain,
That e'er trod the Arcadian plain,' etc.

"The site of Smollett's house, which was shown to us, belongs to the Smollett family. At Renton we saw the monument erected to the memory of Smollett. There are two country seats on the banks of the Leven near the entrance of Loch Lomond, built in the style of the ancient baronial castles which give additional beauty to the surrounding scenery. The one on the western bank is called the Castle of Ballychewan.

THE OLD BUCHANAN HOUSE, SCOTLAND.

"At Ballach we again took steamboat to go up Loch Lomond. A short time after entering the Lake we came to several islands, one of which, Inch Murrin, is considerable in size. Inch Crinie, is a place of confinement for all disorderly wives, of whom there are generally some undergoing the usual course of penance."

He saw Buchanan House.

"In a bay, on the right hand going up the lake, is situated Buchanan House, the seat of the Duke of Montrose. Opposite to his grounds is Clare Inch, an island which formerly (as well as all the possessions of the Duke of Montrose here) belonged to the Lairds of Buchanan, and was their *cri de guerre* or slughorn."

The old mansion house of Buchanan was burnt down in 1850. Buchanan Castle, the present seat of the Duke of Montrose, lies about a mile to the West of the village of Drymen. The Castle was commenced in 1854 and completed in 1857.

Continuing, he says:—

"We had a distant view of the monument which has been erected in the Parish of Killearn to George Buchanan. We stopped a few minutes at Luss on the opposite side of the Loch. We touched at Tarbet after having at 2 P.M. visited and descended into Rob Roy's cave, which has been celebrated by Scott in one of his novels.

"At 4 P.M. landed with Capt. Sanders at Row Ardennan at the foot of Ben Lomond. At the inn, where we dined and slept, we saw a record inscribed on the window of the intemperance of Kean, the actor. In our passage from Tarbet from the Lake to Row Ardennan, the melancholy gloom of the Loch and its surrounding scenery was heightened by a funeral procession in boats which was proceeding across the Loch to Tarbet to perform the last solemn rite over a young lady.

"At 7.30 A.M., (Tuesday, 4 July, 1820), commenced the ascent of Ben Lomond with Capt. Sanders and arrived at its summit at 5 minutes past 10. The weather being tolerably clear, the view was the grandest and most extensive I ever witnessed. To the south was Dumbarton Castle, and the Clyde. S.W. by S. we saw the Firth of Clyde and the Islands of Arran and Bute. About west the Pass of Jura, and to the north of them the Isle of Mull. Immediately around us was a most majestic assemblage of lakes and mountains and islands. On the W. side of Ben Lomond is Loch Lomond, whose silver bosom is bespangled with Inch Murran, Inch Crain, etc., and other islands. Beyond Tarbet we saw the extremity of Loch Long. At the eastern foot of Ben Lomond is Loch Katrine, rendered classical by the writings of Scott. S.E., Loch Ard and the Loch of Menteith. S. by E. the smoke of Glasgow; S.E., Stirling. About E., the Firth of Forth. W. by N. are the mountains of Ben Voirlich and Ben Cruachan. N., Ben Nevis, the highest mountain in Great Britain. E., Ben Ledi and Ben Venue, the Pindus and Olympus of the great Scottish Bard. Ben Ard, N.N.E., Ben More.

"At the foot of Ben Uird, or Blairvocky Hill, is Blairvocky, the land which belonged to Buchanan of Blairvocky, my ancestor, who emigrated to Ireland.

"We sat on the summit of the mountain one hour and twenty minutes. From our guide, who was a shepherd, I learnt the following song, which exhibits by its beauty the superior taste of the lower order of Scotch:—

I.

"Lowland lassie wilt thou go,
　　Where the hills are clad wi' snow,
　Where beneath the icy steep,
　　The hardy shepherd tends his sheep,
　Ill or wae shall ye betide
　　I'll row ye in my highland plaid.

II.

Soon the voice of cheerie spring;
    Will gar a' our plantings ring;
Soon our bonnie heather braes,
    Will put on their summer claes.
On the mountain's sunny side,
    We'll lean us on my highland plaid.

III.

When the summer decks the flow'rs
    Busks the glens and leafy bow'rs,
Then we'll seek the caller shade,
    And lean us on a primrose bed,
And while the burning hours preside,
    I'll screen ye in my highland plaid.

IV.

Then we'll leave the sheep and goat,
    I will launch the bonnie boat,
Skim the loch in cantie glee,
    Rest the oars to pleasure thee
When chilly breezes sweep the tide,
    I'll row ye in my highland plaid.

V.

Lowland lads may dress them fine,
    Woo in words more saft than mine,
Lowland lads hae mair o' art
    A' my boast's an honest heart,
Whilk shall ever be my pride,
    To row ye in my highland plaid.

IV.

Bonnie lad ye've been sae leal,
    My heart would break at our fareweel,
Long thy love has made me fain,
    Take me, take me for thy ain,
Across the firth away they glide,
    Young Donald and his lowland bride."

"At 11.25 A.M., we commenced our descent and arrived at Row Ardennan at 1.15 P.M. Two men whom we met during our descent performed the journey up and down the mountain in 2 hours and 40 minutes which appeared incredible to the guides. They went without a guide."

Returning to Glasgow, he proceeded to Edinburgh and found the surrounding country very picturesque. He arrived at the Star Inn, Prince's Street, on the 5th July, 1820.

"The streets," he says, "are very handsome in the New Town. View from the Calton Hill, on which is a monument to Lord Nelson, much in the shape of a lighthouse, in my opinion bad taste. This view includes the Firth of Forth, the lower parts of the old town and all the New Town. The Regent bridge has been finished very lately, and is a great ornament to the City."

He goes on to say:—

"Castle of Edinburgh situated on a lofty rock. The Regalia of Scotland in a room in the Castle were lately discovered in a chest in which they had been deposited in the last century at the Union, consisting of a crown, sceptre and sword of state. In High Street we visited the house formerly inhabited by Knox, the great reformer, The uniformity of the street is interrupted by the projection of this house. At the corner of the house is a small sculpture of Knox in his pulpit. There is a small stone inscribed with the following words:—

'THEOS — DEUS — GOD.'

"Holyrood Palace is situated in a low spot at the foot of Arthur's Seat, a mountain. It is a plain building in the shape of a quadrangle with a court inside and a cloister. The principal curiosities of this place are the State bed chamber of Queen Mary, as also her private bed chamber and bed—The small room in which she was sitting with the Duchess of Argyll and Rizzio when the favorite was seized and dragged from her presence—The door at which Darnley and the other conspirators entered her bed chamber. Holyrood Abbey in its present state is the most beautiful ruin I ever beheld One of the cloisters or aisles is nearly perfect and the beautiful window in now entire, having been of late restored—it fell with the rest of the building under the weight of the stone roof. Here may be seen, now stopped up, traces of the doors through which Darnley ascended to murder Rizzio, and that through which Mary descended into the Chapel. In one corner of the Chapel is the vault containing the remains of many Scottish Kings. Here also repose many of the nobility of Scotland."

In the Court of Session at Edinburgh he saw Francis Jeffery, Cranstoun and Tom Clarke and Sir Walter Scott, Prothonotary of the Court.

In these words does he eloquently record his impressions of Scotland:—

"Thus being about to take leave of Scotland, it is my duty to admit that no country has ever interested me so much and was so undeserving of the short stay which I made in it. Caledonia, how great are thy attractions when we regard the rugged grandeur of thy highlands, the fertility and beauty of thy Lothian, the intelligence of thy sons and the beauty of thy cities! Who that has trod thy soil could view without emotion the fields immortalized by thy heroes resisting the progress of a hostile and ambitious neighbour! The same feelings gave rise to the following beautiful sentences of Johnson on landing at Icolmkill:—

" 'We were now treading that illustrious island which was once the luminary of the Caledonian regions, whence savage clans and roving barbarians derived the benefits of knowledge and the blessings of religion. To abstract the mind from all local emotion would be impossible if it were endeavored, and would be foolish if it were possible. Whatever withdraws us from the powers of our senses, whatever makes the past, the distant or the future, predominate over the present, advances us in the dignity of thinking beings. Far from me and far from my friends, be such frigid philosophy, as may conduct us, indifferent and unmoved, over any ground which has been dignified by wisdom, bravery or virtue. The man is little to be envied, whose patriotism would not gain force, upon the plain of Marathon, or whose piety would not grow warmer among the ruins of Iona.'

"Cicero in the beginning of his V Book de fin. boni et mali, has put these sentiments into the mouths of his philosophic disputants:—

> "'Tum Piso, Natura ne nobis hoc, inquit, datum dicam, cum errore quodam, et cum ea locavideamus, in quibus memoria dignos viros acceperimus multos esse versatos, magis moveamur quam si quando eorum ipsorum aut facto audiamus, aut scriptum aliquid legamus? Velut ego nunc moveor, venit enim mihi Platonis in mentem.'

'Well may the traveller exclaim in the language of the great, Tully: 'Quacunquo enim ingredimur in aliquam historiam vestigium ponuis.'"

On his way back to England he passed through Berwick and Alnwick, where he viewed the Castle of the Duke of Northumberland, which he says

" is a very extensive building and one of the most ancient and perfect of its kind in all England. The battlements sur-

---

(1) "Then," said Piso, "shall I say that this is implanted in us by nature, or by some mistake, that when we see those places which we have heard that men who deserve to be had in recollection have much frequented, we are more moved than when we hear even of their actual deeds, or than when we read some one of their writings? just as I am affected now. For the remembrance of Plato comes into my mind."

(2) "For wherever we step we place our feet on some history.".

mounted with stone statues in every attitude make the castle seem as if besieged. One of these statues over a gateway is a representation of George Buchanan in rather an unseemly posture in conformity to a vulgar anecdote of that personage and the King of England. At a short distance from Alnwick is a fine stone monument, at the top of which is the Lion of the Percy raised to the memory of the late Duke of Northumberland by his tenants."

At York he,—

"took a survey of the celebrated Cathedral of York; certainly equal to anything of the kind which I have seen—with difficulty I found an entrance into this most solemn and magnificent of temples; remained some time traversing its aisles contemplating the majestic grandeur of the internal architecture."

On his way to London, which he reached on the 11th July, 1820, he,—

" passed many crosses, besides that of Waltham, raised by Edward I. to commemorate the places at which the body of his queen stopped on its way to the place of sepulture. Went to the Crown Tavern in Bow Lane; the coach was greatly retarded by the crowds of people who had assembled to see the ascent of the grasshopper to the top of the steeple of Bow Church."

CHAPTER VIII.

1820.

IN LONDON — GUILDHALL SESSIONS OF THE KING'S BENCH — AT BULLODE'S — BRITISH GALLERY — DINES AT RICHMOND — LEAVES LONDON AND SAILS FOR NEW YORK — SOME OF THE CELEBRATED MEN HE SAW ON HIS TRAVELS.

On the 12th July, 1820, he says:—"Was employed some part of the day in discovering the residence of Mr. James Buchanan," and the next day, "left the Crown, removed to 8 Northumberland Street, Strand, where my cousin lived." This was his future father-in-law, James Buchanan, then British Consul at New York, who had sailed for England on the 9th May, 1820, in the Manchester Packet via Halifax. He had stopped five days at Halifax, and arrived in London on the 9th June, 1820. He returned from England by Liverpool in the "Nestor," on the 3rd October, 1820, and arrived at New York on the 2nd November, 1820.

The time was now rapidly approaching when he should leave to return to Canada and settle down to the practice of his profession.

Neglecting no opportunity to improve his mind and forensic studies, he went to the Guildhall Sessions of the Court of King's Bench presided by Chief Justice Abbott. He saw Haydon's picture of Christ's Entrance into Jerusalem, and Gericault's picture of the Wreck of the French Frigate Medusa, both at Bullude's. At the British Gallery in Pall Mall he saw chiefly portraits, a good marble bust of Cromwell, and the Death of Lord Chatham. He dined at Mr. Scott's, Bedford Row, and with Robert Hayes and Sanders went to Richmond and from there to Hampton Court in a gig.

"Passed through Bushey Park. The gardens at Hampton are very fine and well laid out. The palace has a fine front but the remainder of the building is of brick and is poor in appearance. The collection of paintings is large; among them are the celebrated cartoons of Raffaele. After having returned to Richmond, dined there and walked in the Park, we took stage for London."

His friends Shortt and Goodman, whose names so frequently recur in the Journal, were his school fellows at Dr. Wilkie's school. W. T. P. Shortt took his M.A. at Worcester College, Oxford. He wrote several curious books,—"Collectanea curiosa antiqua Dunmonia, or an essay on Druidical remains in Devon," "Sylva antiqua Iscana, or Roman and other antiquities of Exeter." He also wrote a History of Canada in Greek in contractions, and "A Visit to Milan, Florence." After leaving college he was gazetted to the 34th Regiment of Foot. Dr. Goodman returned to Canada and practised his profession at St. Catharines, Upper Canada.

Having said farewell to his friends in London, he left there on Saturday the 29th July, 1820. At 11 p.m. on the 1st August he embarked on board the " Amity " bound for New York, where he arrived on Sunday, the 3rd day of September.

While on his travels he assiduously attended the Courts and public assemblies of Great Britain, Ireland and France. At Westminster he saw Chief Justice Abbott, afterwards Lord Tenterden, presiding in the King's Bench with Judges Bayley, Holroyd and Best, and heard at the Bar, Sir James Scarlett, afterwards Lord Chief Baron Abinger, Sir John Campbell, afterwards Lord Chancellor, Sir John Jervis, and Peake and Pullen. At Doctor's Commons he saw Sir William Scott on the Bench and heard Dr. Lushington at the Bar. In the Four Courts at Dublin he heard Plunket, Bushe and Burton in the Chancery Court and Scott and others in the King's Bench. In the Court of Sessions at Edinburgh, he heard and saw Jeffrey, Cranstoun and Tom Clarke and the Prothonotary, Sir Walter Scott. In the House of Commons he saw Speaker Sutton and heard Brougham, Tierney, Lord Archibald Hamilton, Col. Davis and Joseph Hume. At Glasgow he heard the eloquent Dr. Chalmers in the pulpit. And on the stage he saw Macready and Kean, the comic Liston, Talma and Garcia. In the London hospitals he heard lectures by Abernethy, Millington, Sir William Blizzard, Astley Cooper and Headington.

CHAPTER IX.

1820-1825.

HE REMOVES TO MONTREAL AND BEGINS PRACTICE WITH JAMES STUART — SIR JAMES STUART — THE BENCH AND BAR OF LOWER CANADA IN 1820 — HIS SISTER'S MARRIAGE — HIS BROTHER GEORGE ARTICLED TO MR. PERRAULT — JOSEPH FRANCOIS PERRAULT — ALEXANDER'S MARRIAGE WITH MARY ANN BUCHANAN — THEIR RELATIONSHIP — PERSONS PRESENT AT THE WEDDING — HIS SUCCESS AT THE BAR — HE FORMS A PARTNERSHIP WITH SOLICITOR-GENERAL OGDEN — HON. CHARLES RICHARD OGDEN.

It was not long after his return to Canada, that he came to live in Montreal, where he now began to practise that profession, in which he became so distinguished. On the 24th May, 1821, he took out his first writ in the Court of King's Bench at Montreal, and during that year he was counsel in a number of cases.

In the October Term of that year, he figures as plaintiff, having, through O'Sullivan & Grant, sued Zabdiel Thayer for legal services. He obtained judgment on the 10th October, 1821, for £25.1.10, for "fees and disbursements of office."

In the beginning of the year 1822, he entered into partnership with Mr. James Stuart. The practice of partnership among advocates, derived from that of the Courts of England, was introduced about that time. Michael O'Sullivan and J C. Grant in 1821, were the first to inaugurate this system. Then came the firm of Stuart & Buchanan, and these examples were speedily followed by Ogden & Gugy, Beaubien & Badgley, Viger & Driscoll, Lacroix & Walker, Bédard & Mondelet, Clark & Bedard, McMillan & Rossiter, Sewell & Griffin, and others,

The firm of Stuart & Buchanan took out their first writ on the 19th January, 1822.

His partner, Mr. James Stuart, had been Solicitor-General, but having been dismissed from his office in 1809, by Sir James Craig, for being discourteous and for not having defended the policy of the Executive Government, although not now a member of the Assembly, was in active opposition to the Government. Kingsford says of him, "Mr. Stuart's superior talents would have gained him pre-eminence in any situation, and he was restrained by little scruple in the exercise of them." At this time he was forty years old, having been born in 1780. He had been admitted to the Bar in 1801, and practised at Quebec until 1805, when "at the early age of twenty-five he was appointed Solicitor-General of Lower Canada," and removed to Montreal. In 1825, he became Attorney-General, which office he held until 1830, when he was suspended by Lord Aylmer upon the report of the Standing Committee of Grievances of the Assembly recommending a petition to the King petitioning him to dismiss the Attorney-General for exacting fees on Commissions issued on the King's demise, for arrogance, and a number of other trivial complaints, and was subsequently removed from his office by Lord Goderich, the Colonial Secretary, for having exacted fees for the renewals of the Commissions of Notaries and others on the death of the King, and having, contrary to the law, inserted in the text of the Commissions "during pleasure." He was appointed Chief Justice of Lower Canada in 1838. He was created a Baronet in 1842, and died in 1853.

"Few public men," says Kingsford, "have left behind them so unenviable a reputation for haughtiness and reserve. His ability and his knowledge as a lawyer remain unimpeachable. It was said of him that he once declared that he had never read a book unless with the view of obtaining information practically of use to him. His application was great, and any subject which as a duty he studied he mastered. But he was without generous sympathy with literature, and his speeches attracted by power and force rather than by literary grace and polish. He was one of the last to whom Ovid's well-known lines could be applied:

" Ingenuas didicisse fideliter artes
Emollit mores, nec sinuit esse feros."

The partnership of Stuart & Buchanan lasted until about April, 1825, when Mr. Stuart on his appointment as Attorney-General returned to Quebec.

In the year 1820, the Bench of Lower Canada was composed of Chief Justices Monk, at

Montreal, and Sewell, at Quebec, and puisne Judges Reid, Foucher and Pyke, at Montreal, and Kerr, Bowen and Perrault, at Quebec. The Hon. Pierre Bédard was Provincial Judge at Three Rivers. Judge Ogden, who had not sat on the Bench for some years, being absent in England on leave, had just resigned, being replaced by the Advocate-General George Pyke.

The Attorney-General was Norman Fitzgerald Uniacke, and the Solicitor-General, Charles Marshall. Uniacke, son of the Hon. Richard John Uniacke, of Halifax, sometime Attorney-General of Nova Scotia, had received this appointment on June, 20, 1809, but not having given satisfaction, he was suspended in the following year by Sir James Craig. Chief Justice Sewell and Judges de Bonne and Kerr being asked to report as to his fitness for that position, reported that they considered the Attorney-General's knowledge of Criminal Law very superficial, his knowledge of the Civil Law defective, that he possessed little acquaintance of the French language, and that they did not consider him qualified for the office. Chief Justice Monk and Judges Panet and Ogden reported that they had hardly had a chance to judge of his efficiency, but they did not think he quite came up to what the Attorney General should be. Having obtained leave of absence, Uniacke went to England and being reinstated in his position returned to Montreal and held it until 1825, when he was appointed Judge of the King's

Bench in Montreal. In September, 1818, as the result of an accident in Montreal, his left leg was amputated. He sat on the Bench until 1834, when he resigned and was succeeded by Samuel Gale. He returned to Nova Scotia where he was named Judge of the Superior Court. He died on 11th December, 1846, at Halifax.

The Solicitor General, Charles Marshall, who was an Englishman and a barrister of the Inner Temple, was appointed to that office on 12th June, 1817. Sir John Coape Sherbrooke, having in 1816 dismissed Stephen Sewell for his action in publishing certain libellous documents to discredit the Government, complained to the Home Office that he could not fill the office of Solicitor General from the Bar here, and asked that a lawyer be sent from the English Bar to fill the office. Marshall, on the recommendation of Lord Chief Justice Vicary Gibbs, was sent out, and arrived in Quebec in the month of June, 1817. He was required to reside in Quebec (the Attorney General living at Montreal) and the inadequacy of his salary led to employing him in the Criminal business of the Courts. Previous to coming to Canada, he appears to have contracted an unfortunate marriage, but he did not bring his wife to Canada, nor allow her to join him here. In 1822, Uniacke, whom Marshall had hoped to succeed in his office as Attorney General, having declined to resign his office, he (Marshall) obtained leave of absence and returned to England, and does not appear to have come back to Canada.

The Advocate General was George Vanfelson, appointed on the 28th January, 1819. "He was given a dinner by the Gentlemen of the Bar on the 6th February, 1819, at Mailhot's Hotel (at Quebec) on his appointment."

In 1820 the only King's Counsel were David Ross, of Quebec, Alexis Caron and C. R. Ogden. The following gentlemen were subsequently appointed to this rank in the order named: J. T. Taschereau in 1821, the first French Canadian to receive this rank of distinction; Pierre Vezina, of Three Rivers, in 1824; J. R. Vallières de St. Réal, in 1825; Stephen Sewell, who had been Solicitor General, in 1827; A. W. Cochran and Joseph Bédard in 1828; Michael O'Sullivan, Frederic Auguste Quesnel and Philipe Panet, in 1831; Dominique Mondelet, in 1833; A. D. Bostwick, of Three Rivers, James Charles Grant, who died the year after his appointment, Alexander Buchanan and Jean Francois Joseph Duval, in 1835; and in 1836, Henry Black, of Quebec, was the last to receive the patent of King's Counsel. These names represented the leaders of the Bar of Lower Canada during the years 1816 to 1835. But mention must be made of the following lawyers, who, although not honored with this mark of distinction, were eminent at the Bar: Andrew Stuart, at one time Solicitor General; Louis Plamondon, John Fletcher, afterwards a Judge for St. Francis; Louis

Moquin, and B. C. A. Gugy, at Quebec, and Samuel Gale, Denis B. Viger, Jean R. Rolland, Toussaint Peltier, William Walker, C. C. S. de Bleury, C. S. Cherrier, and Louis Hypolite Lafontaine, at Montreal.

The Duke of Richmond, from whom Alexander had received his commission of advocate, died in August, 1819, and was succeeded by the Earl of Dalhousie, who held office of Governor General for eight years until 1828.

On the 3rd November, 1820, Alexander's sister Jane was married to Captain William Hall. They were married at Quebec by the Revd. James Harkness, of St. Andrew's Church, and Mr. J. F. Perrault signed the Register. The following letter speaks for itself:—

Monsieur & Ami, QUEBEC, le 31, 8re, 1820.

J'ai réglé le compte de votre sœur sur le même pied que j'ai établi le vôtre & il lui revient les sommes suivantes à prendre sur

Intérêt à compter du 9, 9vre, 1820. M. John White, appliqué sur la maison de feu votre père...............	£1000.
Intérêt à compter du 28, 8re, 1820. M. John Ross, sur le prêt de £500, son 1/3........................	166.13. 4
M. J. Fr. X., fils, les effets achetés a l'encan de feu votre père........	58.13.11
Intérêt à compter du 1, 9re, 1820. Moi même pr. reliquat de compte de tutelle...........................	246.13. 7
Total	£1472. 0.10

ce qui donnera une rente annuelle de £88.6.5½ à votre sœur, si vous jugez convenable de laisser ces differentes sommes à intérêt comme vous m'avez paru désirer d'en faire une clause dans son contrat de mariage, Je vous envoye ce détail pour l'etablir plus certainement correctivement.

J'ai l'honneur d'être avec considération,
Votre affectioné serviteur et ami,

J. F. Perrault.

M. Alex. Buchanan,
Avocat, Présent.

By her contract of marriage referred to and passed "at the dwelling house of the above named Joseph Francois Perrault in the said City of Quebec, in the afternoon of the 3rd November, 1820" her brother Alexander, Andrew Stuart, Advocate, and Henry Black, Advocate, who were all parties to the deed, were appointed Trustees to receive certain claims and invest the proceeds for her benefit.

The venerable Perrault evidently had a desire to have his wedding present to Jane placed on record and be known to posterity, for the deed solemnly sets forth "and the said Joseph Francois Perrault, for and in consideration of the affection which he beareth towards the said Jane Buchanan doth hereby give unto the said Jane Buchanan in token thereof, a tea pot, cream ewer and sugar dish, all of silver plate, hereof accepting the said Jane Buchanan by and with the authority of the said Joseph Francois Perrault."

On the 19th July, 1821, Alexander Buchanan, on the advice of a family council of himself and John Buchanan, brothers, and William Hall, brother-in-law, Andrew Stuart, Jos. Fr. X. Perrault, junior, Edward Burroughs and Henry Black, friends of George Buchanan, was appointed by Mr. Justice Bowen tutor to him to pass his articles of clerkship for the profession of the law with Mr. J. F. Perrault. The application to the Court for the necessary authority to pass the indentures was made by Mr. Perrault and recites that George Buchanan, minor, of the age of sixteen years in August, 1821, has had a liberal education, which puts him in a position to aspire to the profession of advocate, attorney, and solicitor in this Province, or of Prothonotary— that it is necessary to pass a *brevet* to this effect with some qualified person of the profession—that his revenues are only annually £30, and consequently too slight to provide for his keep and board, and that it will be necessary to find some one of the profession who would be willing to charge himself with his "logement, chauffage et nourriture" for his work, and permit him to retain his thirty pounds current for his keep, without touching his capital of £500—and therefore, if some one of the Bar wish to accept this condition that Mr. Perrault be authorized to pass the deed of apprenticeship of George Buchanan with such person, if not, that there be named a tutor to pass with him articles. The articles were signed at Quebec on the 31 July, 1821, at which time Alexander is described as of Montreal.

Mr. Perrault whose, name occurs so frequently in these proceedings, was for many years Prothonotary of the Court of King's Bench at Quebec. He was born in 1753, and commenced the study of the law in 1790, with Maitre Mézières, advocate, at Montreal. He had almost completed his term of apprenticeship with M. Mézières, when that gentleman died. The Legislative Council having rejected a bill dispensing with the six months that remained to be completed, he was on the 8th May, 1795, appointed with David Lynd, Prothonotary of the King's Bench and Clerk of the Peace and Sessions at Quebec. He died on the 5th April, 1844, aged 91 years.

The account of tutorship rendered by Mr. Perrault is interesting as showing life in Quebec in the early part of the century.

The very first item is "pr. autant que Jane a perdu au jeu chez M. Vanfelson, o.2.6," yet Jane was only sixteen at the time. She had evidently come out in society in 1816, for in that year there is an entry "donné à Jane pour souliers, rubans, gands, et à elle pr. le bal de la reine £1.0.0." In 1817 she went to a ball at the Chateau, and in 1818 to a ball at Mr. Duchesnay's. In the latter year she went into mourning for the Princess Charlotte. These items explain themselves:— in 1818, "donné à Jane 4/- neuf pr. marquerau wist." In 1819, "donné à Jane pr. payer le charetier qui l'amene du bal du chateau, o.2.9." In August, 1819, she was given £2.10.0. for her trip to Varennes in the steamboat as far as Sorel, 7/6 for her half of a caleche from Sorel to Varennes, the same to return from Varennes to Sorel, and £2.5. for the steamboat to come down. In March, 1820, M. Baby gave a ball to which she went. Jane was educated at the Ursuline Convent, at Quebec, where she made her first communion as a Catholic, but on her marriage to Captain Hall, she returned to the Protestant Church.

The account also contains the expenses for George:—

In 1816 he was taking lessons in dancing. He also went to a French school in Quebec. In May, 1817, the sum of £27.1.9 was paid to Mr. Wilkie for six months' school tuition for George; in November of the same year £28.8.0, and in February following £14.5.0; 11 May, 1818, £12.12.6 for one quarter, and in November, £21.13.2. During the summer of 1817, Alexander went on a trip to Brandy Pots. Jane was in Montreal and George went to Rivière Ouelle, probably on a visit to the Perraults.

Previous to the 1st of April, 1819, Mr. Perrault settled George's affairs with his brother Alexander, and on that date appears to have opened a new and special account for him.

In 1821, George was attending the dancing school of M. Provendie, mtre. de danse, and in

1822, that of M. Rod, who charged ten shillings a month. About July, 1822, having taken lessons in navigation from Capt. Wm. Hutton, for which he paid £2.0.0., he appears to have left Canada on a sea voyage, and seems to have been a long time absent for his name does not appear again until 1828, when apparently he returned, for on the 7th June of that year there is an entry of two pounds having been paid him for his voyage to Montreal.

On the 22nd October, 1829, Mr. Perrault settled his account, at which time George was presumably in Quebec.

On the 22nd July, 1822, by deed of "déliverance de legs," passed at Montreal, "Alexander Buchanan, Esquire, of the said City of Montreal, Advocate, acting as well for himself and for and in the name and on behalf of his brother John Buchanan, of Hawkesbury, in the Province of Upper Canada, Gentleman, duly authorized to this effect by Letter of Attorney, and Jane Buchanan, wife of William Hall, also of said Montreal, Master of the Steamboat "New Swiftsure," hereunto authorized by her said husband, also party hereto, universal residuary legatees of the late John Buchanan, Esquire, in his lifetime of the City of Quebec, in the said Province, Surgeon," transferred to George Buchanan, accepting by Francois Xavier Bender, of Montreal, Advocate, the sum of £500, as the last instalment of the price of £3,500. currency due by John White for the house and premises situated in Parloir Street, in the Upper Town of the City of Quebec. The sale of this property led to a lawsuit. In 1823, Alexander Buchanan, John Buchanan, William Hall, and Jane Mary Buchanan, his wife, brought an action in the Court of King's Bench at Quebec, against John White and James McCallum for £2,000., two instalments of the purchase price of £3,500., currency, due 9th May, 1819, and 9th May, 1821, and against Joseph Francois Perrault for a deliverance of all the real and personal property of their father Dr. John Buchanan. The Court of King's Bench, on the 20th of June, 1823 gave judgment in favor of the Plaintiffs. In this case Stuart & Black acted for the Plaintiffs and Mr. Vallières de St. Réal for the Defendants. This judgment was confirmed in the Provincial Court of Appeals on the 20th November, 1823, and by the Privy Council on the 28th April, 1828.

On the 31st January, 1824, Mr. Buchanan's name is found as godfather to the son of his partner, James Stuart, who was named Charles James, and became Sir Charles James Stuart, Baronet.

---

(1) Sir Charles Stuart, Baronet, died on the 25th February, 1901, at 98 Eaton Square, London, aged 77 years. He was buried at Brompton Cemetery. His only sister, Mary Stuart, died on the 2nd of March, 1901, at her late brother's residence. The following appeared in "The Times" of March 1st, 1901:—

"Sir Charles Stuart, second Baronet, died at his residence in Eaton Square, on Monday, aged 77. Educated at University College, Oxford, where he graduated in 1845; he was called to the Bar at the Inner Temple in 1848, and succeeded his father, who was Chief Justice of Lower Canada, in 1853. Sir Charles Stuart, is

On the 2nd of March, 1824, Alexander Buchanan married Mary Ann, the eldest daughter of James Buchanan, British Consul at New York.

The following statement of James Buchanan shews the exact relationship which existed between Doctor John Buchanan and himself:—

"My daughter, Mary Ann," James Buchanan writes, "married Alexander Buchanan, Q.C., whose father was Physician to the Forces at Quebec, whose grandfather and my father were cousins by my mother's side, his father named John, the grandfather Alexander, and resided at Fintona."

Mary Ann Buchanan was born at Farmhill, near Omagh, on the 11th June, 1802, and was thus twenty-two years old at the time of her marriage.

The wedding took place at the Manhattan Bank House, Bowery Hill, at New York, They were married by the Reverend Doctor Jonathan Mayhew Wainwright, Rector of Grace Church, New York. Doctor Wainwright afterwards became Rector of Trinity Church, Boston, and then Bishop of New York.

Among the relations and guests present were Mr. and Mrs. James Buchanan, their children, Robert Stewart, John Stewart, Oliver William (only 4 years old), Jane, Sarah, Elizabeth, Maria,

---

himself succeeded by his brother Major-General Edward Andrew Stuart, who was born in 1832, served in the Crimea where he was severely wounded, and in the China war of 1860, was Lieutenant-Governor of Chelsea Hospital from 1855 to 1860, and is Colonel of the Royal Scots (Lothian Regiment)."

MARY ANN BUCHANAN.

Isabella, and Amelia, and their friends Emily Neilson, Elizabeth Neilson, Caroline Black, Matilda Few, Catharine F. Stuyvesant, E. M. Munroe, Susan de Lancey, Juliana Gouverneur, Julia M. Lambert, Margaret Turnbull, Martha Glover, M. P. Carey, S. E. Perkins, Mr. and Mrs. Cadwallader D. Colden, Thomas William Moore, David R. Lambert, M. Munroe, Thomas Proctor, Thomas G. Carey, Samuel Glover, Francis Stoughton, James Munroe, Junior, Peter Stuyvesant and Thomas Frost.

Alexander Buchanan was now fast making a name for himself in his profession, in which he was eminently successful and soon took his place as a leader at the Montreal Bar.

About October, 1824, he entered into partnership with the Hon. Charles Richard Ogden, then Solicitor-General.

Ogden, who was a son of Judge Isaac Ogden, was the senior of Alexander Buchanan both in years and at the Bar by seven years. He was born in 1791, and, having studied law at Montreal, was admitted to the Bar in 1812. In 1816, not four years after his call to the Bar, he was appointed a King's Counsel, being the fourth lawyer of Lower Canada to receive that honour. He first practised at Three Rivers, and in 1818 was appointed to act as Attorney-General and Solicitor-General for the District of Three Rivers. In 1824 he was appointed Solicitor-General of Lower Canada, when he removed to Montreal and "entered into partnership with Mr. Buchanan of that City. The firm soon became eminent in the profession, and the members of it enjoyed a very large and lucrative practice." In 1833, Mr. Ogden was advanced to the office of Attorney-General, when he removed to Quebec. He was Attorney-General until 1842, when he went to England, where he died in 1866.

CHAPTER X.

1825–1835.

THE FIRM OF OGDEN & BUCHANAN — OF BUCHANAN & ANDREWS — HIS CASES — THE BROTHERS-IN-LAW CLUB — FOUNDATION OF THE ADVOCATES LIBRARY — HE IS ITS FIRST SECRETARY — REPORT OF COMMITTEE AS TO THE STUDY FOR THE BAR — THE MONTREAL COMMITTEE — HE IS MASTER OF ST. PAUL'S LODGE — DEATH OF WILLIAM BUCHANAN OF YAMASKA — MARRIAGE OF ANN BUCHANAN TO HENRY McFARLANE.

The firm of Ogden & Buchanan did an active business until 1833, when, as has been said, Mr. Ogden left Montreal to live at Quebec. About March, 1832, Henry Ogden Andrews had become a partner in the firm of Ogden, Buchanan & Andrews, and when Mr. Ogden retired, the firm became Buchanan & Andrews and remained so until 1841, when the firm of Buchanan & Johnson came into existence. In 1851, Mr. Buchanan was in partnership with John Bleakley and H. O. Andrews, the firm then being Buchanan, Bleakley & Andrews.

Mr. Buchanan conducted many important cases involving grave questions of law, and not a few of these cases went to the Privy Council. But owing to the absence of any regular reports of the decisions of the Courts of Lower Canada during his practice, only very slight information is obtainable concerning his cases. The case of Dorion vs. Dorion was among the first of importance in which he was engaged. This was an action *petitio haereditatis* by which the Plaintiffs claimed that the Defendants had taken possession of the Estate of Jacques Dorion, without any legal authority for so doing. Stuart & Buchanan were for the Plaintiffs and Mr. B. Beaubien and Mr. Samuel Gale appeared for the several Defendants. The case was argued in the King's Bench in Montreal in 1822, and that Court, in 1824, decided that the property, of which no disposition had been made in the Will of the Testator, belonged to the Plaintiffs. The Plaintiffs were not satisfied with this judgment and appealed to the Court of Appeals at Quebec, which Court, in 1828, reversed the judgment; Stuart & Buchanan for the Appellants, Mr. Beaubien with Mr. Vallières de St. Réal for the Respondents. The case then went to the Privy Council and there both the former judgments were reversed and the case sent back in order that certain parties might be added to the record. This case was before the Courts as late as 1857, when it was finally decided in the Superior Court in Montreal. By that time the parties originally in the case as well as their counsel had all passed away, and Mr. C. S. Cherrier, Q.C., and Mr. A. A. Dorion (the late Chief Justice Sir Antoine Dorion) acted for the representatives of the Plaintiffs, and the firm of Leblanc and Cassidy for the Defendants.

The first mention of Buchanan's name in the law reports is in 1823 on the Appeal of John Scott and others and the Phœnix Assurance Co. This appeal arose out of an interlocutory order of the Court of King's Bench at Montreal, in an action of covenant upon a policy of insurance by which that Court assumed the power of compelling the parties to submit the matters in contest between them to arbitrators, thereby enforcing the specific execution of the clause or condition in the policy under which the parties had agreed that, in case any difference or dispute should arise touching any loss or damage, such difference was to be submitted to the judgment and determination of arbitrators.

Buchanan for the Appellant argued that in three distinct points of view the Court below had acted unwarrantably in referring the matters in issue between the parties to arbitrators:—

1. That considering the terms in which the condition was couched it appeared, evidently, to have been the intention of the parties that the submission to arbitration should be dependent on the free will of the parties, but if the parties did submit, that the award to be made should be obligatory.

2. That even a submission to arbitration is a revocable instrument and is assimilated to a power of attorney; *a fortiori*, an agreement to submit can-

not bind irrevocably. And a party refusing *stare compromisso* could be made liable only to a penalty agreed upon, or to assessed damages. In accordance with which is the principle of the French law declaring that the courts cannot decree a specific performance.

3. That the King cannot, by an agreement between any two or more of his subjects, be divested of his prerogative of judicial supremacy the exercise of which he had delegated to his courts of justice. That those courts have accordingly held that a mere agreement of persons to submit matters in dispute between them to arbitration cannot oust the courts of their jurisdiction, nor deprive the contracting parties of their right of resorting to the royal tribunals for the adjustment of their controversies.

John Fletcher, afterwards Judge Fletcher, followed on the same side and Thomas Gugy with Andrew Stuart represented the Respondents. On the 20th of January, 1823, the Court of Appeals presided by Chief Justice Sewell maintained the Appeal and held that under a clause or condition in policies of insurance, that in case of any dispute between the parties it should be referred to arbitration, the courts are not ousted of their jurisdiction, nor could they compel the parties to submit to a reference in the progress of the suit.

The case was then tried on the merits in the Court of King's Bench, and on the 20th of June, 1825, that Court, composed of Judges Reid, Foucher and Pyke gave judgment in favor of the Plaintiffs, but this judgment, being appealed to the Court of Appeals, was, on the 20th of January, 1826, reversed, and the Plaintiffs' action dismissed on an objection raised for the first time when the case was in Appeal, on the ground that the certificate called for in the policy of insurance was insufficient. From this judgment the Plaintiffs appealed to the Privy Council, but unsuccessfully, for that body, on the 13th May, 1829, confirmed the judgment of the Court of Appeals dismissing the action. In the Privy Council, Mr. Brougham argued the Appeal.

The next case mentioned in the law reports, is that of Fleming & the Seminary of Montreal, which excited great interest. The proper title of the case was Messire Jean H. A. Roux et al vs. William Fleming. The facts were as follows:—

In 1821 the Gentlemen Ecclesiastics of the Seminary of Montreal brought action against William Fleming, of Lachine, complaining that he had illegally erected a windmill at Lachine and that as Seigneurs they had the exclusive rights to operate windmills on the Island of Montreal, and asked that he be ordered to demolish this windmill. The Seminary was represented by Stephen Sewell, and Stuart & Buchanan acted for Fleming.

In 1822 the Court of King's Bench maintained the Plaintiffs in quiet and peaceable possession and enjoyment of the right of Banalité in the

Seigniory of the Island of Montreal, and ordered the Defendant to demolish the windmill in such manner only as to prevent the windmill from grinding wheat or grain of any sort or kind into flour or meal. This case was of great importance, as the corporate existence of the Seminary of Montreal was involved and its competency to exercise Seigniorial rights over the Island of Montreal denied, and from the judgment of the Court of King's Bench, Fleming appealed to the Court of Appeals.

The Appeal was argued in the Court of Appeals at Quebec in the term of January, 1824, before the President of that Court, Sir F. N. Burton, Lieutenant-Governor, Chief Justice Jonathan Sewell, and the Honourables John Richardson, A. L. J. Duchesnay, H. M. Percival, Oliver Perrault, W. B. Coltman and William Smith, and five days were taken up with the hearing, but no decision was rendered, and on the 20th of January, 1824, the Court being then equally divided, ordered a rehearing. In the term of January, 1825, Mr. Louis Moquin for the Respondents obtained a rule upon the Appellants to show cause why the opinions of two members of the Court, namely, Chief Justice Sewell and the Honourable William Smith, brothers-in-law, who were in favor of maintaining the Appeal and dismissing the action, should not be reckoned as one, and why judgment should not accordingly be rendered by an affirmance of the judgment of the Court below. Bédard and Vallières de St. Real, Counsel for the Respondents, argued in support of the rule, which Buchanan for the Appellant resisted, and on the 18th of January, 1825, the Court "having taken time to consider of its judgment made an order that the Respondents should take nothing by the rule."

The case seems to have there dropped, as there is no record of a rehearing having taken place. The late John Fraser, in his Pen and Ink Sketches refers to the case and says:—

"FLEMING'S WINDMILL. — This old windmill is a standing monument to the memory of a determined, stubborn Scotchman—'that indignant spirit of the North,'—in resisting the pretensions of the wealthiest, the greatest corporation in Lower Canada, to prevent him building his mill.

When the late Mr. Fleming commenced the building of his mill for the manufacture of oatmeal, the gentlemen of the Seminary of St. Sulpice, as Seigneurs of the Island of Montreal, claimed that they alone had the right of building mills of any description. Mr. Fleming thought differently; he admitted if they controlled the water privileges their charter gave them no control over the 'winds of Heaven' nor of any other power a man may utilize for the purpose of running his mill.

A long lawsuit was the result, the late Mr. Buchanan, K.C., was Mr. Fleming's legal adviser. We forget exactly how this case ended. It is all in the law reports. We believe, however, that the Seminary, after a long contest, allowed the matter to drop and permitted Mr. Fleming to finish his mill. The old mill stands firm and solid with its four wings but without any sails, as it has not been used for the past thirty years. It looks like a Martello tower and may stand for centuries; a monument to the memory of a determined Scotchman."

In 1827 Ogden & Buchanan took out an action which was destined to go to the Privy Council This was the celebrated case of Donegani vs. Donegani.

In the year 1794, Jean Donegani the elder, and his wife, both of them Italians by birth, emigrated from Moltrazio, in Lombardy, to Lower Canada. They brought with them four children, viz: three sons, Jean the younger, Joseph and Daniel, and one daughter, Thérèse. All these children had been born in Italy. Thérèse married Joseph Donegani, and she had by him three children, Jean Antoine, Joseph and Guillaume Antoine, who were all born in Canada, and became her heirs at her death, in 1807. Jean Donegani, the elder, and his wife, having amassed considerable property, returned to Moltrazio, and died there in 1809, having by his will and codicil, both made at Montreal, left a legacy of £500 to his daughter Thérèse, and the residue of his real and personal property to his wife for life, and after her death one half of it to his son Joseph, and the other half equally between his other two sons Jean and Daniel.

In 1815, upon the death of his mother, Joseph Donegani took possession of the real estate at Montreal. In February, 1827, Jean Antoine, Joseph and Guillaume Antoine Donegani, the children of Thérèse Donegani brought their action in the Court of King's Bench at Montreal, as the grandchildren and sole heirs at law of Jean Donegani against their uncle Joseph Donegani for the recovery of this property which they claimed by reason of their birth within the dominions of His Majesty, and their being the only legal heirs of their grandfather, to the exclusion of their uncle Joseph Donegani, and their other uncles, whose character of aliens, they contended, rendered them incapable of taking any portion of the property of their deceased parent, either by right of inheritance or by devise.

The arguments of the Counsel in the King's Bench as given in the report of this case are very interesting. Buchanan argued for the Plaintiffs and the brilliant William Walker with Mondelet for the Defendants.

The Court of King's Bench maintained the Plaintiffs' action, holding that an alien can purchase and acquire, as also dispose of his property by deed of sale, deed of gift *inter vivos* or otherwise, but he could not devise by last will, and the legal right to the entire estate devolved to Jean

Antoine Donegani and his brothers as lineally descended from the grandfather.

Joseph Donegani appealed from this judgment to the Court of Appeals of Lower Canada, which, in 1832, affirmed it with costs. In the Court of Appeals Duval and Vallières de St. Real, both of whom were afterwards Chief Justices, acted for the Appellants and Ogden and Buchanan for the Respondents. He then appealed from the latter judgment to the King in Council. In the Privy Council Joseph Donegani was represented by Sir John Campbell, K.C., and Dr. Lushington, and Jean Antoine Donegani and his brothers by Coltman, K.C., and Jacob, K.C., and in 1835, the appeal was dismissed with costs, and the principle that the *droit d'aubaine* became the law of Lower Canada, with regard to aliens, on the ancient French Law being established there was affirmed. The Judges in the Privy Council were Vice-Chancellor Sir Lancelot Shadwell, Mr. Baron Parke and Mr. T. Bosanquet, Chief Judge of the Court of Bankruptcy.

In the Appeal of Russell and Field in 1833, he acted for the Appellants. This was an action instituted by the Appellants against the Respondent, to which was pleaded the pendency of another suit between the same parties, and for the same cause of action, in the State of Vermont. This plea was maintained by the judgment of the Court below, which gave rise to the appeal. In the King's Bench the Plaintiffs had been represented

by Fisher & Smith, and the Defendant by John
Boston, but, in the Court of Appeals, Buchanan
& Andrews acted for the Appellants and W. K.
McCord for the Respondent. The Appeal was
argued by Buchanan and the grounds upon which
this judgment was impugned were, that whether
such respect should be shown to litispendance in
a foreign country, as to suffer it to bar or suspend
a suit, was a question of public law, and so should
be decided by the laws of England, as a paramount
authority throughout the Empire. According to
the principles of English jurisprudence, litispendance in a foreign country, or even in one of the
colonies, could not be pleaded in any way to an
action in the courts of Westminster Hall. Upon
the supposition that this were a case to be governed
by the practice of the French courts, litispendance in a foreign country could not be pleaded,
as France was distinguished from most of the
states of Europe by her showing no regard for
foreign jurisprudence. Viewing the plea of litispendance abroad, in its true light, as ascertained
by force of obligation, but *ex comitate* the basis
of that country, which is reciprocity, would fail
in the present instance, as in the state of Vermont,
and the other United States of America, litispendance in a foreign country or even in a sister state
could not be pleaded to an action brought
there. The Court of Appeals reversed the judgment of the Court below and held that litis-

pendance in a foreign state is no bar to an action instituted in this Province. The unfortunate Respondent, William H. Field, quite a young man, had an unhappy ending. He had been arrested for debt at the instance of Messrs. Hector Russel & Co., in January, 1833, and was detained in the Montreal gaol, where he committed suicide in December, 1833.

On the appeal of William Maitland and John Molson, in which judgment was rendered in 1830, Stephen Sewell, K.C., was Counsel for the Appellants, and Solicitor-General Ogden and Buchanan for the Respondents. This was an action resulting from a collision between the steamboats "New Swiftsure" and "Hercules."

In 1845 we find him with F. G. Johnson, Counsel for the Appellant in the appeal of Lemesurier vs. Hart Logan. The Court decided in favor of his contention that, upon the sale of goods by admensuration which may happen to be destroyed before measurement, the loss is cast upon the seller.

The last case of importance mentioned in the reports is the case of The Quebec Fire Assurance Co. vs. Molson and St. Louis which arose out of the destruction in 1843 of the Church at Boucherville, from fire caused by sparks from the chimneys of the steamboat "St. Louis" belonging to John Molson. This case was decided in the Privy Council in 1851.

In the year 1827 Dr. Wilkie started a newspaper, "The Star," at Quebec. Amongst those who contributed articles to this paper were Andrew Stuart, Judge Fletcher and Alexander Buchanan. "The Star," the first number of which appeared in December of that year, lasted for three years. The following extract is from a note to "A View of the Civil Government and Administration of Justice in the Province of Canada While it was Subject to the Crown of France," which is reprinted in the first volume of the Lower Canada Jurist:—

"On what ground the VIEW was attributed in 'The Star' to Chief Justice Hey, I know not; but as the proprietor and chief editor of that paper —the late Rev. Dr. Wilkie—was no ordinary man in literature, was scrupulously exact in every statement of facts, and ranked among the contributors to and supporters of his paper, such men as the late Andrew Stuart, Judge Fletcher, Alexander Buchanan, and one or two living legal characters of almost equal note, whose means and opportunities of obtaining correct information, on all such subjects, were of the best description, I think it highly probable, that the point of authorship of the VIEW being in Chief Justice Hey, was clearly ascertained, before it was allowed to be stated in so positive a manner in a paper of such high repute and generally acknowledged correctness as 'The Star.' It is possible, however, that the VIEW and PLAN embodied in it, may have formed the Report adopted by Governor Carleton and his Council, from which both the Chief Justice and Attorney General Maseres dissented."

F.G.

Jan., 1857.

Alexander Buchanan belonged to the Brothers-in-Law Club at Montreal, composed exclusively of lawyers, hence its name. It existed from about 1827 to 1833, and among its members were: Samuel Gale, William Walker, William Badgley, John S. McCord and Henry Griffin. The Club was essentially a social and convivial association, each member being obliged to provide a certain number of bottles of wine. The bets and fines were also paid in wine. The following is an extract from a charming article entitled "The Old Clubs of Montreal," which appeared in "Harper's Weekly" for the 16th February, 1901, written by the late Mr. William McLennan, Notary, of Montreal.

"After the Beavers, the Grey Beards, and the Bachelors came the Brothers-in-Law, the last of the old dining clubs. This was the outcome of a dinner at a tavern at Cote des Neiges on the last day of February, 1827, when a number of lawyers proposed and founded the Order, fifteen in number, to dine together six times during the year. The members sent their contributions of food and wine before them, being especially careful as to the quality. The entrance fee was six bottles.

"In the minutes we find that Mr. Walker, Q.C., having lost a wager of a hat or six bottles of wine, at the option of the winner, the late Judge Gale, the latter generously presented the result to the club, whereupon it was resolved that the loser should be held 'to procure a hat of the shape worn by Spanish cavaliers, to be worn by the president of the day during the transaction of public business, and to be thereafter considered the property of the society.

"When the late Judge McCord 'positively declared his inability to sing he was permitted to escape on drinking two bumpers.' Henry Griffin, first Notary of the Bank of Montreal, presented the Club with a snuff-box on the 20th June, 1829. John Molson, Sr., presented the club on the 10th March, 1832, with a leg of mutton raised on Boucherville Islands; 'never was such a leg seen on this side of the Atlantic—in truth 'twas 'Mister John's Leg.' Before it was half consumed the Brothers-in-Law were unanimously of opinion that the man who can raise such mutton is worthy of a seat at His Majesty's Council for the Province of Lower Canada.

"Their last meeting was held on the 20th February, 1833. Only four members were present, and the secretary, paraphrasing King Henry, remarks, 'The fewer men, the greater share of honor,' and adds, 'The delinquent members were considered too bad to be fined.' "

In the month of February, 1828, was founded the Advocates Library under the patronage of the Honorable James Reid, Chief Justice of the District of Montreal, on the suggestion of Stephen Sewell, K.C., who drafted the original prospectus of the Association which was signed by Chief Justice Reid and four puisne Judges of the Court of King's Bench for the District of Montreal. The Officers of the Association were:—

Stephen Sewell, K.C.	President.
Joseph Bédard, Esq.	Vice-President.
Charles R. Ogden, Esq., Sol. General	
Alex. Buchanan, Esq	Managing Committee.
John S. McCord, Esq	
Alex. Buchanan, Esq	Secretary.
Fred. Griffin, Esq	Treasurer.

By the laws of the Government of the Advocates Library each original member was to pay towards the purposes of the institution the sum of ten pounds currency. Each member was obliged "on the last juridical day in October Term of each year to pay to the Treasurer of the Society the sum of £2.10.0 currency."

On the dissolution in April, 1828, of the Students Law Library Association, which had been established a few years before, the books which formed their library were presented gratuitously to the Advocates Library.

Chief Justice Reid, having by letter dated the 18th August, 1830, to the Advocates Library, made certain suggestions as to the qualifications of candidates for admission to the Bar, a Committee composed of Stephen Sewell, K.C., Solicitor-General Ogden, K.C., Hon. Dominique Mondelet and Alexander Buchanan were appointed in October, 1830, to report on a system of education for the study of the profession of the Law and Regulations for the admission to the study and practice of the law. The Report of this Committee was drafted by Alexander Buchanan and is signed by the members of the Committee.

The Report is in the following terms:—

"The Committee appointed on   day of October instant, having taken into consideration the suggestions contained in the Honorable the Chief Justice's letter of the 18th August, 1830, addressed to S. Sewell, Esq., beg leave to report their sentiments upon the subjects thus submitted for their enquiry.

The undersigned conceive that at this period any formal or express regulation, having for its object a scrutiny into the qualifications of persons presenting themselves as students to any of the members of this Association, would appear invidious in the eyes of the rest of the Bar, and excite umbrage in our brethren of the profession who have not chosen to become associates in this institution. At the same time they feel conscious that none of the members of this institution would so far lose sight of their own respectability and be so regardless of their duty to the profession as to become instrumental in rearing to the Bar persons likely to reflect disgrace upon the profession, or as to withhold any uniform information by which the unworthiness of a candidate for the study of the Law might be made known to the gentlemen at whose hands instruction may be sought by such individual.

The second matter for enquiry is how far it may be expedient to draw up a plan or system of study to be observed by the young gentlemen studying under the auspices of the members of this institution, and to take measures for ascertaining occasionally the progress made by such pupils.

That such a regulation is practicable little doubt can be entertained; yet the undersigned conceive that it would be more advisable to leave such advocate to prescribe the course of study to be followed by his pupils which must in many instances be varied according to the education, knowledge and capacity of individuals. And they would add that the main advantages of such a regulation will naturally flow from the adoption of modes of instruction of a more public nature as hereafter recommended.

The Honorable the Chief Justice further suggests that a system should be arranged for the examination of candidates coming forward to the profession to be varied according to circumstances.

Without the participation of the rest of the Bar which constitutes a majority of that body, the undersigned think that the establishment of any express regulation co-extensive with the suggestion of the Hon. the Chief Justice might excite in our other brethren of the Bar a feeling of hostility against our institution, which it should be our desire to prevent if possible. It cannot, however, be dissembled that if an understanding could be produced among the brethren of our institution by which a more strict examination of candidates for the Bar shall be had, some benefit to the profession may result, although the undersigned are of opinion that the respectability of the profession and that science among its members would be more effectually promoted by an examination into the education and qualifications of an individual before he becomes a pupil than by canvassing his proficiency in legal learning when he is on the eve of being called to the Bar, and they cannot but regret that the state of the profession, from the want of that examination which can only be the offspring of incorporation, precludes the possibility of subjecting the would-be pupil to this test.

The last suggestion of the Hon. Chief Justice consists in recommending the translation into English of some approved work on the Civil Law, giving a certain portion of the work to such of the members as might be willing to undertake it so that at the appointed meetings it might be examined and approved; the Chief Justice at the same time expressing his fear that it might be impracticable to get up anything in the shape of lectures.

The Committee cannot but highly appreciate the motives that prompted the Hon. the Chief Justice to recommend to the institution the adoption of means for encouraging the study of the Civil Law which constitutes the basis not only of our jurisprudence but of the codes of most civilized nations, without a competent language of which professional education in this country must be deemed incomplete. They therefore think that this institution should pursue measures to promote the study of that branch of the Law; but they humbly conceive that the plan proposed by His Honor the Chief Justice of parcelling out notes upon the Civil Law for translation would hardly attain the desired end; nor would the unequal and heterogeneous admixture of style in composition thus written redound much to the credit of the institution.

With all due deference to the opinion of the Chief Justice the Committee humbly lay before this institution their thoughts upon the best modes of reaching the object brought to its consideration by the letter of the Chief Justice, which they embody in the following propositions:—

1. That the style and name of the institution be altered by adding to the original name "Advocates Library" the words "and Law Institute."

2. That the institution under its new name do by all means in its power promote the science of the Law by the delivery of prolections or lectures upon its various departments, the writing of dissertations and of translations, and by offering honorary distinctions or rewards for contribution of essays upon subjects to be chosen and given out at stated periods.

3. That the subjects of the lectures to be established be as nearly as possible made to fall within the following classification: 1. Natural Law; Roman Law; 2. French Customary and Ecclesiastical Law; 3. Criminal Law of England and Constitutional Law; 4. English Law of Real Estate property, and 5. the Law of Practice and Evidence, which five departments include every possible topic of legal discussion.

4. That once in every year a medal or other mark of distinction be offered for the best essay upon any given subject relating to jurisprudence, and that all persons, advocates or students in this Province be permitted to compete for the same.

5. That the members of the institution, as soon as circumstances may permit, do cause prolections upon the said several classes to be pronounced by such of the associates as may be willing to undertake the honorable and useful task, and that no persons but the members of this institute, and their pupils shall be admitted on the occasion of such prolections.

6. That for the purposes of enabling this Institute to effect the said intentions, a fund be formed to defray its necessary expenses to be raised by an annual subscription of 15 shillings, and first payable on the 1st January next.

7. That this institute be under the direction and management of the respective officers governing the Library for the time being.

All of which is nevertheless submitted."

On the 28th December, 1832, Alexander Buchanan was installed Worshipful Master of Saint Paul's Lodge, No. 514, now No. 374 on the Registry of England, held at Montreal. He had been Secretary in 1829, Junior Warden in 1830, Senior Warden in 1831. In 1834 he was one of the Permanent Committee.

It may be interesting to know that five others of the family have been members of that Lodge, viz:—

> Alexander Carlisle Buchanan (brother-in-law) in 1833.
> Wentworth James Buchanan (son), in 1855.
> Alexander Buchanan (grandson), in 1892.
> Arthur William Patrick Buchanan (grandson) in 1894.
> Rupert Charles Buchanan (grandson), in 1903.

William Buchanan, the Consul's brother, who lived in the Parish of St. Michel d'Yamaska, where he had steam mills, died of cholera at Montreal, on the 16th August, 1834, aged 44 years.

The following is taken from "A Topographical Dictionary of the Province of Lower Canada," by Joseph Bouchette, published in London, in 1832, in the 3rd volume under the name "YAMASKA."

"In front of the seigniory are the isles du Moine, aux Raisins, &c. In the mouth of the river is the large island St. Jean, entirely covered with wood, some of it is of good quality. At the head of the island are the extensive steam mills of W. Buchanan, Esq., the power of which is applied to the manufacture of flour, barley and oatmeal, and to the sawing of timber. Mr. Buchanan resides on the island and occupies a neat lodge, very agreeably situated at the forks formed by the Yamaska and the branch falling into Bay de la Valiere." He had married in June, 1814, Anne Hazlett, daughter of George Hazlett, of Londonderry, Ireland. This George Hazlett was of the same family as William Hazlett, the author, and John Hazlett the miniature painter. The name was originally Haslett, but the Hazletts' father, the Rev. William Hazlett, seems to have changed the orthography about 1783. Anne Hazlett died in Ireland, leaving a daughter Ann, who was born in 1816. Alexander Buchanan, on the death of her father, was appointed her Tutor upon the advice of a Family Council held in Montreal, on the 19th August, 1834, composed of Alexander Carlisle Buchanan, the younger, cousin, Hugh Taylor, advocate, James Scott, advocate, John Jones Day, advocate, and Henry A. Stone.

At this time Ann Buchanan was eighteen years of age and living temporarily at Alexander Buchanan's. On the 22nd of that month she was married at Montreal, to Henry McFarlane, of London. The Register was signed by A. Buchanan, A. C. Buchanan and Henry A. Stone. By the marriage articles of Henry McFarlane and Ann Buchanan, her uncles John Buchanan and George Buchanan, of Omagh, were appointed her Trustees, and the articles are signed by Henry McFarlane and Anne Buchanan, her uncle A. C. Buchanan, her cousin A. C. Buchanan, Henry A. Stone and Alexander Buchanan. There is attached a letter of attorney from Asaph Stone, of New York. After the marriage Mr. and Mrs. McFarlane left for England, intending to live in London. They afterwards settled at Rocky Hill, New Jersey, and left issue John Buchanan McFarlane and others, of Rocky Hill, New Jersey.

Alexander Buchanan was at one time an officer of the original St. Patrick's Society of Montreal. Mr. D. R. McCord writing in the "Old and New," said:—

"The St. Patrick's Society was founded on the feast of its patron Saint in the year 1834. It was then undenominational. Its objects were stated to be the advancement and welfare of Irishmen, assisting their immigration to and promoting their settlement in this province. The by-laws are thirty-four in number, and contain no allusion to stated religious services.

The first office bearers were as follows:—

John Donellan and A. Buchanan, respectively president and vice-president; T. A. Begley and C. Sweeney, the re-

cording and corresponding secretaries. I know nothing of
the first named gentleman. In 1819, there was a gardener
of the name located in Sanguinet street. The president
might have been his son, and in a superior social position
in the succeeding generation, if we may judge by his
associated office bearers. A. Buchanan was subsequently
a leader at the Bar and a man of cultivation. His father
was a surgeon in the army, and his sons are with us in the
persons of Wentworth, a retired general manager of the
Bank of Montreal, Mr. Justice Buchanan, late of the Super-
perior Court, Brock Buchanan, also of the same monetary
institution as the first named. He derives his patronymic
from the hero and victim of Queenstown Heights, to whose
regiment his grandfather was at one time attached, and
the saint the object of our present enquiries who terminated
the serpent worship—let us say—is not forgotten in the
name of our confrere of the present generation. Mr. Begley was of the Department of Public Works, unless my
memory play me false. Campbell Sweeney was a north of
Ireland man—as was also the president. He was the brother
of Robert who was out in the well-known rencontre of
honor with Major Ward of the Royals. A son of the corresponding secretary when last I saw him was in the service
of the said Corinthian pedimented treasury on the Pacific
slope. Three, at least, of the officers were thus Protestants."

CHAPTER XI.

1835-1840.

HE IS APPOINTED A K.C. — PRESIDENT OF ADVOCATES LIBRARY — CHAIRMAN OF COMMISSION TO ENQUIRE INTO CASES OF PERSONS IN CUSTODY — APPOINTED JUDGE OF COURT OF REQUESTS — THEIR JURISDICTION — ON CIRCUIT — HIS WIT — RELATIONS WITH GOVERNORS-GENERAL — HON. CHARLES BULLER — EDWARD GIBBON WAKEFIELD.

On the 19th June, 1835, he was appointed King's Counsel for the Province of Lower Canada. Up to this time King's Counsel had been appointed only to act in the Districts in which they practised. He and James Charles Grant, who was appointed the same day as he was, were the first two to receive this appointment.

James Charles Grant, K.C., was the son of John Grant, of Lachine, an agent of the North-West Company. He was admitted to the Bar on the 14th January, 1814, and in 1820, formed a partnership with Michael O'Sullivan, the firm being known as O'Sullivan & Grant. He was appointed a King's Counsel on the 19th June, 1835, and died on the 25th November, 1836. On his death the following appeared in the Montreal Transcript. :—

"We scorn to flatter the living, although, if we find on public grounds reasons for approbation, we express it; not to do so would be pusillanimous, it would be to fear the envious more than we respect the good. With Mr. Grant's political opinions we have nothing to do. He had the distinction of the silk gown, as King's Counsel, and in his general practice as an Advocate he was zealous and sagacious. In his private relations he was, as regarded his own family, a kind and affectionate relative—as regarded the man he considered his friend, he was social, hospitable, sincere—as regarded the generality of mankind he was kind-hearted, liberal, nay generous almost to a fault—yet, much as we know of his spontaneous generosity, no one ever heard him sully a noble act by the slightest allusion to it. That glow of charity which alike warms the heart of him that gives, and of him that receives, burned indeed within his own bosom, but was one of those beauteous flowers "born to blush unseen." Few men have been more deeply regretted, for few have been so highly respected."

In England, the appointment of counsel for the Crown has always been a matter of prerogative in this sense, that it has been personally exercised by the Sovereign, with the advice of the Lord Chancellor, the appointment being made by letters-patent under the sign manual. In early times the appointment was accompanied by a fee or retainer of moderate amount, but that formality has long since fallen into abeyance.

In consequence of the death of King William IV., the commissions of King's Counsel were vacated at the expiration of eighteen months after his death, and on the 20th September, 1838, a new patent appointing him one of Her Majesty's learned in the Law was issued, and on the 4th January, 1839, he took the oath of office as such.

In 1837, the Hon. Michael O'Sullivan,[1] then Solicitor General, F. A. Quesnel, Dominique Mondelet and Buchanan were the King's Counsel at Montreal.

In 1836, he was elected President of the Advocates Library. He held this office five times, —that year and in 1838, 1841, 1842 and 1843.

On the 17th July, 1835, he was appointed with Tancred Bouthillier, of Montreal, and John Simpson, of Coteau du Lac, Commissioners to fix the line between the Provinces of Upper and Lower Canada.

His brother, John Buchanan, died at Niagara in the month of December, 1837, at the early age of thirty-seven years, leaving a widow and two

---

[1] Michael O'Sullivan was born in 1786, and was admitted to the Bar of Lower Canada on the 6th April, 1811. He was appointed K.C. in 1831, and Solicitor General in 1833. He practised at Montreal until the 25th October, 1838, when he was appointed Chief Justice for the District of Montreal. He died on the 7th March, 1839, at Montreal, and was buried in Notre Dame Church. He was Lieutenant and Adjutant in the militia for the District of Beauharnois, and was present at the Battle of Chateauguay in 1813, of which he wrote an account signed "Un Temoin Oculaire." In 1819 he fought a duel with Dr. Wm. Caldwell, "at six o'clock Saturday morning the parties, with the seconds, having met near the Windmills, five shots were fired by each gentleman; two of them dangerously wounded Mr. O'Sullivan, Dr. Caldwell receiving a shot in the arm which is much shattered."

children—a son, Alexander Grant, and a daughter, Jane Louise.

On the 30th November, 1838, he was appointed with George Weekes, John Bleakley and Duncan Fisher, Commissioners to enquire into the cases of the State Prisoners confined in the Montreal Gaol. He was the Chairman of the Commission for which he received £315 sterling.

On 12th April, 1839, he was appointed Commissioner or Judge of the Circuit Court of Requests for the District of Montreal, and on the 19th of that month, took the following Oath of Office before Monk & Morrogh, Prothonotaries of the Court of King's Bench for the District of Montreal, and Commissioners Per Dedimus Potestatem:—

I, Alexander Buchanan, do swear that I will truly and faithfully and according to the best of my knowledge and ability perform the duties of the office of Commissioner of the Court of Requests in and for the District of Montreal.

Dated at Montreal, this nineteenth day of April, one thousand, eight hundred and thirty-nine.

A. BUCHANAN.

His salary as Commissioner was £600 sterling per annum. He probably sat for the first time at Vaudreuil, on the 2nd September, 1839. These Circuit Courts of Requests for the Districts of Quebec, Montreal and Three Rivers were established by an Ordinance enacted on the 11th April, 1839. The Commissioners for Quebec and Three Rivers were A. R. Hamel and P. B. Dumoulin, respectively. The Commissioners had jurisdiction to hear, try and determine, in a summary way, all civil suits or actions purely personal wherein the amount claimed, or the thing in dispute did not exceed the sum or value of £10 sterling. Only barristers of ten years standing at least could be Commissioners of these Courts, and such Commissioner being appointed a Justice of the Peace, was the Chairman of the Quarter Sessions in the District in which he was Commissioner of the Court of Requests. In certain matters the Commissioners had the same power as a Judge of the Court of King's Bench. The sittings of the Court of Requests, for the District of Montreal, were held at Vaudreuil, Terrebonne, L'Assomption, Berthier, Vercheres, St. Denis, West Church, in the Township of Shefford, Chambly, Dorchester, commonly called St. Johns, and at Chateauguay.

These Courts were abolished on the 1st January, 1842, by an Act passed on the 18th September, 1841, and were replaced by District Courts.

By the acceptance of this office, he could only act for the Crown, but that this was very remunerative may be seen on referring to the returns of money warrants from which it would appear that between 1838 and 1846, he was on different commissions as well as acted for the Crown in criminal prosecutions and customs cases. His account for services as Queen's Counsel in 1840 was £180.0.0 and his account for legal services for criminal prosecutions performed for Government from October, 1840, to April, 1841, was £140.19.4.

In April, 1841, he resigned as Commissioner of the Court of Requests and Chairman of the Quarter Sessions of Montreal.

He was very witty. His was a dry and sarcastic but still kindly wit. Many anecdotes are told of him. Travelling on the steamboat from Montreal to Quebec to attend the Court of Appeals, which in those days always sat at Quebec, a number of judges and lawyers were on board, on their way there for the same purpose, when one of the party with Buchanan pointed out Judge Day sitting apart as was his habit, and remarked that the Judge appeared to be thinking of some case, when Buchanan exclaimed, "D..n it! He thinks he is thinking." Another,—the Gugys were noted for their wickedness and Buchanan in the course of a speech which he was delivering, summed up their quality and quantity in the following terms: "When," said he, "the Gugys are in hell, then will the reign of Satan be overthrown."

On another occasion, when holding Court in the Townships, he was sitting in a case in which the defendant, who was a retired colonel as well as a local magistrate, was sitting on the bench with him. Judge Buchanan asked him whether he owed the debt and received an indignant denial, "Go into the box," said the Judge, "and be sworn." But this the colonel declining to do, judgment was entered against him.

It is said that he once saved a confrère from conviction. He secured a verdict of acquittal and wrote on the indictment, "Legally acquitted, morally guilty."

With the different Governors-General, Lord Durham, Lord Sydenham, Sir Charles Bagot, and Sir Charles Metcalfe, he was on terms of friendship. He knew intimately the brilliant Charles Buller and Edward Gibbon Wakefield, who had come to Canada as Secretaries to Lord Durham. Buller was a friend of Carlyle, who wrote an Essay on his death, which took place in his forty-second year, in 1848.

Of him Carlyle writes:—"A very beautiful soul has suddenly been summoned from among us; one of the clearest intellects and most ærial activities in England has unexpectedly been called away. Charles Buller died on Wednesday morning last, without previous sickness, reckoned of importance, till a day or two before . . . To a singular extent it can be said of him that he was a spontaneous clear man. Very gentle, too, though full of fire, simple, brave, graceful. What he did and what he said came from him as light from a luminous body, and had thus always in it a high and rare merit, which any of the more discerning could appreciate fully . . . . . To many, for a long time, Mr. Buller merely passed for a man of wit, and certainly his beautiful natural gaiety of character, which by no means meant levity, was commonly thought to mean it and did for many years hinder the recognition of his intrinsic higher qualities. Slowly it began to be discovered that under all this many-colored radiancy and conversation there burnt a most steady light; a sound, penetrating intellect, full of adroit resources and loyal by nature itself to all that was methodic, manly, true,—in brief a mildly resolute, chivalrous and gallant character capable of doing much serious service."

Wakefield, who had an extraordinary career, was born in 1796, and educated at Westminster School and the Edinburgh High School. "He followed the tradition of his family in making a youthful and surreptitious marriage. His father was first married at seventeen and afterwards contracted a secret alliance in Paris. One of his brothers ran off with an Indian princess. But of all the Wakefields it was Edward Gibbon who most notoriously distinguished himself in the field of matrimony. He eloped with Eliza Susan Pattle, a wealthy ward of Chancery, before he was of full age, and he carried through the enterprise with considerable dash and ingenuity." Being left a widower, he abducted, in 1826, Miss Turner, an heiress, and his trial took place at the Lancaster Assizes, in 1827. Sergeant Cross and Brougham were Counsel for the prosecution, the conduct of the case chiefly falling upon the latter. The Wakefields secured Scarlett, the ablest advocate of the day. Wakefield was found guilty and sentenced to three years imprisonment in Newgate. The effects of his incarceration in Newgate were "Punishment by Death in the Metropolis," which resulted in the reformation of the criminal law of England, and in this way "a term of imprisonment suffered by a man of genius availed to reshape the code of England." His "Letter from Sydney" is also due to his imprisonment.

He was released from Newgate in the month of May, 1830, and eight years later came to Canada with Lord Durham. He is generally supposed to have had some hand in Lord Durham's celebrated Report.

In 1842, he was elected a member in the Assembly of Lower Canada for Beauharnois, but left Canada, never to return, early in 1844. He wrote "England and America," and "The Art of Colonization," and has been called "A Maker of Colonies." He died in England in 1862. He was a powerful magnetizer and was very fond of using his power of magnetism on all occasions.

CHAPTER XII.

1840-1845.

HIS PARTNERSHIP WITH F. G. JOHNSON, AFTERWARDS SIR FRANCIS JOHNSON, CHIEF JUSTICE OF THE SUPERIOR COURT — PRESIDENT OF SEIGNIORIAL TENURE COMMISSION — PRESIDENT OF COMMISSION TO REVISE ACTS AND ORDINANCES OF LOWER CANADA — REPORTS OF THE COMMISSION.

In the year 1841 he formed a partnership with Francis Godschall Johnson, who in later years was to become Chief Justice of the Superior Court for the Province of Quebec, and attain the honor of knighthood. Johnson, who was then only twenty-four years old, had been admitted to the Bar in 1839.[1] The firm of Buchanan & Johnson lasted until the 27th December, 1845, when it was dissolved by mutual consent. A year or so later Mr. Buchanan associated John Bleakley and Henry Ogden Andrews with him, the firm being Buchanan, Bleakley & Andrews.

In the Canada Gazette appeared the following, dated at Quebec the 30th June, 1842:—

"His Excellency the Governor-General has been pleased by an instrument bearing date the thirtieth day of June, to revoke the Commission issued on the twenty-ninth day of March, appointing George Van Felson, Esquire, Chief

---

[1] For an account of his life see the Appendix.

Commissioner, and John Samuel McCord, and Nicholas Benjamin Doucet, Esquires, Joint Commissioners to enquire into the State of the Feudal Tenure in that part of the Province heretofore Lower Canada, and to appoint Alexander Buchanan, Esquire, Queen's Counsel, Joseph André Taschereau,[1] Esquire, advocate, and James Smith,[2] Esquire, advocate, to be Joint Commissioners to enquire into the Law and other circumstances connected with Seigniorial Tenure as it obtains in that part of the Province heretofore Lower Canada."

Alexander Buchanan was the President of this Commission. Their report dated the 29th March, 1843, is entitled,—

"Report of the Commissioners appointed in pursuance of an address of the Honorable the House of Commons of 17th Sept., 1841, to enquire into the state of the Laws and other circumstances in connection with the Seigniorial Tenure and its obtaining in that part of the Province of Canada heretofore Lower Canada, laid before the Legislative Assembly by Message from His Excellency the Governor-General on the 4th October, 1843."

His remuneration for this Commission was £500.

On the 16th March, 1842, Sir Charles Bagot, then Governor-General, appointed a Commission to revise the Acts and Ordinances of Lower Canada and to consolidate such of them as related to the same subject and which could be advantageously

---

(1) Joseph André Taschereau was admitted to the Bar in 1828, and became Police Magistrate of Quebec. In 1845 he was appointed Solicitor-General and in 1847 Circuit Judge at Quebec.

(2) James Smith was admitted to the Bar in 1828; appointed Attorney-General in 1844, and Judge of the Court of Queen's Bench at Montreal (now the Superior Court) in 1847.

consolidated. This Commission was composed of the Hon. Charles Richard Ogden, then Her Majesty's Attorney-General for Lower Canada; the Hon. Charles Dewey Day, then Her Majesty's Solicitor-General for the same; Alexander Buchanan, Q.C., the Hon. Hughes Heney, Advocate, and G. W. Wicksteed, Advocate, their appointment being consequent upon an address of the Legislative Assembly, dated the 28th August, 1841. The subsequent elevation of Mr. Day to the bench, and Mr. Ogden's absence in England prevented their taking part in the execution of the work, which, however, was completed by Mr. Buchanan and Mr. Wicksteed, on account of the death of Mr. Heney, which took place at Three Rivers on the 13th January, 1844, and the public statute law then in force, which had been scattered over a great number of volumes, from the time of the Conquest up to 1841, was ascertained and collected into one volume, entitled, "The Revised Acts and Ordinances of Lower Canada." The reports of the Commissioners, three in number and dated respectively the 21st March and the 24th November, 1843, and the 1st July, 1845, are well worthy of perusal, and it may here be remarked that in their report of the latter date they advocated the codification of the laws twenty years before they were actually codified.

Mr. Wicksteed, who was a nephew of Judge John Fletcher, was born in 1799. He came to Canada in 1821, was admitted to the Quebec Bar in 1831, and became a Q.C. in 1854. He was subsequently appointed Law Clerk of the Senate and died in Ottawa in 1895.

Alexander Buchanan was appointed on the 7th June, 1842, Justice of the Peace for the Districts of Montreal, St. Francis, Three Rivers and Quebec.

CHAPTER XIII.

1845-1851.

HE IS SENIOR Q C. — REFUSES CHIEF JUSTICESHIP — COURT HOUSE DESTROYED BY FIRE — CROWN PROSECUTOR FOR MONTREAL — HIS FEES AS SUCH — HE TAKES PROMINENT PART AT MEETINGS OF THE BAR — LECTURES ON WILLS — ELECTED A MEMBER OF THE COUNCIL FOR MONTREAL SECTION OF THE INCORPORATED BAR OF LOWER CANADA — HIS DAUGHTER ELIZABETH'S MARRIAGE — HIS DEATH — HIS LEGAL ADVICE EAGERLY SOUGHT AFTER — ADMIRATION OF STUART, FLETCHER AND BLACK, Q.C. FOR HIM — MEREDITH Q.C.'s TRIBUTE — HIS WRITTEN LEGAL OPINIONS — HIS VALUABLE LIBRARY — HIS CHARACTER AND PERSONAL APPEARANCE — STUDENTS IN HIS OFFICE — HIS WILL — HOUSES OCCUPIED BY HIM — MRS. BUCHANAN'S DEATH — THEIR FAMILY.

From the year 1840, Mr. Buchanan was the senior Queen's Counsel at Montreal. A writer in the "Old and New" columns of the Montreal Gazette, of the 9th June, 1894, says:—

"Silk gowns were rarer in those days than at present. In 1843, according to a published authority, there were only four Q.C.'s of whom Mr. Buchanan was senior; the others were Henry Driscoll, Come S. Cherrier, and Duncan Fisher; about a year later appears the name of William Collis Meredith. The first four have long since passed away. Last year public and private regrets were recorded when the pale reaper claimed as his own the Chief Justice, the fifth on the above list."

There is good authority for the statement that Mr. Buchanan was twice offered and declined the Chief Justiceship.

On the 18th July, 1844, the old Court House at Montreal which had been built in 1800 was destroyed by fire, the Advocates Library sustaining some damage, but the Court records were all saved. After the destruction of the Court House, the old gaol then occupied as barracks by the militia was vacated by them and fitted up. A Montreal paper of that year says:—

"The Court of Queen's Bench opened this morning (16th September) in one of the rooms in the upper storey of the old gaol. The Court was presided by Mr. Justice Rolland assisted by Mr. Justices Gale and Day. The new Attorney-General, Mr. Smith, robed in his silk gown (1), was at the Clerk's table, as well as Messrs. Buchanan, Driscoll, Cherrier and Meredith, the Queen's Counsel; the Sheriffs, Clerks and other Officers of Justice all being at their posts. The repairs made to the room were only finished on Saturday night and several things yet remain to be done, such as seats for the Jury and for the public. But the space is so limited that it is difficult to imagine where they will be placed, for there is no more room for the pleaders and the public, the room being already completely occupied by the seats for the Judges and the Advocates."

---

(1) This was a hit at Mr. James Smith, who had just been, appointed Attorney-General, and as such had been made a Queen's Counsel.

The old Government House, now the Chateau de Ramezay, was used as a Court House until 1856, when the present Court House was completed.

During the years 1840, 1841, 1842, 1843, 1844, 1845 and 1848 he was Counsel for the Crown in Criminal cases, or as it is now called Crown Prosecutor, at Montreal. In a Return of the names of Gentlemen, who have been employed as Queen's Counsel or Counsel for the Crown in the Province of Canada, since the Union, his name appears for Canada East, with the amount of his Fees, as follows:—

Alexander Buchanan, Queen's Counsel,

1841	£322. 0. 0
1842	797.18 .4
1843	572 .2. 8
1844	479.16. 8
1845	898.13.11
1846	....
1847	....
1848	157. 5 0
1849	....
Total	£3,327.16. 7

In 1846, his account for costs in suits for Customs duties at the instance of the Collector at Montreal, amounted to £195.18.6.

On Saturday, the 10th April, 1847, the Court of Queen's Bench at Montreal was closed on account of the sudden indisposition of Judge Day. For some time Judge Gale had been unable, through illness, to sit. This left only Judge Rolland but as the law required that two judges should always be on the Bench during the Superior Term, the Court was forced to adjourn.

The Bar was very indignant at seeing the Bench deserted and in the afternoon a meeting was held in the Advocates Room in order to make a protest to the Executive.

The following members were present:—La Fontaine, Cherrier, A. Ouimet, F. Pelletier, Cartier, Robertson, Bethune, Fleet, Godard, Letourneux, Buchanan, MacDonell, Loranger, Ibbotson, Beaudry, Taylor, Buchanan (G. C. V.), Hubert, Moreau, Ross, LeBlanc, Audy, Day, Easton, Rossiter, G. Ouimet, Scott, Tailhades, Coursolles, Bouchette, Hart, Salmon, Conoll, Roy, Armstrong, Lafrenaye, MacIver, Poitras, LeBlanc, Burroughs, Johnson, A. R. Cherrier, Belinge, Rochon, Papin, Fenwick, Berthelot, J. A. Morin, Radiger and MacKay. Toussaint Peltier was in the Chair, and R. MacKay, acted as Secretary.

Moved by Mr. Buchanan, seconded by Mr. Johnson, and Resolved:—That the Bar of Montreal believes it to be its duty to express the regret which it feels at seeing that since the death of the Hon. Chief Justice Vallières de St. Real, the number of the Judges of the Court of Queen's Bench for this District has remained incomplete, and that the Bench is composed in such a way that there has been no quorum for the administration of justice on account of the accidental illness of one Judge as happened this morning."

In the case of the Queen against James Carroll, who was tried for murder, at Montreal, on the 8th February, 1848, before Judges Rolland and Day, the Attorney General Badgley and Mr. Buchanan, Q.C., prosecuted for the Crown, and B. Devlin defended the prisoner, who was convicted on the 10th February. In a report of this case it is said, "Mr. Buchanan, Q.C., then prayed for judgment, upon which the prisoner was sentenced to death." This sentence was subsequently commuted to imprisonment for life in the penitentiary.

At a meeting of the Bar in Montreal, held on the 5th May, 1848, a committee composed of Toussaint Peltier, Alexander Buchanan, Q.C., William C. Meredith, Q.C., A. Aimé Dorion, Christopher Dunkin and Romuald Cherrier, were appointed to communicate with the Bars of the different districts for the purpose of ascertaining their views as to taking steps to incorporate the Bar of Lower Canada and with the committees to be appointed by the different districts, to prepare a draft of an Act of Incorporation to be submitted to the legislature.

At a meeting of the Bar of Montreal, held on the 30th December, 1850, A. Buchanan, Q.C., C. S. Cherrier, Q.C., and G. E. Cartier, were appointed a Committee to report on the legality or illegality of the Advocates Tariff recently promulgated by the Judges of the Superior Court for the Province of Quebec. At a subsequent meeting Henry, Stuart, S. C. Monk, Robert MacKay and T. J. J. Loranger were added to the Committee, who made the following Report.

"The undersigned forming the majority of the Committee charged to decide on the legality of the tariff promulgated by the Judges on the 17th December, 1850, are of opinion:
That the tariff of fees for the Superior Court of Lower Canada is incomplete and illegal.
That the former tariff for the Superior Court is not repealed and still remains in force in virtue of 12 Victoria, ch. 38, sec. 100.
That the new tariff promulgated for the Circuit Court is valid and repeals all other tariffs formerly in force for the said Circuit Court."

A. Buchanan.
S. C. Monk.
Henry Stuart.
R. MacKay.
T. J. J. Loranger.

Early in February, 1851, it is announced that on Monday the 17th of February, Alex. Buchanan, Esq., Q.C., will lecture on Wills and Successions before the members of the Law Students Society.

At the annual meeting of the Bar of Montreal held in May, 1851, the following were elected officers of the Bar:—Toussaint Peltier, Batonnier; F. Griffin, Syndic; J. A. Berthelot, Treasurer; P. A. Lafrenaye, Secretary; and A. Buchanan, C. S. Cherrier, J. J. Day, G. E. Cartier, S. C. Monk, Henry Stuart, T. J. J. Loranger and A. A. Dorion, Council of the Bar.

At a meeting of the Corporation of the Montreal English Hospital in May, 1851, he was elected one of the Governors of that institution for the ensuing year.

On the 11th June, 1851, his eldest daughter, Elizabeth Jane, was married in Christ Church at Montreal, by the Revd. D. Robertson, Chaplain to the Garrison, to George Blicke Champion Crespigny, Captain in the XXth Regiment of Foot, then stationed at Montreal. Frederick Horn, Colonel, and William P. Radcliffe, Lieutenant of the XXth Regiment, and Alexander Buchanan signed the Register.

He died at his house No. 7 Cornwall Terrace, St. Denis St., Montreal, on the 5th November, 1851, at the early age of fifty-three years. His funeral which took place on Saturday afternoon the 8th November, was largely attended by the Bench and Bar as well as by the public. Judge Rolland, Judge Aylwin, and Judge J. S. McCord, the Hon. Peter McGill, the Hon. John Molson and Sheriff John Boston, Q.C., were the pall bearers.

The Montreal Transcript of the 8th November, 1851, said:—

"It is with sincere regret that we have to record the "death of Mr. Alexander Buchanan, Q.C. The deceased "gentleman was one confessedly at the head of the pro- "fession which he adorned, in learning and in intelligence. "As a feudist and a publicist, he has left no equal. His was "a finely cultivated and nobly informed mind. Without "much fluency of speech, he was earnest and logical; and, "perhaps, if he spoke less, it was because he reflected more.

"Mr. Buchanan was a man who would have adorned any "society whatever. Learned, thoughtful, and unpresuming; "to ask his opinion was as nearly as possible to get at the "truth. It is to be regretted that beyond a few detailed "consultations, he has left so little memorials of his great "powers."

The Montreal Gazette of the same date said:—

"THE LATE A. BUCHANAN, Q.C.—The funeral of this "much lamented gentleman took place on Saturday after-"noon. The Hon. Messrs. Justices Rolland, Aylwin and "McCord, the Hon. Messrs. McGill and Molson, and Mr. Sheriff "Boston bore the pall, and several of the Judges and a "large number of the Bar followed his remains to their "last resting place. The profession which he so much "adorned in his lifetime, could not but have felt that they "were honoring themselves in paying this slight tribute of "respect to his memory. He will still live in the remem-"brance of those who had the good fortune to know him. "We all feel that a master spirit has gone from among us, "and may scarcely hope to possess so ripe a scholar or "jurist again for long years to come."

Even a paper so inimical to his nationality and to his party as "La Minerve" is obliged to acknowledge that "conscientious studies, an unerring judgment and great assiduity for work had raised Mr. Buchanan to the first rank of jurists of the Canadian Bar. Few men have been so much esteemed as Advocates, and few men have had, in private life, so many friends."

He was great as a consulting Counsel, and his advice was eagerly sought after, few cases going to Appeal without his opinion having been obtained on one side or the other. The distinguished Andrew Stuart, under whom he had studied, and John Fletcher and Henry Black, Q.C., both of whom became judges, were his intimate friends and had the greatest reverence for his opinions and the deepest admiration for him, whom they held to be the most thorough Roman lawyer at the Bar.

In 1844, Mr. Meredith, Q.C., afterwards Chief Justice Sir William C. Meredith, in the course of an opinion expresses the high esteem in which Alexander Buchanan was universally held, when he says,—

"It is not without some diffidence that we express our "opinion, on the foregoing case, which has been submitted "for our consideration; that opinion being at variance with "a judgment which has been pronounced by Mr. Buchanan. "But notwithstanding the sincere regard which we enter-"tain for the views of that justly eminent lawyer, yet we "must say, that we are unable to discern any reason "sufficient to reconcile our minds to the judgment to which "we have already made allusion.

And Mr. Meredith concludes,—

"Such is our view of the matter, but even taking it for "granted that it is well founded, we apprehend that there "would be some difficulty in inducing the magistrates to "adopt it, opposed as it is to the opinion of Mr. Buchanan."

He exemplified in his person the truth of that well-known remark made by a celebrated man that "there seldom yet has been an able and "determined man who did justice to the law, to "whom it, did not, in turn, at one time or another, "amply do justice."

It may not be inappropriate to give an extract from an address delivered by the Honorable Francis G. Johnson, on the occasion of his installation to the Chief Justiceship of the Superior Court for Lower Canada, on Saturday the 25th January, 1890, in the Court House at Montreal:—

"With more than the number of years commonly "allotted to man stretching behind me, of which time half "a century has been passed in the profession of the law, "and half of that again on the Bench, I have something to "remember, though it may not be so easy to tell it as it "impresses me: for if not within these very walls yet within "those of the old Court House which they have replaced, "and on this very spot, or very near to it, indeed, I have "seen Chief Justices Reid, O'Sullivan, Vallières and Rol-"land on the Bench—men whose names will surely live in "the annals of our profession; and at the Bar I have heard "Buchanan and Walker, and Driscoll, and Meredith, and "Drummond, and Lafontaine, and Dorion, and Loranger, "and Papin, and many others, some passed into the shadow-"land, and one or two still with us, like our venerable "friend, who has so kindly joined in the chorus of your "good wishes for me to-day."

It is greatly to be regretted that he did not accept the office of Chief Justice, for he would have adorned it, and he would have been enabled to show his powers to the full, thus perpetuating his great knowledge of the law in his judgments, which would have then been placed on record. As it is, without these, his name is yet remembered at the Bar, and his reputation as a great lawyer still stands and will go down to future generations of lawyers.

His written opinions alone would entitle him to rank as a jurist, and stand foremost in the annals of the Bar of Lower Canada.

He left but two manuscript volumes of the many Opinions given by him. These Opinions, written in a chaste literary style, are examples of his great erudition and of his happy command of language.

The following selections are taken from these Opinions.

Thus, on the question whether the public could legally claim any right in or upon certain property bounded in front by the River St. Lawrence, he says:—

"For a long period of time the question respecting the property of the banks and shores of navigable rivers was one much cultivated and involved in doubt.

It seems, however, to have been at last the settled opinion of modern and more enlightened Jurists in France, that the property of the banks and shores of navigable rivers resides in the proprietors of the adjoining lands, subject to the exercise by the public of the servitude of use for the purposes of navigation and intercourse.

The jurisprudence, in truth, merely revived in France the principles of the Roman Law on the same subject which were in vigor in that country, at an early day before the servile favorers of the Royal Domain had endeavored to introduce a contrary rule.

The language used by the Sovereigns of France in their Ordinances on this subject implies a recognition of the titles individual to this species of property, while the main object of these enactments was to limit that property and to define the rights of the public upon it, &c."

He concludes another opinion with this sentence:—

"In considering the above questions we have had cause to lament the poverty of our jurisprudence on the subject of fire insurance. No causes similar to that under consideration as to the construction of these policies and of their conditions seem to have as yet occurred as subjects of judicial decision and coming at our conclusions we have been constrained to advert to general principles of law and to analogy."

He was a man of the highest and purest integrity. His manners were graceful, engaging and courteous, and he had a kind disposition. In appearance, he was tall, of an erect and dignified carriage and fine presence. His face was interesting and attractive. His forehead broad and well developed, and his complexion fair, his hair brown and thick. He was extremely particular about his dress. For some years previous to his death he walked stiffly from the effects of a fractured ankle.

In his political opinions, he was a Tory of the home school but seems to have steadfastly kept aloof from the violent and discordant political discussions of those days.

In conclusion, it is not going too far to apply to him the delightful language of Brougham writing of a great jurist: "There has seldom," he writes, "if ever, appeared in the profession of the law any one so peculiarly endowed with all the learning and capacity which can accomplish, as well as all the graces which can embellish, the judicial character, as this eminent person . . . . His judgment was of the highest caste; calm, firm, enlarged, penetrating, profound . . . His vast superiority was apparent when, as from an eminence, he was called to survey the whole field of dispute, and to marshal the variegated facts, disentangle the intricate mazes, and array the conflicting reasons which were calculated to distract or suspend men's judgment. If ever the praise of being luminous could be justly bestowed upon human compositions, it was upon his judgments, and it was the approbation constantly, as it were peculiarly, appropriated to these wonderful exhibitions of judicial capacity." . . .

"His learning, extensive and profound in all professional matters, was by no means confined within that range. He was amply and accurately endowed with a knowledge of all history of all times; richly provided with' the literary and the personal portion of historical lore; largely furnished with stores of the more curious and recondite knowledge which judicious students of antiquity and judicious students only, are found to amass; and he possessed a rare facility of introducing such matters felicitously for the illustration of an argument or a topic, whether in debate or in more familiar conversation. But he was above the pedantry which disdains the gratifications of a more ordinary and every day curiosity. . . . . . Above all, he was a person of great classical attainments, which he had pursued and, indeed, improved from the earlier years of his life . . . and hence, as well as from the natural refinement and fastidiousness of his mind, he derived the pure taste which presided over all his efforts, chastening his judicial composition and adorning his exquisite conversation. Of diction, indeed, he was among the greatest masters."

Among those who studied in his office were William Foster Coffin, author of "1812," and at one time Joint Sheriff of Montreal; Samuel Cornwallis Monk, afterwards a Judge of the Court of Queen's Bench; Christopher Dunkin, afterwards a Judge of the Superior Court; Sydney R. Bellingham, who died in Ireland in 1900, aged 92 years, and the late John Monk, advocate.

In his Will, made at Montreal, on the 16th October, 1851, in the presence of Henry Ogden Andrews, advocate, John Monk, advocate, and Hanbury L. MacDougall, he gave directions that his estate should be sold and the proceeds invested in good and sufficient securities. He left to his wife the use of the interest of the proceeds during her lifetime, and after her death, he gave to his youngest child Mary, the sum of Two thousand pounds, and as to the rest of his estates he left them in equal shares between all his children. He appointed his "said wife and son George Charles Vidua, and my friend Hugh Taylor, of Montreal, Esquire, Advocate, Trustees for the purposes aforesaid, and also Executrix and Executors of this my last will and testament."

His Will was probated on the 13th December, 1851, on the petition of the Executors through their attorney, F. G. Johnson.

He was one of the best classical scholars of his day. A great lover of books, he had collected a remarkably large and rare library containing many first editions. "He was," wrote one a few years ago, "a lover of letters. Canadian bibliophiles can point to their choicest specimens of Canadiana bearing on the title page the well known signature of this gentleman." His library passed through the great fire of 1852, and was sold in that year. Among the rarer editions were the following selection:—

Roman Civil Law.

Accursii, Glossæ ad Institutiones, 1 vol. 8vo.—("very rare and valuable.")
Brissonii, de Formulis Juris Civilis Romani, Francofurti, 1592, 1 vol. 4 to ("rare and valuable.")
Brissonii, Opera Minora, Lugd. Bat, 1749, in vellum, ("Scarce.")

Corpus Juris Civilis, cum comment: Accursi glossatum, Ludguni, 1612, 6 vols. folio, ("a very valuable edition.")

Corpus Juris Civilis, Gothofredus, Amstel, 1663, 2 vols. folio, "Entre toutes ces ditions, on préfère celle de 1663, parce qu'elle est mieux executée; parce que le texte Grec des nouvelles manque dans plusieurs des éditions nouvelles; enfin parce que les additions faites dans les temps postérieurs, ne l'emportent pas sur le prix d'une édition d'Elzevir." *Le Camus Bibl: de Droit*, 287. Sells at Paris for 141 francs, see Brunet."

Cujacii, Opera Omnia Fabrotus. Paris 1658, "a rare edition of this valuable work. The Edition of 1795 sells for £14 14 0 sterling; see Bohn. This edition is in excellent condition. "Le célèbre Jurisconsulte Cujas, est, sans contredit le premier des interprètes du Droit Romain." *Dupin.*

Corvinus, Enncleatio Juris Civilis sec. ord. Inst. (Elzevir 1664.)

Digesta et Institutiones Justiniani, (Gothefredus 1583) 1 vol. 8 vo.

Evarardi, Loci Argumentorum Legales, (Lugduni 1568) 1 vol. 8 vo.

Grotius, de Belli et pacis jure, 1670, 1 vol. 8 vo.

Gothofredi, (Jacobus) Opera minora juridica, 1 vol. folio, Ludg. Bat. 1773 in vellum (rare).

Gothofredi (Theophilus) 1 vol, 4 to. Genevæ, 1620. Greek and Latin in vellum, very rare.

Leyseri, Meditationes ad Pandectas, Lipsæ, 12 vols. in 10, 4to, "Cet ouvrage, fort estimé des jurisconsultes Allemands, est peu commun en France." *Brunet.* "A valuable edition, in vellum."

Novdt, Opera Omnia, 2 vols. folio, Lugd. Bat. 1767.

Pacii, Analysis Juris Civilis, sec. ord. Instit. (1601) 1 vol. 18 mo.

Petiti Leges Atticæ, 1 vol. folio, Paris, 1685.—"a great body of Philological and Juridical learning." *Bohn.*

Respublica Romana, 1 vol. 24 mo. (Lug. Batava. Elzevir, 1629.)
Strykii, Opera Præstantiora, 1 vol. folio, "rare edition."
Zonchœius, Quæstiones Juris Civilis (Oxon, 1660) 1 vol. 18 mo.

English Law.

Fortescue's de Laudibus Legum Anglicæ (very scarce) 1 vol. 8 vo.

English Literature.

Austin's Hæc Homo, wherein the excellency of the creation of woman is described. London, 1737, (rare and very curious) 1 vol. 24 mo.

Digby, Sir Kenelm, the Sympathetic Powder, a discourse in solemn assembly at Montpellier, by Sir K. Digby, Knight. London 1769, 1 vol. 12 mo. (rare and very curious.)

Jonson, Ben, Works of, London, 1631 1 vol. folio. "Very scarce and valuable."

Jones Secret History of Whitehall from Charles II. to the abdication of James II., London 1697. "A very curious and scarce work." 1 vol. 24 mo.

Little's Poems, London, 1804, 1 vol. 12 mo. very scarce.

Milton's Minor Poems, London, 1645. ("Very rare") 1 vol. 12 mo.

Maurice, Prince of Nassau, Heroic Acts of, 1 vol. 4 to. ("very scarce.")

Magica Adamica, or the Antiquities of Magic by Enger, Philadelphia, London 1650, 1 vol. 36 mo. "very rare and curious."

Ramesey, W. Gent. and Student of Astrologie. Astrologie restored, London 1651, 1 vol. 4 to. "A very curious and rare work."

Systemia Agriculturæ, of the Mystery of Husbandry Discovered, to which is added the Kalendarium Rusticam, by J. W. Gent. London 1669, 1 vol. 24 mo. "Very curious and rare."

Testament, New (Geneva) 1557, Rare, 1 vol. 8 vo.

French Literature.

Comines, Phil. de, ses Mémoires. Paris 1576, 2 vols. 36 mo. "An extremely rare edition. An edition of 1648 sold for 80 francs at Didot's."

L'Art de Vérifier les dates des Faits Historiques, des Chartes, des Chroniques et autres ancien Monumens, depuis la Naissance de Notre Seigneur. Paris, 1783, 3 vols. folio. "Ouvrage très estimé et dont les exemples se sont vendus jusqu'à 300 francs et plus cher. Ordinairement vendu, Fargeau, 650 francs." *Brunet.*

Nouvelles Pensées sur la cause de la Lumière, 1 vol. 8 vo. "Very curious and scarce."

Rabelais, Oeuvres de, (Edition Jacob) 1 vol. 18 mo. and Geneva 1782, 4 vols. 24 mo.

Sevigniana, (1656) 1 vol. 24 mo.

Traité sur les Perruques, 1 vol. 18 mo. "Very curious work; it contains the autograph of the celebrated Archbishop Bossuet."

Italian Literature.

Davila Historia, delle Guerre Civili di Francia, 1 vol. 4 to., Venetia, 1692. In vellum.

Soave, Pietro, Istorica del Concilio Tridintino, 1 vol., 4to. Geneva, 1660. "A rare and valuable edition."

Dutch Literature.

Valentyn, Oud en Nieuw Oost Indien,—A collection of voyages to the East Indies (in Dutch) with numerous plates of Natural History, views, portraits, charts, &c. Amst. 1726. "Cette collection est fort curieuse." *Brunet.* "This work is scarce and little known." *Dibin.* "A copy sells for £15 15 0 strlg." *Bohn.*

Greek Literature.

Aristotelis Opera, 4 vols. 12 mo. Greek and Latin. (Pacii 1587).

Antoninus Liberalis (Xylandri), 1 vol. 16 mo.—Basil 1568.
"Xylandri, not being satisfied with his first attempt of editing this author, caused the present edition to be published, which is, in every respect, a more valuable one, and is nearly as rare as the former." *Dibdin.*
Apthonii, Progymnasmater, 1 vol. 36 mo. Greek and Latin, 1627,—"scarce."
Aelianus de Animalibus, 1 vol. 36 mo. Greek and Latin, 1616.
Casaubon, Athenai Diepnosophista, 1 vol. folio, Lugduni, 1557,—"scarce and valuable."
Dinneri Epicthetorum Græcorum Farrago, 1 vol. 16 mo. 1607.
Demosthenis Oratio de Corona, Greek and Latin, Cramoisy, 1648, 1 vol. 16 mo.
Epicteti, Stoici Philosophi Enchiridon, 1 vol. 8 vo. Wolfius Londini, 1670,—"rare."
Florelegii Variorum Epigrammatum, 1 vol., 1604.
Herodiani Historia, 1 vol. Greek and Latin, Oxon: 1678. "Very correct and beautiful." *Dibdin.*
Homeri Ilias, 1 vol. 8 vo., Greek and Latin, Heyne, 1819.
Heliodori, Aethiopico, 1 vol. 16 mo. Frankfort, 1631.
"Recherchée et peu commune." *Brunet.* "Valued by him at 30 frs."
Hippocratis Aphorismata, 1 vol. 24 mo. Greek and Latin, 1633.
Longini de sublimitate, 1 vol. 12 mo. Amstel, 1733.
Plutarchii Opera Omnia, 6 vols. 8 vo. Greek and Latin, Stephanus 1572;—"very rare. Brunet says:—"Edition non moins remarquable par sa belle exécution que par son exactitude,les exemplaires ainsi complets, sont très recherchés." Vendu £12 15 0. Dibdin says:— "This is the first edition of the entire works of Plutarch."
Dr. Harwood says:—"This is the most correct work of that great man (Stephanus) ever published."
Pindari Olympia, &c., et Anacreontis Carmina, 2 vols. 36 mo. Greek and Latin, H. Stephanus 1586.

Sophoclis Tragediæ, 2 vols. 16 mo. (Foulis 1745.)
Suidæ, Lexicon, 1 vol. folio, Froben Basil, 1544,—"This is an exceedingly valuable and scarce edition—worth £15."
Scriptores de re accipitraria, 1 vol. 4 to. (1612).
Tragediæ Selectae, 2 vols. Greek and Latin, (Stephanus, 1567).
Testamentum Novum, 2 vols. 24 mo. Elzevir, 1624.
Xenophontis Cyropaedia, 1 vol. 8 vo. (Paris, 1538).
Xenophontis Memorabilia, 1 vol. 8 vo. (Oxon. 1749).
Zosimi Historiæ, 1 vol. 12 mo. Greek and Latin (Oxon, 1679).

LATIN AUTHORS.

Ansonii, Opera, 1 vol. 36 mo. Amstel, "rare."
Amelil, Sex. Vict. Hist. Romanae. 1 vol. 8 vo. Schotti, Leipsic, 1670, "very rare."
Aeliani, Variæ Historiæ, 1 vol. 36 mo. Geneva, 1593,—rare—Greek and Latin.
Apuleii Madravrensis Platonici, Opera omnia quæ exstant (Wechliana, 1621)—"very rare and valuable"—1 vol. 24 mo.
Allus Gellius, Noctes Atticae, 1 vol. 24mo. (Amstel, 1651, Elzevir)—"valuable and scarce edition."
Bœthius de consolatione philosophicae, 1 vol. 24 mo. Leipsic, 1751. "Cette edition est très recherchée." *Brunet.*
Ciceronis Opera, 2 vols. 4 to. (Vander: a: a: Amstel, 1692).
Ciceronia Opera Rhetorica, 1 vol. 18 mo. (Gryph. Lugd. 1555)—scarce.
Concionies et Orationes, 1 vol, 24 mo. Elzevir, 1662. "La plus belle et moins commune des quatres éditions de ce recueuil qu' ont donnés les Elzevirs—vendu 75 frs." *Brunet.*
Gœzii, Rei Agrariæ Scriptores, 1 vol. 4 to. 1674.—very scarce.
Horatii, Opera cum notis, Bond. 1 vol. 24 mo. 1767. "A fine edition, copied from Elzevir of 1676."
Juvenalis et Persii, Satyræ, 1 vol. 4 to.—"valuable edition" (Baskerville).

Justini Hist, ex Trogo Pompejo, cum notis, Isaaci Vossii, (1722) 1 vol. 16 mo.
Livii, Historiae, (Ruddiman, 1751) 4 vols.
Lucani, Pharsalia, (Didot) 1 vol. folio—"valuable edition."
Lactantii, Opera, 1 vol. 36 mo. (Lugd. 1593)—"very rare."
Macrobii Opera, 1 vol. 36 mo. (Lugd. Gryph. 1585))—"scarce and valuable."
Plinii, Historia Naturalis, 3 vols. 24 mo. 1635, Elzevir.
Quintiliani Opera, 1 vol. folio (Paris, Constellier, 1725.)
Stephani Thesaurus Linguæ Latinæ, 4 vols. folio—a very valuable work.
Senecæ Opera, 1 vol. folio, (Paris, 1619).
Senecæ Opera, 1 vol. 18 mo. (Crispin, 1614).
Suetonii Opera, 1 vol. 26 mo. (Amstel, 1612)—"rare."
Senecæ Tragediæ, 1 vol. 36 mo. (Amstel, 1678, Elzevir)—"rare."
Statii Opera, 1 vol. 36 mo. (cum notis Gronovii Amstel, 1653, Elzevir). "Dr. Harwood calls this a very scarce edition."—*Dibdin.*
Silius Italicus de secundo Bello Punico, Amstel, 1628, 1 vol. 36 mo.
Taciti Opera, 1 vol. 36 mo. (Gryph. Lugd. 1584)—"scarce and valuable edition."
Terentii Comediæ, 1 vol. 36 mo. (Amstel 1630).
Valerii Maximi, Opera, 1 vol. 16 mo. (Lugd. Gryph. 1538) "rare edition."

Modern Greek and Latin Authors.

Alexandri ab Alexandro, geniales dies, 2 vols. 8 vo. (Lugd. 1673).
Beroaldi, Phil. Orationes, 1 vol. 12 mo. (Gauthier, Paris, 1509)—"scarce."
Beroaldi, Flores Poetarum, 1 vol. 36 mo. 1556—"also scarce."
Buchanan, (George) Opera Omnia, 2 vols. folio, (Edin. Ruddiman, 1715).
Buchanan (George) Poemata, 1 vol. 24 mo. (Amstel 1687).

Bacon de Augmentis Scientiarum, 1 vol. 36 mo. (Lugd. Bat. 1652)—"scarce."
Biblia Sacra, 1 vol. 16 mo. (Londini, 1656).
Concilii Tridentini, Celebrati Canones et Decreta, 1677 "rare"—18 mo.
Lavata de Spectris, 1 vol. 24 mo. Lugd. 1687—"Curious and scarce."
Lucianus Mortuorum Dialogi (Greek and Latin) 1 vol. 24 mo. (Paris, 1656).
Mureti Orationes, 1 vol. 36 mo. (Paris 1578) "a rare edition."
Spelmanni Glossarium Archæologicum, 1 vol. folio (ed. 1687).
Skinneri Etymotogicon, 1 folio, 1671
Scoti (Dun) Quæstiones ad Aristot. Logica. 1 vol. 16 mo. (Edition of 1600).
Vossii Rhetoricæ, 1 vol. 16 mo. (Edition of 1567).
Valla (Laurentius) de Linguæ Elegantia, 1 vol. 18 mo. (1658).
Weckerum de Secretis, 1 vol. 24 mo. (Basil 1642) "Curious and rare."

In the year 1827 he was living near what was then known as St. Mary's Foundry. Later he occupied a house on Notre Dame Street near the old Water Works, in 1832, where his son Alexander Brock was born. From this house he removed to the large house owned and at one time occupied by Sir James Stuart, situated at some distance east, also on Notre Dame Street, and which was still standing in 1892, being then used as a carriage factory. About 1838 he moved into the large and comfortable house which he had built at Côte à Barron, now known as Sherbrooke Street. It still stands at the corner of

HOUSE ON SHERBROOKE ST., MONTREAL.

Sherbrooke and Cadieux Streets, fronting on the former. The grounds which surrounded the house extended down the slope to Ontario Street, then a creek. They are now covered by houses and divided up by streets, and the stables have been torn down. Here he lived until 1849, when he leased it to Lieutenant-General Sir William Rowan, K.C.B., Commander of the Forces, and went to live at No. 7 Cornwall Terrace, St. Denis Street.

The Côte à Barron house was subsequently occupied by Lieutenant-General Sir William Eyre, and then by Sir John Michel, and in 1852 it was sold to Mr. Bruyère, a partner in the large and wealthy firm of Masson, Bruyère, Thomas & Co.

In 1849 Cornwall Terrace was the fashionable row of houses in the city. In 1850 Sir James E. Alexander, A.D.C., lived in No. 1; Col. Dyneley, R.A., C.B. (whose wife was a sister of Lord Ellenborough), in No. 2; J. B. Greenshields in No. 3; John Ostell in No. 4; Henry Jackson in No. 5; E. S. Freer in No. 6; and Mr. Buchanan in No. 7.

After her husband's death Mrs. Buchanan continued living at No. 7 Cornwall Terrace until 1852, when the Terrace was destroyed in the great fire. The family then moved to Bleury Street above Ontario Street, and after that, in 1854, to No. 49 Champ de Mars. In 1855, Mrs. Buchanan with her daughter, Mary, went to live in England. In 1857 she returned and lived first at Woodstock, and afterwards, at Quebec, with her son Brock. She died on the 18th July, 1862, at Saco, Maine.

They had issue:

I. George Carlo Vidua Buchanan, was born on the 20th October, 1825, at Montreal. He was named after Count Vidua, an Italian friend of his father's, who had visited him at Montreal. His god-parents were Maria Froste, William Buchanan, and Henry Black by his proxy George Stuart. He went to Black's School on St. Helen's Street, at Montreal. In 1840, he began the study of the law in the office of Henry Black, Q.C., at Quebec. While there he lived with his uncle, Alexander Carlisle Buchanan. Returning to Montreal he entered the office of C. S. Cherrier, Q.C., and Mr. Antoine Dorion, afterwards Chief Justice of the Queen's Bench, and at that time practising together, but leaving them he completed his law studies in the office of John Rose, Q.C., afterwards Sir John Rose, Bart., and was admitted to the Bar on the 14th November, 1846. He practised for some years at Montreal in partnership with Mr. John Monk, the firm being Monk & Buchanan, and then removed to Sweetsburg in the Eastern Townships, at which place he ever afterwards practised. He was at one time in partnership with the Hon. L. S. Huntington and for many years with the Hon. G. B. Baker, the firm being Buchanan & Baker. In 1862 he was appointed Crown Prosecutor for the District of Bedford, which office he held until his appointment to the Bench. In 1864 he was appointed by the Quebec Government Commissioner to settle the much disputed question relating to

HON. G. C. V. BUCHANAN.

titles of Bolton lands and acted in such capacity for three years. He was appointed a Queen's Counsel on the 28th February, 1873; a Commissioner for consolidating the General Statutes of the Province of Quebec in 1877, and on the 28th February, 1881, he was raised to the Bench as Judge of the Superior Court for the District of Bedford, in the place of Mr. Justice Dunkin, and was sworn in on the 21st March, 1881. In 1885 he was appointed Revising Officer. In the month of January, 1887, he resigned his seat on the Bench. The Legal News noted his retirement in the following terms:

"Under the pressure of many losses, we have "omitted to notice particularly the retirement of "Mr. Justice Buchanan of the Superior Court. "It was rumoured at first that his withdrawal was "only temporary and that after a period of rest he "would probably be able to resume the duties of "his office. We regret that this information proves "to be without foundation and that Mr. Justice "Buchanan has been compelled, by the condition "of his health, to place his resignation in the hands "of the Government. Mr. Buchanan, who was "assigned to the district of Bedford, was a Judge of "great accomplishments and personally very much "esteemed. Many of his judgments have appeared "in this journal, and bear evidence of his ability "as a jurist. He has also sat from time to time " in the Court of Review in this City, and his "presence will be greatly missed by his colleagues "and by the profession generally."

He married on the 17th November, 1863, Abbie Louise Snow. He died at Montreal on the 3rd July, 1901. He left issue:—

(1) Mary Maud, married on 1st January 1896, to George G. Foster, K.C., of Montreal; and has issue: (1) George Buchanan, born 17th August, 1897; (2) Ruth Elizabeth.

(2) Florence Geraldine, died on 25th March, 1886, aged 16 years, at Sweetsburg;

(3) Charles Ernest, born 15th June 1871.

II. Elizabeth Jane Buchanan, born on the 24th October, 1827, at Montreal. Her sponsors were Hon. John S. McCord, Mary Griffin, wife of the late Frederick Griffin Q.C., of Montreal, and Mary Irwin, by her proxy Maria Froste. On the 11th June, 1851, she was married at Montreal to Captain George Blicke Champion Crespigny, XXth Regiment, of Foot, second son of Charles Fox Champion Crespigny, Esquire, of Harefield House, Uxbridge, Middlesex, England. In 1854 Captain Crespigny was appointed to the School of Musketry at Hythe, England, with the brevet rank of Lieutenant-Colonel from 1859. He died on the 30th June, 1893, aged 78 years, at Folkestone. Mrs. de Crespigny ([1]) died on the 30th April, 1897, at the same place. They had issue:—

(1) George Harrison Champion de Crespigny, of Burton Latimer Hall, Kettering, Northampton-

---

([1]) In 1876 Colonel Crespigny took up the "de," which for some reason had been dropped by his father.

shire, born on the 9th July, 1863, gazetted 14th May, 1884, Lieutenant in the Northamptonshire Regiment. He was appointed Captain in the 3rd Battalion Northamptonshire Regiment (Militia) in 1892, Honorary Major in 1898, and Major in 1903. On the 1st December, 1890, he married Gwendoline Blanche, daughter of W. C. Clarke-Thornhill, of Rushton Hall, Northants. Fixby, Yorkshire, and Swakeleys, Middlesex, J. P. for Co. of Northampton. He has issue:—

(1) George Arthur Oscar, born 25th November, 1894.
(2) Mildred Frances.
(3) Gwendoline Sibyl.

(2) Julia Constantia, died on 7th September, 1876, aged 24 years, at Les Avants, Montreux, Switzerland.

(3) Georgiana Elizabeth.

III. Wentworth James Buchanan, born 11th December, 1828, at Montreal. His sponsors were C. R. Ogden, Anne Amelia Monk, and R. W. Harwood. He was educated at the High School at Montreal, and in 1847 entered the Commercial Bank of Canada, leaving which he entered in 1853 the service of the Bank of Montreal. In 1858 he was appointed Agent at Woodstock, Ont., and held in succession the post of Manager at Brantford, Cobourg, Hamilton, Toronto, and at Montreal in 1874. In 1879 he was appointed Assistant General Manager, and in 1881 General Manager of the Bank of Montreal. He retired on the 31st October, 1890. He married Agatha, youngest daughter of Major Arnold R. Burrowes, Grenadier Guards. He died at Montreal, on the 2nd of July, 1905. He left issue:—

 (1) Claude Wentworth, of Montreal, born 22nd May, 1872.

 (2) Fitzherbert Price, B. Sc., of Montreal, born 16th March, 1874.

 (3) Richard Trevor, of Woodlands, P.Q., born 18th November, 1876; married in 1905 Constance Hale, of Lennoxville, and has issue:—

  (1) Mary Ada (Minda).

  (2) Alice Agatha, married to Frank H. Weir, of Montreal, and has issue.

IV. William Robert Buchanan was born on 22nd September, 1830, at Montreal, went to to Australia and thence some years afterwards to the Sandwich Islands. He married twice, having issue by both marriages, and died in January, 1902, at Honolulu. He married, first, Miss Muselwhite and had issue, Gertrude, died unmarried; Charles A.; William; Amy, married to Mr. Hope; and Helen, married to Mr. Brundage; secondly, Emma C. Brickwood, and had issue; Wentworth M.; Irene Martha, married to William H. Cornwell, Jr.; Grace, married to Allen Dunn; May, married to Henry N. Almy; Alexander, and Agnes Judd.

WENTWORTH J. BUCHANAN.

V. Alexander Brock Buchanan, of Montreal and Murray Bay, was born on the 10th January, 1832, at Montreal, in his father's house on Notre Dame Street, which stood almost opposite the Donagana Hotel, now used as the Notre Dame Hospital. He was baptized on the 16th March following by the Rev. John Bethune, Rector of Christ Church, of Montreal. The Sponsors were James C. Buchanan by his proxy, Alexander Buchanan, W. Guild and Sarah Blackwell by her proxy, Margaret Jamieson. In September, 1843, on the opening of the High School of Montreal, he went to that school, where he remained until 1847 when he went to Brantford and entered the establishment of Mr. Ignatius Cockshutt, general merchant. In August 1850, with his uncle, William Oliver Buchanan, he set out for Charleston, Kanawha Co., Virginia, where he was engaged at the coal mines. He returned to Montreal in 1852, and in May of that year went into the office of Mr. Jesse Joseph, and in the following May into the office of Gillespie, Moffatt & Co. On the 1st May, 1856, he entered the service of the Bank of Montreal. In April, 1857, he went as Accountant to Bowmanville, Ont.; in 1858 as Accountant to Cobourg; in 1859 as Accountant to Quebec; in September 1863 he was appointed Agent at Cornwall; in December 1866, Agent at St. Catharines, Ont., in January, 1869, he was acting Agent at Simcoe, and in May, 1869, he returned to the Head Office at Montreal. He was appointed

Secretary of the Bank of Montreal in 1876, and Inspector of Branch Returns in 1896. On the 1st September, 1898, he was granted one year's leave of absence, and on the 1st November, 1899, after more than forty-three years of active service in the Bank of Montreal he retired on his pension. It was chiefly due to his efforts that the Pension Fund Society of the Bank of Montreal, of which he was one of the charter members, and the first secretary, was founded, On the 12th May, 1857, he married Elizabeth Ann, daughter of Francis Best and of Emily Atkinson, his wife, of Montreal, who had come with her parents to Canada in 1842. They were married by the Rev. John Bethune, Dean of Montreal, in St. John's Chapel, Gosford Street, Montreal. Mrs. Brock Buchanan was born on the 22nd April, 1834, at Killyman, in County Armagh, Ireland, and was baptized on the 24th May, 1834, by the Rev. H. Revel, Curate Assistant of Killyman. Her mother, Emily Atkinson, who was born in 1807, was the daughter of Joseph Atkinson, Esq., of Crowhill, near Portadown, Co. Armagh, and was married on the 27th November, 1828, in the Parish Church of Tartaraghan, Co. Armagh, by the Rev. Henry Stewart, in the presence of her father, Joseph Atkinson, and Joseph Willis, to Francis Best, who was born in 1804.

They had issue:—

(1) George Reid, born on the 6th March, 1858, at Bowmanville, C.W., and died on the 16th January, 1861, at Quebec.

ALEXANDER BROCK BUCHANAN.

2. Alexander Buchanan, late of Vancouver, B. C., born on 1st September, 1861, at Quebec; married at Montreal on 25th November, 1903, Anna Mary, daughter of the late Hon. James O'Brien, of Montreal.

3. Rupert Charles Buchanan, of Montreal, born on 7th June, 1867, at St. Catherines, C. W.; married on 22nd April, 1896, at Quebec, Mary Jane, daughter of William McLimont, of Quebec, and has issue:

(1) Alexander Ronald, born 16th July, 1901.
(2) William Henry Keith, born 4th June, 1903.
(3) Nancy Greaves.

4. Arthur William Patrick Buchanan, K.C., of Montreal, born on 4th November, 1870, at Montreal; matriculated from the Montreal High School into the first year of the Faculty of Arts, McGill College, in September, 1887; graduated LL.B. in Laval University on 29th April, 1893, and admitted to the Bar of the Province of Quebec on the 8th July, 1894; appointed K. C. in 1908; married at the Parish Church of Stoke Poges, Bucks., Eng., by the Rev. Vernon Blake, Vicar of Stoke Poges, on the 2nd June, 1897, to Berthe Louise, elder daughter of the late William Quirin, and of Isabelle Mercer, his wife, of Boston, Mass.; admitted a member of the Buchanan Society, of Glasgow, Scotland, on the 1st November, 1900; practises with Mr. W. J.

White. K. C., the firm being White & Buchanan. He has issue:

(1) Erskine Brock Quirin, born on 21st March, 1898, at Montreal.
(2) Audrey Isabel Patricia.

5. Albert Edward Clarence Buchanan, born on 4th November, 1870, at Montreal.

1. Elizabeth Emily (Lemmy) died on 26th January, 1880, at Montreal.
2. Frances (Lily) married on 15th April, 1899, by the Rev. Canon Norton, D.D., at Christ Church Cathedral, Montreal, to Arthur Hamilton Buchanan, Manager of the Bank of Montreal at Spokane, U. S. A., son of the late Alexander Carlisle Buchanan, of Quebec.
3. Ethel (Cherry) died on 23rd September, 1898, at Montreal.
4. Gwendoline, died on Sunday, the 26th July, 1896, on her 19th birthday, at Montreal

VI. Margaret Lucy, born on 13th May, 1834, and died on 27th March, 1837.

VII. Frederick Albert, born on 17th February, 1836, and died on 27th October, 1842.

VIII. Mary Alexandrina, born on 25th October and died on 20th November, 1841.

IX. Mary, born on 10th October, 1842, married on 10th November, 1876, at St. Thomas's, Portman Square, London, to Richard Mainwaring Williams, M.A., St. Peter's College, Cambridge,

MRS. ALEXANDER BROCK BUCHANAN.

clerk in Holy Orders, Rector at that time of Edmondshaw, Dorset, and later of Harnhill, Cirencester, in Gloucestershire, Eng. She died on the 17th June, 1901, at Harnhill. She had issue:

(1) Herbert Mainwaring, born on 9th June, 1879, Lieutenant in the Army Veterinary Department.

(2) Gwladys Louisa.

(3) Marjorie Mary.

Buchanans of that Ilk.

Buchanans of that Ilk.[1]

For our knowledge of the history of the Family of Buchanan, we are indebted to William Buchanan of Auchmar. His very interesting Essay upon the Family and Surname of Buchanan, first published in the year 1723, and written in quaint language, is of the greatest authority. Our gratitude is due to the author for the splendid result of his labour and research, in which we possess so complete a record of the Family of Buchanan and of its various branches.

The author, the sixth Laird of Auchmar, married on the 4th June, 1696, Jean Buchanan, daughter of John Buchanan, Laird of Carbeth, and died in 1747.

In the preface to his book, the author says that in some cases, where authentic records could not be had, he had been obliged to take up with the best attested and most generally received traditional accounts; yet for the most part he says that he is supported in what he says by ancient charters of uncontested authority.

---

[1] The above is chiefly compiled from "A Historical and Genealogical Essay upon the Family of Buchanan," by William Buchanan of Auchmar, first published in the year 1723, and reprinted in 1820, and from "Strathendrick," by the late Mr. John Guthrie Smith, F. S. A., Scot., in which the section on the Buchanan genealogies was prepared by Mr. A. W. Gray Buchanan from genealogical trees and memoranda written by Mr. Guthrie Smith.

The following is the account which he gives of the origin of the family:—

"Sueno, or Canutus, at this time (1014) King of England and Denmark, his birth-day approaching, which all the Danish officers and soldiers in Ireland resolved to solemnize with great jollity, Turgesius, the Danish General, sent orders to all the Danish officers in Ireland to repair to Limerick, being their principal garrison and his residence, to assist at the solemnity, fearing nothing that the Irish would or could do in such low circumstances. The general at the same time sent orders to the Irish nobility and gentry, to send to Limerick against the King's birth-day a thousand, or, as others say, two thousand of the most beautiful of their daughters, to dally with the Danish officers at that festival. Of this the Irish King getting intelligence, resolved to send the desired number of the most clear-complexioned youths that could be found, clothed in women's habit, with long Irish skiens, or daggers, below their clothes, with orders that, so soon as they went to bed with their several paramours, being generally drunk on such occasions, they should stab them with these concealed daggers, and afterwards seize upon their guard-house, where their arms were laid by, and if matters succeeded, to give a signal by kindling a large fire upon the town wall; the Irish King with a small party being ambushed in a wood near by, in expectation of

"the event. These Irish viragoes put their orders
"into execution to the utmost, and having given
"the concerted signal to the King, introduced
"him and his party to the town, who, without
"any mercy or resistance, killed all the Danes
"in the garrison, being destitute of sense, officers,
"and arms, reserving their General Turgesius
"for further punishment, which was inflicted
"upon him by drowning, which then, and as yet,
"is reputed the most ignominious death among
"the Irish. Most of all the other Danes through-
"out the kingdom were shortly after cut off.
"This massacre was a kind of parallel to another
"of that nature committed on the Danes in Eng-
"land some little time before this, by command
"of Ethelred, the English King. But, as that,
"so also this, fell short of the success projected
"thereby. For no sooner was the Danish King
"of England informed of his countrymen's
"disaster, than he sent a powerful army into
"Ireland, which with the utmost rigour did pro-
"secute all who had any hand in this late tragedy;
"so that most of them fell victims to the rage
"of their inveterate enemies, and those who did
"not were necessitated to abandon their native
"country. Among the number of those was"—

I. Anselan Buey Okyan, or Fair Okyan, son to Okyan, provincial king of the south part of Ulster, who left Ireland about the year 1016, and went to Scotland, where he entered the service of Malcolm, King of Scotland, and for his services against the Danes received the grants of several lands in the north part of Scotland, is said by Auchmar to be the first Laird of Buchanan. The account of the origin of the surname of Buchanan in general, and of six of the first principal men of that family successively in particular, is founded by Auchmar upon probable and uncontroverted tradition.

"Anselan Okyan," says Auchmar, "not only " was recompensed for this service by King Mal-" colm with lands of considerable value, but also " with very splendid arms. The arms assigned " by that king to this Anselan upon account of " his descent, and more especially upon account " of his heroic achievements, are, in a field or, a " lion rampant sable, armed and langued gules, " holding in his paw a sabre, or crooked sword, " proper, which arms that surname retained " always without the least addition or variation, " until that addition obtained upon a very honour-" able occasion, at the battle of Bauge."

Anselan, the first Laird of Buchanan, married the heiress of Denniestoun, and was succeeded by his son,

 II. John, whose son and successor was

 III. Anselan, whose son and successor was

 IV. Walter, whose son and successor was

 V. Girald, or Bernard, whose son and succcessor was

 VI. MacBeath, whose son and successor was

 VII. Anselan, the seventh Laird, who was

seneschal to the Earl of Lennox. In the year 1225, he obtained from Malduin or Maldoven, third Earl of Lennox, a charter of an island in Loch Lomond called Clarines or Clareinch, which charter was confirmed by King Alexander II. in the year 1231. Of Clareinch, Auchmar says—

"The Isle of Clareinch was the slugorn, or call
" of war, proper to the family of Buchanan;
" such like being usual in all other families in
" these times, and for some following ages. So
" soon as this call was raised upon any alarm,
" the word Clareinch was sounded aloud from
" one to another, in a very little time, throughout
" the whole country; upon hearing of which all
" effective men belonging to the Laird of Buchanan,
" with the utmost diligence, repaired well armed,
" to the ordinary place of rendezvous, which,
" when the lairds resided in that island, was upon
" a ground upon the shore opposite thereto.
" That which in these more modern times came
" in place of the slugorn was the fire-cross, being
" a little stick with a cross on one end of it, the
" extremities of which were burnt, or made black
" by fire. This cross, being once set a-going,
" was carried through with such despatch, as in
" a few hours would alarm the people of a vast
" extent of ground."

"The name of Buchanan," he says, "was
" so numerous in heritors, and the castle of
" Buchanan so centrally placed in respect of the
" interests and residence of these heritors, that the

"Laird of Buchanan could, in a summer's day, call fifty heritors of his own name to his house, upon any occasion, and all of them might with conveniency return to their respective residences against night, the furthest of them not being above ten miles from Buchanan."

Anselan had three sons, Gilbert, his successor, (2) Methlen, ancestor of the McMillans, and (3) Colman, ancestor of the MacColmans.

VIII. Gilbert Buchanan, who is said to have been the first to assume the surname of Buchanan. The ancient surname of the family was MacAusland or Macausland. As to the meaning of the name Buchanan, the author of "Strathendrick" says:—

"The Rev. J. B. Johnston derives the place name Buchanan from the Gallic bog chanan, 'low ground belonging to the canon.' The surname also takes in Gallic the form 'Mac-a-chanonaich,' 'son of the canon,' but nothing seems to be known as to the canon to whom this refers, history and tradition being alike silent on the point."

Gilbert Buchanan, who was also seneschal, or chamberlain, to the Earl of Lennox, was Laird about 1274, and was succeeded by his son,

IX. Sir Maurice Buchanan, who had three sons, Maurice, his successor, (2) Allan, who married the heiress of Lenny, and (3) John, ancestor of Buchanan of Auchneiven.

X. Sir Maurice Buchanan lived about 1320. "There is a traditional account," says Auch-

mar, "that king Robert Bruce, after his defeat
"at Dalree, near Straithfillan, by Macdougall,
"lord of Lorn, and his adherents, came all alone,
"on foot, along the north side of Loch Lomond
"(being the most rugged way of any other of this
"kingdom), the day after that battle, to the castle
"of Buchanan; where, being joyfully received,
"and for some days entertained, he was secretly
"conveyed, by the earl of Lennox and Buchanan,
"to a place of safety. This report is the more
"probable, in regard there is a cave near the shore
"of Loch Lomond, in Buchanan parish, termed
"the King's Cave; it being reported, that king
"Robert lay over night in that cave, in his journey
"towards Buchanan." He married a daughter of
Sir Walter Menteith of Rusky and had a son,

XI. Sir Walter Buchanan, who, according
to Auchmar, "seems to have been a very active
"gentleman, and made a very bright figure in his
"time, having made a very considerable addition
"to his old estate by the purchase of a great
"many other lands." He lived to a great age,
and had only one son, John,[1] who married the
heiress of Lenny, and died before his father. This
John had three sons, (1) Sir Alexander Buchanan,
who slew the Duke of Clarence at the battle of
Bauge in 1420, and was himself slain at the battle
of Verneuil in the year 1424, being never married.
(2) Sir Walter Buchanan, who succeeded to the

---

(1) Auchmar designates this John the 12th Laird of Buchanan.

Estate of Buchanan, and (3) John of Ballachondachy, ancestor of the Buchanans of Lenny.

The author of the book Pluscarden gives the following account of these two battles:—

"In the year 1420 envoys were sent by
"Charles VII. king of France, to the governor
"of Scotland, the duke of Albany, for succour
"against Henry V., who was then invading the
"kingdom of France with a great host of men-
"at-arms, seizing and ravaging everything. So
"the governor called together the three estates
"of the realm, and despatched his son John, earl
"of Buchan, with whom was Archibald Douglas,
"eldest son of the earl of that ilk and nephew
"of the said duke, with ten thousand men-at-
"arms splendidly equipped at the expense of the
"said king of France; and ships were sent both
"from France and from Spain to the said king-
"dom of Scotland to bring the said nobles to the
"said kingdom of France. They were welcomed
"with the greatest rejoicings, and the chief leaders
"of the army were given fine places to live in,
"to wit, the castle of Chatillon to the earl of
"Buchan, the castle of Dunleroi to Archibald
"Douglas, earl of Wigtown; the castle of Lan-
"geais to sir Thomas Seton, and the castle of
"Concoursault to sir John Stewart of Darnley,
"together with their respective lands and domains
"and most wealthy towns and fortresses. Now
"these, until the battle of Bauge, were not thought
"much of, but were called by the French only

" mutton-eaters and wine-bibbers and consumers,
" and of no use to the king and kingdom of France,
" until and up to the time that the battle of
" Bauge was fought chiefly by the Scots, where
" the whole nobility and the flower of the English
" chivalry fell in battle, on Easter Eve, during
" an eight days' truce and armistice agreed upon
" by the chiefs, namely, the said lords of Scotland
" and the duke of Clarence of England, out of
" reverence for Christ's passion and the taking
" of the sacrament. Yet on the eve of the said
" Easter Festival, while the Scots thought no
" evil, nay, were utterly free from falseness and
" deceit, and were playing at ball and amusing
" themselves with other pleasant or devout oc-
" cupations, all of a sudden the English chiefs
" treacherously rushed upon them from an ambush
" while they were almost unarmed. But by God's
" mercy some men of note were playing at a pas-
" sage over a certain river, and they caught sight
" of their banners coming stealthily in ambush
" through the groves and woods. So they hastily
" gave the alarm at the top of their voices, and
" defended the passage for a while with bow and
" spear; else all the chiefs of Scotland, thinking
" no evil, would have been taken unawares and
" destroyed with the edge of the sword. But
" the English chiefs, fully armed *cap-a-pie*, pre-
" sumptuously thinking they would utterly bear
" down and defeat the Scots in the twinkling
" of an eye, left their archers behind in their too

"great haste; and thus they were routed by the
"Scots, who were lightly armed and almost with-
"out armour. For the latter are most mighty
"men at a sudden charge and very good with
"the spear; and they came pouring in at the word
"with great shouting, roused and emboldened
"by the bad faith of the English and strong in
"their own good faith, and thereby rendered
"braver; and with so impetuous an onset did
"they assail and bear down the English chiefs
"with spears and maces of iron and lead and
"keen-edged swords, that they bore down and
"felled to the earth both the chiefs and their
"comrades, as well as their standard-bearers,
"banners, attendants, pennons, flags and stan-
"dards, and at the first shock slew the flower
"of the chivalry of the English army, the duke
"of Clarence, brother to the king of England,
"and other generals and earls and magnates,
"knights and barons, with many other lords;
"and, when they had despatched their followers
"who were present, the others behind them, who
"were coming to the fight, were quickly put to
"flight. This was at the hour of Vespers. Further-
"more the chiefs of Scotland and their army
"pursued the fugitives as far as the bridge of a
"certain town which is called Le Mans, eight
"leagues off, killing some, capturing some and
"smiting down others, until interrupted by the
"night, when they escaped in the woods and
"groves."

"There was the king's brother the duke of
"Clarence slain, as stated, and the earl of Kyme,
"the earl of Riddesdale and the lord de Roos,
"together with the lord Grey of Codnor and many
"other barons, to the number of twenty-six
"territorial lords; and there were taken the earl
"of Somerset, brother of the queen of Scotland,
"the wife of King James I., and the earl of Hunt-
"ingdon. Somerset was taken by Lawrence
"Vernor, a Scot, and by sir John Sibbald, knight
"of Scotland; and also the brother of the said
"earl of Somerset. The lord of Fewant was
"also taken there, as well as many other lordlings
"of whom there is no mention. Nor do I find
"any positive account of who killed whom in
"such a general *mêlée*; but the common report
"was that a highland Scot named Alexander
"Macausland, a native of Lennox, of the house-
"hold of the lord of Buchan, killed the said duke
"of Clarence; for, in token thereof, the afore-
"said Macausland brought with him to camp a
"golden coronet of the finest gold and adorned
"with precious stones, which was found on his
"helmet upon his head in the field; and he sold
"it for a thousand nobles to the lord Darnley,
"who afterwards left that coronet to Robert
"Houston in pledge for five thousand nobles he
"owed him. Note that few Scotsmen and French-
"men died, not more than eighteen, of whom
"two were Frenchmen, men of quality, namely,
"Charles Boutillier and the brother of the lord

"des Fontaines. On the day following Easter
"Sunday news reached the king of the French
"that all the Scots ran away, and that the French
"gained the field and the victory and the honour;
"whereat the king of France, who was at Tours,
"marvelled greatly. But on the fourth day
"after the battle the Scottish chiefs presented
"themselves with their prisoners, two earls of
"England and five or six great barons, before
"the king of the French at the said city, while
"the French had no prisoners. Then the king
"publicly broke forth in these words, saying,
"'Ye who were wont to say that my Scots were
"of no use to me and the kingdom, and were
"worth nothing save as mutton-eaters and wine-
"bibbers, see now who has deserved to have
"the honour and the victory and the glory of
"the battle.'

"The Dauphin of France, seeing the summer
"was passing away and winter approaching,
"and looking to the good luck of the Scots and
"relying on their help, after mature deliberation
"sent the aforesaid earl of Buchan, Constable
"of France, into Scotland to bring back a larger
"army of Scots. He brought back with him
"Archibald, earl of Douglas, second of that name,
"together with ten thousand men-at-arms and
"many other nobles, knights, barons, lords and
"others, splendidly appointed, some of whom
"landed in Brittany, some at La Rochelle, at
"the Feast of Fasten's Even in the year 1423.

" The king of France was defunct, and his son
" the Dauphin Charles not as yet crowned, as
" divers cities stood in his way between him
" and the place of his coronation, the city of
" Rheims. He was indeed king, although not
" crowned; but he had few supporters in the
" kingdom, owing to the difference between him
" and the duke of Burgundy on account of the
" murder of the duke of Orleans; and therefore
" he was in great want of money. Still the king
" bestowed upon the said earl of Douglas the
" duchy of Touraine, and the other lords he grati-
" fied according to their rank, so that, what with
" gifts and with promises, they were content to
" live and die in the cause of the king against the
" English. At length the brother of the defunct
" king of England, the duke of Bedford, then
" regent in France, and with him the earl of
" Salisbury and the duke of Gloucester with a
" large train of men-at-arms, laid siege to the
" castle of Ivry in Perche, and it was arranged
" with them that, failing succour within forty
" days, the aforesaid castle was to be surrendered
" to them. So the chiefs of the Scots, seeing
" this, prepared with all alacrity and speed to
" have an encounter with them. And it came
" to pass thus. When this earl of Douglas and
" duke of Touraine had been made lieutenant-
" general of the king of France, and invested
" with the ducal coronet at Bourges in Berri
" with the utmost magnificence, and had after-

"wards posted guards in his castles and towns,
"he got ready on the appointed day; and with
"him were the said earl of Buchan, constable
"of France and son-in-law of the said lord duke,
"as well as the whole nobility of Scotland who
"were there at the time; and of Frenchmen
"there were the counts de Harcourt, d'Aumale,
"de Tonnerre, de Narbonne, and many French
"nobles; and these all fell in the battle, so that
"hardly any noble either of Scotland or of France
"escaped from the aforesaid, but was either
"taken prisoner or slain. There, on some level
"ground near the town of Verneuil, between the
"said castle of Ivry and the aforesaid town, died
"the said duke of Touraine, together with the
"constable of France, his son-in-law, and James
"Douglas, his second son, a most gallant knight,
"and the nephew of the king of Scotland, and
"other barons and knights, to the number of
"fifty lords of distinction, and a great host of
"others, both nobles and bowmen, whose num-
"bers it is impossible to fix with certainty, though
"they are set down at seven thousand Scots
"and five thousand Frenchmen. Now the man-
"ner and cause of the loss of the battle were as
"follows. The French army did not come quite
"in time on the appointed day for the recovery
"of the castle, but on the following day; and
"thus the castle was surrendered to the English,
"and the French army at Verneuil in Perche,
"which was held for the king of England, made

"ready and gave the assault and took the town.
" Then they posted their army all round and en-
" camped, thinking the English army would
" return to Normandy. At length French scouts
" came in great haste, saying that the whole
" chivalry of the English were approaching
" quickly in three separate lines of battle, and
" were about to charge them. On hearing this
" the Scottish chiefs fell to wrangling among
" themselves as to which of them should take
" precedence, and much jealousy was stirred up;
" and thus disunited, divided, not thoroughly
" one in heart, they marched upon the field of
" battle. The Frenchmen, however, who were at
" one among themselves, formed another line,
" while the Lombards and Germans were in re-
" serve in a third line.

" The French troops being thus drawn up,
" the English in like manner were drawn up in
" three lines of battle, in the first of which was
" the earl of Salisbury, in the second John duke
" of Bedford, and in the third Frenchmen, Bur-
" gundians, and strangers. The Scots first charged
" the vanguard of the English, where was the
" earl of Salisbury, and made the greatest havoc
" of them. Bringing some of them to the ground,
" killing some and putting others to flight, they
" drove them back splendidly, forcing them to
" retreat upon the second column or line of battle.
" On seeing this, the Lombards and Germans
" and Gascons, who had armour on their horses

"as well as on their bodies and were all mounted,
"being unwilling to dismount, and thinking the
"victory declared for the French, began to fall
"upon the baggage behind and rear-guard; for
"they were as it were a flying column appointed
"to succour the others in time of need. And in
"fact at the first onset they charged the English
"archers and broke their ranks; and, on others
"coming up, they made a gap through them,
"and passed on to the booty, while the others,
"in their terror, took to flight and joined the
"column of the duke of Bedford, where they
"rallied. And thus the English lords, inspirited
"by their arrival, renewed their battle cries,
"and, massing themselves in one body, returned
"and charged the ranks of the French and Scots,
"who, as already stated, were foolishly divided
"among themselves and allowed gaps in their
"line. Wherefore the English, caught between
"the lines of the Lombards and the French, so
"that they had either to defend themselves or
"die in battle, made an effort, pushed between
"their lines, and finally gained the victory,
"cruelly and mercilessly killing all the lords and
"nobles. The Lombards, however, after they
"and their followers had taken the spoil, seeing
"the result of the battle, the cruel slaughter
"and the flight of the French, retreated in a body
"without returning, and did not draw rein until
"they reached the river Loire, where they divided
"the spoil. And thus their plundering occasioned

"the loss of the battle. After the victory, however, the field was pillaged, and heralds sought out the bodies of the lords, to wit of the duke of Touraine, of the earl of Buchan, who was also the constable, and of James Douglas, the said duke's son; and their bodies were taken to Tours in a wagon, and were buried in one and the same grave in the cathedral church of the said city, in the middle of the choir. But the duke of Bedford, after gaining this victory, amid his pomp and vainglory was smitten with most loathsome leprosy on his return to Rouen, and expired, leaving the government to the earl of Salisbury, who began to exercise the office of regent in the most overbearing manner."

XII. Sir Walter Buchanan, married Isobel Stewart, daughter of Murdoch, Duke of Albany, and Governor of Scotland. He had three sons:—

(1) Patrick, his successor;

(2) Maurice, who was Treasurer to Princess Margaret, daughter to King James I. of Scotland, and wife of the Dauphin of France, afterwards Louis XI., and who accompanied her to France, and was present at her death in the year 1430. This Maurice Buchanan is supposed by Mr. W. F. Skene to be the author of the Liber Pluscardensis.

"He was," says Skene,[1] "a master of arts,

---

[1] Liber Pluscardensis, edited by Felix J. H. Skene. Preface, page 21.

"as appears by the title of Maitre, but must
"have been quite a young man, and in Sir John
"Stewart's (of Darnley) suite, and therefore
"must have been in the town of Orleans when
"Joan of Arc raised the siege, and entered the
"town in May, 1429, only three months after
"Sir John Stewart's death. Maurice of Buchanan
"must have seen her, and known her, and may
"have been present at her death. After this he
"returned to Scotland; for Bower, in narrating
"the voyage of the Princess Margaret to France
"in 1436, under the charge of the Bishop of Brechin
"and the Earl of Orkney, gives a list of her suite.
"In this list he gives the names of six knights.
"Then follow, ' Magistri Johannes Stewart, prae-
"positus de Methven, et Maurice de Buchanan,
"thesaurarius Delphinissae, clerici.' If Maurice
"of Buchanan was treasurer to the Dauphiness,
"he occupied a position that must have brought
"him into continual and close intercourse with
"her. He was also, as we see, a cleric, a Scots-
"man, and a Highlander of Lennox, and this
"combines in his person all the conditions indi-
"cated by the work itself."

"Pluscarden was a Cistertian Priory founded
"by Alexander the Second, and Spottiswood,
"in his account of it, adds, 'It is commonly
"reported that the famous Book of Pluscarden,
"seen and perused by George Buchanan, was
"penned here.' I am indebted to Mr. Stuart
"for a passage in the history of the Abbots of

" Kinloss by Ferrerius, which bears that during
" the tenure of the abbacy by John Flutere,
" seventeenth Abbot from 1445 to 1460, the White
" monks were ejected from Pluscarden, and
" Black monks, or Benedictines, introduced.
" These monks seem to have come from Dun-
" fermline, for in the chartulary of Dunfermline
" there is, in 1454, a commission by the Abbot of
" Dunfermline to the Prior of Pluscarden, in
" which it is called ' a cell of Dunfermline,' and
" ' a convent now of the order of St. Benedict; '
" and 1456, another commission by the Abbot
" of Dunfermline to William de Boyis, his sacris-
" tan, to visit the Priory of Pluscardyn, with a
" view to its reformation,—a commission which
" ended in the usual way, for in 1460 we find
" the Abbot confirming a deed granted by William
" de Boyis, Prior of the Priory of Pluscarden.

" In the following year, 1461, the author writes
" his history at the command of the Abbot of
" Dunfermline, which would be intelligible enough
" if he had then retired to Pluscarden, at that
" time a cell of Dunfermline, and under the Abbot's
" jurisdiction.

" The conclusion I come to is, therefore, that
" the Liber Pluscardensis, or Book of Pluscarden,
" is the correct name of this work, and that it
" was probably compiled in the Priory of Plus-
" carden, in the year 1461, by Maurice Buchanan,
" who was a cleric, and had been treasurer to
" the Dauphiness."

(3) Thomas Buchanan, ancestor of Carbeth.

XIII. Patrick Buchanan, who married one Galbraith, heiress of Killearn, Bamoir and Auchinreoch, had (1) Walter, his successor, and (2) Thomas Buchanan, ancestor of Drummikill, and a daughter Anabella married to James Stewart of Baldorrans.

XIV. Walter Buchanan, who married the daughter of Lord Graham, had two sons:

(1) Patrick Buchanan,[1] who married the daughter of the Earl of Argyle, was killed at the battle of Flodden in the year 1513, in the lifetime of his father and left two sons, (1) George, who succeeded his grandfather, and (2) Walter Buchanan, ancestor of Spittal.

(2) John Buchanan, of Arnpryor and Gartartan, ancestor of the family of Arnpryor.

XV. George Buchanan, who succeeded his grandfather, Walter Buchanan of that Ilk, married, first, Margaret Edmondstone, daughter of the Laird of Duntreath, by whom he had (1) John,[2] who died before his father, married, first, Elizabeth Levingstoun, daughter of Lord Levingstoun, and had George, his successor; secondly, Helen Chisholme, daughter of William, Bishop of Dunblane, by whom he had a daughter, Elizabeth, married to Mr. Thomas Buchanan of Ibert, Lord Privy Seal; second, Janet Cunninghame, daughter

---
(1) This Patrick Buchanan is designated by Auchmar as the 16th Laird of Buchanan.
(2) Auchmar calls him the 18th Laird of Buchanan.

of Cunninghame of Craigens, and widow of the Laird of Houston. He had by this marriage, (2) William, ancestor of Buchanan of Auchmar, and a daughter Margaret, first married to Cunninghame of Robertland, secondly to Stirling of Glorat, and thirdly to Douglas of Mains. George, Laird of Buchanan, was Sheriff-Principal of Dumbartonshire, and died 15th February, 1560–61.

XVII. Sir George Buchanan, succeeded his grandfather, George, Laird of Buchanan, in 1561. He married Lady Mary Graham, daughter of John, Earl of Menteith, and had John and two daughters, (1) Helen, who married Alexander Colquhoun of Luss, and (2) Susanna, who married John Macfarlane of that Ilk.

XVIII. Sir John Buchanan, who married Annabel Erskine, daughter of Adam, Commendator of Cambuskenneth, son of the Master of Mar, had, (1) George, his successor, and (2) Walter Buchanan. This Sir John Buchanan "was," says Auchmar, "accounted the worst, if not the "only bad one of all the Lairds of Buchanan;" and by his frequent travels into foreign nations and other extravagances had involved his estate in such an immense debt that his grandson at first found it inconvenient to enter as heir.

XIX. Sir George Buchanan, was Colonel of the Stirlingshire Regiment, and lost a great many of his regiment and kinsmen at the battle of Ennerkeithing, in which he was taken prisoner, and died in 1651. Of him Auchmar writes:

"George, third of that name, Laird of Bu-
"chanan, father to the late laird, who being
"colonel of the Stirlingshire regiment, during the
"whole of the civil wars in the reign of king
"Charles I., was with his regiment (most of the
"officers and a good many of the soldiers thereof
"being of his own name) at the battle of Dunbar,
"as also at the fatal conflict of Ennerkeithing; at
"the last of which, Buchanan, with Sir John
"Brown, colonel of Midlothian regiment, with
"their two regiments, stopped the passage of the
"English army over Forth for some days, and
"would have continued so to do till relief had
"come from the king's grand army, then encamp-
"ed at Stirling, had not major general Holborn,
"commander in chief of that party of the Scot-
"tish forces (biassed as was thought with Eng-
"lish gold) commanded these brave gentlemen to
"abandon their post, and allow the English free
"passage, which when effected, the general drew
"on these two regiments with that of brave Sir
"Hector McLean, mostly composed of his own
"name, to an engagement with the best part of
"the English army; Holborn himself, with his
"regiment of horse, wheeling off without firing
"one shot, and leaving these three regiments of
"foot to the mercy, or rather merciless rage of the
"enemy, they after a most valiant resistance,
"even much greater than could be expected
"from their number, were in the end over-
"powered, and mostly cut to pieces. The laird of

"McLean, with most of any account of his name, was killed, as also a vast number of the name of Buchanan, the laird himself with Sir John Brown, and some few other officers, being made prisoners, in which condition Buchanan continued unreleased till his death in the year 1651."

Sir George married Elizabeth Preston, only daughter of Sir George Preston of Craigmillar. He had one son, John and three daughters, (1) Helen, who married Sir John Rollo of Bannockburn, (2) Agnes, who married James Stewart of Rosyth (3) Jean or Janet, who married John Leckie of that Ilk.

XX. John Buchanan, last Laird of Buchanan, who married, first, in 1653, Lady Mary Erskine, daughter of Henry, Lord Cardross; and second, in 1677, Jean Pringle, daughter of Mr. Andrew Pringle, a minister. By his first wife he had a daughter, Elizabeth, married to James Stewart of Ardvoirlich, by whom he had a daughter, Janet, married to Henry Buchanan of Leny. In consequence of the extravagances of his grandfather, Sir John Buchanan, the last Laird succeeded to a greatly encumbered estate, and being compelled to compromise with the creditors he entered upon the estate as singular successor. He died in December, 1682, and his estate was purchased from his creditors by James, third Marquis of Montrose.

As given by Auchmar, the paternal arms of the family of Buchanan are:—

Or, a lion rampant sable, armed and langued gules, within a double tressure, flowered and counterflowered with flower-de-luces of the second.

Crest, a hand coupee holding up a ducal cap, or duke's coronet, proper, with two laurel branches wreathed surrounding the crest, disposed orleways proper; supported by two falcons garnished Or.

Ancient motto above the crest:—*Audaces Juvo*. Modern motto in compartment:—*Clarior Hinc Honos*.

The Buchanans of Blairlusk.

James Buchanan, H.B.M. Consul at New York.

The Buchanans of Blairlusk.

I. John Buchanan, of Gartincaber, the first son of the second marriage of Thomas Buchanan, 3rd Laird of Carbeth, and third in direct descent from Sir Walter Buchanan, 13th Laird of Buchanan (who lived about 1443), was born in 1545 and acquired the lands of Gartincaber. He had two sons, (1) George of Gartincaber and (2) William.

II. George Buchanan, of Gartincaber, married Elizabeth Leckie, and had four sons, the eldest, John, to whom his father gave the lands of Blairluisk or Blairlusk.

III. John Buchanan, of Blairlusk, had two sons, (1) George of Blairlusk and (2) William.

IV. George Buchanan, of Blairlusk, was born in 1648, succeeded his father in 1662, and having sold his estate of Blairlusk to his brother, William, went to Ireland. He settled at Deroran in the County of Tyrone, in 1674, and married, in 1675, Elizabeth Mayne, and had four sons : (1) John of Tyrone, ancestor of James Buchanan, H. B. M. Consul at New York from 1816 to 1843; (2) William of Tyrone, from whom the Buchanans of Meadville, Pennsylvania, U.S.A., are said to be descended; (3) George of Munster, from whom the Buchanans of Louisville, Kentucky, U.S.A., are said to be descended; and (4) Thomas of Ramelton in Donegal, said to be the ancestor of James Buchanan, who became President of the United States.[1]

V. John Buchanan, of Tyrone, who was born about 1676; married, in 1703, Catherine Black, and had a son John, and others.

VI. John Buchanan, of Donaghanie, near Omagh, was born in 1704; married first, in 1735, Jane Nixon, and by her (who died in 1736) had one son, (1) John of Omagh; secondly, in 1738, Mary Orr, and had issue, besides a daughter, (2) William, of Deroran, (3) Andrew, and (4) Patrick.

VII. John Buchanan, of Omagh, was born in 1736. He married, first, Jane Long, who died without issue; and, secondly, in 1770, Sarah, daughter of James Sproule, of Granan, near Dromore, Co. Tyrone, and sister of Oliver Sproule, Esq., M.D. He was a Commissioner to value the glebe house upon a death. He died at Omagh, on the 13th October, 1820, aged 84 years. His wife died there on the 30th April, 1822, in her 71st year. They were buried in Donaghanie Church Yard, near Omagh. They had issue:

(I) James Buchanan, H. B. M. Consul at New York, of whom hereafter.

---

[1] "Strathendrick," by J. Guthrie Smith, page 351. James Maclehose & Sons, Glasgow, 1896

(II) Jane, married to James Robinson, brewer, of Londonderry, and subsequently of Niagara, Canada, and had issue, among others, Sarah Jane, married in 1832 to James Jay, of Litley Court, Herefordshire, and a Magistrate for the City of Hereford, and Helena, married to Surgeon Waters, of Birr, Ireland.[1]

(III) John Buchanan of Lisnamallard, Co. Tyrone, born in 1779, and died at Omagh on the 12th January, 1842. He acquired the estate of Lisnamallard in 1828. He married, in April, 1820, Mary Jane, daughter of James Blacker, a Sheriff's Peer and Police Magistrate of Dublin, and had issue:

(1) John Blacker, Acting Clerk of the Peace for the County of Tyrone and Agent of the Earl of Charlemont, d.s.p. 1862;

(2) Jane Elizabeth;

(3) Sarah, d.s.p.;

(4) James, d.s.p.;

(5) George, of Keston Tower, Kent, born in 1827, M. I. C. E.; married, in 1860, Gertrude, daughter of George Armitage, D. L. Yorks, and died, s.p. 7th June, 1897;

(6) Elizabeth, d.s.p.;

(7) William, d.s.p.;

---

[1] James Jay, Esq., of Litley Court, Herefordshire, Magistrate for the City of Hereford; born 1808, married 1832, Sarah, daughter of James Robinson, Esq., and by her had, with other issue, James Albert Buchanan, Captain 3rd Royal Lancashire Militia, born 1838, married 1869, Alice Marianne, daughter of James T. Hill, of Hull, and by her, who died 3rd November, 1907, had issue a daughter.

(8) Mansergh George, d.s.p.;

(9) Alexander Carlisle, of Riverdale, Omagh, and late of Morden, Manitoba, Canada, born in 1834; married, in 1863, Anna Sophia, daughter of D. Wilson, and died leaving issue:

(1) George Alexander, of Morden, married Nora Clutterbuck of Bath, and has issue.

(2) John, who volunteered for active service in South Africa and served in the Strathcona Horse.

(1) Mabel, married to Richard Heckels, and has issue.

(2) Jane Gertrude, married to Arnold Bowen, and has issue.

(3) Florence, married to Gustavus Piggott, and has issue.

(4) Bertha Violet, married to Charles H. Edwards, and has issue.

(10) Colonel Lewis Mansergh Buchanan, C.B., F.R.G.S., F.R. Met. Soc., of Edenfel and Lisnamallard, near Omagh, Co. Tyrone, late Colonel commanding the Fourth Battalion Enniskillen Fusiliers, born 31st December, 1836; joined Royal Tyrone Fusiliers Militia in 1855, and volunteered with 80 men to the Army in the Crimea in 1856; was gazetted to the 88th Connaught Rangers, with which distinguished Regiment he served through the Indian Mutiny, including

COL. LEWIS M. BUCHANAN, C.B.

the actions at Cawnpore under Major General Windham, battle of Cawnpore, capture of Lucknow, operations in the Doab with the Column under Colonel G. V. Maxwell, to whom he was Orderly Officer, and siege and capture of Calpee, receiving medal and clasp; rejoined Royal Tyrone Fusiliers in 1862, and commanded the Battalion from 1887 to 1897. He is the author of " Last Winter in Spain," "Through the Himalayas and Chinese Thibet," and "The Climate of Ulster." He married first, in 1862, Eleanor Margaret, daughter of William Whitla and Elizabeth Buchanan, and by her (who died in 1877) has issue:

(1) Lt. Colonel John Blacker Buchanan, R.A.M.C., born 26th April, 1863; educated at Sherborne and Dublin University; served in the South African War, 1899-1901, and took part in the relief of Ladysmith and was mentioned in the despatches; married 25th October, 1894, Mary Louisa, daughter of Rev. A. A. Harland, Harefield, Middlesex, and has issue: (1) Dora Mary, died June, 1895; (2) Helen Margaret and (3) Evaleen Mary, twins; (4) Mary Elizabeth.

(2) Lewis Ernest, Major Fourth Battalion Royal Enniskillen Fusiliers, born 4th September, 1868; volunteered for active service in South Africa and served in the South African War; married, 3rd December, 1903,

Constance Kate, daughter of Frederick S. Goulding, Brockley, Kent, and has issue:

(1) Joyce E. and (2) Audrey E.

(3) Mansergh George Reginald, born 7th September, 1870.

(4) Calvert James Strong, born 10th July, 1872; served through the South African War with the Rhodesian Horse and was severely wounded.

(1) Ellen Elizabeth, married to William P. Grubb, of Bessbrook, and has issue.

(2) Mary Jane Eleanor, married to Effingham MacDowel, M.D., F.R.C.S., of Sligo, and has issue.

(3) Alice Lilian, married to Charles Hope, of Chatham House, Trowbridge, Kent, and has issue.

(4) Eleanora Agnes, married Sept. 3, 1902, to Colonel Mackenzie Churchill, late Military Secretary, Ceylon, and has issue.

Colonel Buchanan married, secondly, in 1878, Wilhelmina, daughter of George A. Molony, R.M.

(IV) George Buchanan, born in 1782, sometime Hearth and Window Collector at Belfast and Chief Distributor of Stamps for Co. Tyrone, died s.p. in 1869.

(V) William Buchanan, born 14th July, 1785; married in June, 1814, Anne Hazlett, daughter of George Hazlett, of Londonderry, who died in Ireland. He went to Canada and settled at Yamaska, Lower Canada, where he had steam mills. He became a Justice of the Peace for the District of Three Rivers, and died at Montreal on the 16th August, 1834, leaving a daughter, Ann. She was born in Londonderry on the 11th June, 1816, and was married at Montreal on the 22nd August, 1834, to Henry McFarlane, of London, afterwards of Rocky Hill, New Jersey (born in April, 1810, at Boston, and died 11th March, 1887, at Rocky Hill). She died 11th November, 1886. They had issue:

(1.) Henry McFarlane, born 18th June, 1835; d.s.p. 24th October, 1858.

(2) William Buchanan McFarlane, born 3rd May, 1844.

(3) George Elliot McFarlane, born 6th November, 1848.

(1) Anne McFarlane, married Abram Voorhees, of Rocky Hill, N.J., and left issue.

(2) Marie McFarlane, married Claude Chateaux, of Pau, France, and left issue.

(3) Helen McFarlane, married Rev. Lewis Henry Lighthipe, of Orange, N.J., and left issue.

(4) Laura Elizabeth McFarlane.

(5) Flora McFarlane.

(6) Alice Frances McFarlane.

(7) Catherine Estelle McFarlane.

(8) Mary McFarlane.

(VI) Alexander Carlisle Buchanan, born in 1786; went to Canada and became His Majesty's Agent for Emigrants at Quebec. He wrote "Emigration Practically Considered, with detailed Directions to Emigrants proceeding to British North America," published in 8vo. in 1826. A second edition was brought out in 1834. He returned to Ireland, and died s.p. at Omagh, on the 13th April, 1840; and

(VII) Sarah Caroline, born in 1793, was married, first, on the 30th March, 1812, at Omagh, to Captain Joseph Orr, of the East Norfolk Regiment, who resided at Salem, near Londonderry, Ireland (he died on the 6th May, 1826, from the effects of a fall from a horse); secondly, at Cappagh, Tyrone, on the 23rd September, 1829, to James Marks, of New Road, Fitzroy Square, London, and died without issue on the 16th November, 1862, at Kingstown near Dublin, Ireland.

JAMES BUCHANAN,
H. B. M. Consul at New York.

James Buchanan, H.B.M. Consul at New York.

James Buchanan was born at Strathroy, near Omagh, County Tyrone, Ireland, on the 1st February, 1772. When he was two years old his father removed to Omagh, where he received his education. Upon the advice of Mr. Alexander Carlisle, an Irish solicitor, he studied law, and accompanied Mr. Carlisle on circuit to the Liffy Assizes. He states that in the year 1787 he set out for Dublin on horse-back, there being at that time no stages, for the purpose of being formally indentured to Mr. Henry Gower, Solicitor, the Dublin agent of Mr. Carlisle, and having signed his Articles he returned home until the next term. As for the first two years of his clerkship he was only required to attend the Hilary and Trinity Terms, he remained at Omagh acting as Mr. Carlisle's clerk and looking after his business, but the next three years he attended all the Terms.

In 1791, he made the acquaintance of Mr. and Mrs. Francis Tempest Brady, whose son, Maziere Brady,[1] in 1822, married Elizabeth, daughter

---

[1] Maziere Brady, born 20th July, 1786, married 26th July, 1823, Elizabeth Ann (who died 15th June, 1858), daughter of Bever Buchanan, Esq., of Dublin. He became Lord Chancellor of Ireland, was created a Baronet, and died in 1871, being succeeded by his son, Francis William Brady, now Sir Francis Brady, K.C., County Court Judge of Tyrone.

of Bever Buchanan, of Dublin, and became Lord Chancellor of Ireland, and of Richard Robinson, brother of James Robinson, of Dublin, afterwards of Londonderry, brewer, who married his sister, Jane Buchanan. At that time Mr. Brady lived at No. 18 Parliament Street, Dublin, where he carried on the business of lace manufacturer and hatter. This Bever Buchanan died on the 1st January, 1813, aged thirty years, "upon his return from a party at which he had appeared in good health and spirits."

In 1792, upon his admission to the practice of the law, he took lodgings with the Robinsons and occupied their second floor for three years. It was here that, in 1792, he met Miss Sarah Hodgson, whose father lived at Workington, in Cumberland, in England. Through her mother, who was a near relative of Mrs. Brady, he made her a proposal of marriage, which was accepted, and in the month of September, 1794, he went to Cumberland. All arrangements were made for the wedding, which, however, never took place on account of her sudden death. He says:

"I was vain enough to take a man servant "with me, and went to Mr. Hodgson's house, "where I resided with a very interesting family, "two gentlemen and three ladies, and most "respectably connected, where I was handsomely "entertained. The use of a servant then was to "dress my hair, wearing powder, such was es- "sential. After a week or ten days, our marriage

" was fixed, but Sarah having taken cold, a fever
" ensued, which confined her to bed, and as I
" had to be back in Dublin before the first of
" November, to attend Term, the family thought
" she would be able to go to church, and having
" been dressed, I aided her downstairs, but she
" fainted and had to return to bed. I therefore
" determined to proceed by way of Liverpool to
" Dublin, which I did a day or two after; and when
" I reached Liverpool, where her brother, an
" attorney, resided, he next morning received a
" letter of Sarah's death. To describe my feelings
" is out of the question, nor shall I attempt it. I
" deemed it the heaviest calamity that could
" befall me. There was a meekness and total
" absence of vanity on account of her personal
" attractions that rendered her, in the eyes of all,
" more lovely and interesting."

About this time, a contested election of the City of Londonderry was the means of introducing him to the notice of the Government. " Mr.
" Carlisle," he says, " being a freeman of the city,
" and so confined with the gout determined on
" being as it were carried to Derry, and I accom-
" panied him and helped him into bed and to put
" on his clothes. We arrived on the last day of
" the election. The candidates were Sir George Hill
" and Henry Alexander, a nephew of Lord Caledon.
" His (Alexander's) father had been an alderman
" and built a splendid house near the City of
" Derry. Sir George Hill was the son of the

"Collector of the Port. On proceeding to the
"poll Mr. Carlisle had to be borne in an armchair
"over the heads of the people and voted for Mr.
"Alexander, and I believe his was the last vote.
"In a few hours Mr. Alexander came to the Inn
"to return thanks to Mr. Carlisle and to express
"his gratitude that being so ill he should incur the
"risk of the journey, and quite unexpected I,
"of course, was in the room, and having asked
"Mr. Carlisle how he should prove his gratitude,
"Mr. Carlisle replied he had no request as to
"himself, but he came on account of the young man
"present, and any service he should render him
"was all he had to ask. I was not expecting this,
"upon which Mr. Alexander assured me that on
"all occasions he would feel most happy to serve
"me, and I must add, while I deemed it of little
"importance at the time, yet through life he
"faithfully fulfilled his promise."

His income derived from his practice soon permitted him to keep a saddle horse in Dublin and to take additional lodgings at the Black Rock, to which he rode daily.

"Disaffection and rebellion," he says, "was
"fast spreading in Ireland in 1793 and 1794 under
"different names, chiefly among all denominations
"but the Church of England, as only the mem-
"bers of that church were appointed to office and
"to the Magistracy, but the Test Act having been
"repealed, by which I, the son of a Presbyterian,
"was put on the same footing as any other subject,

" I was determined to hold by the Crown though none of my family held any office.

" Having called a public meeting to raise a Corps of Volunteers in Omagh, Mr. Galbraith, Lord Belmore's agent, a magistrate and of great might, felt my assumption a reproach and he set on foot a company. I could take no command as residing in Dublin, but I induced a Mr. Smyley, a gentleman of respectability, and a Mr. Simpson, an active young man in Omagh, to become officers, and selected some influential men to be sergeants. In consequence of these efforts a day was fixed for accepting the service of one or other of the companies. My squad was drawn up before my father's house; Mr. Galbraith's at his home. The officer arrived, and, having briefly heard the facts as to my having started the idea, sanctioned my company, and they were forthwith drilled, clothed, and held their position during all the troubles."

In 1796, he joined the " Attorneys' Corps," which was raised that year in Dublin. Each company was composed of 100 men, and no man under six feet was admitted into the grenadier company. He not being of the required height was placed in the rear guard. The silver plate, a buckle with the letters A. C. and the date 1796 with the arms of Ireland on it, which belonged to him is still in the family.

It was about this time that he bought the house No. 44 William Street in Dublin, which he occupied until he removed to Omagh. This house had belonged to Mr. Henry Alexander.

The Rebellion of 1798 having widely spread, James Buchanan was introduced by Mr. Alexander to Mr. Hamilton, Under Secretary of State, who consulted him as to what should be done to counteract the efforts of the disaffected in the County of Tyrone, and as a result he was vested with authority to take such steps as circumstances might call forth. He relates the part which he played in the Rebellion.

"I proceeded," he says, "on horseback to "Omagh (from Dublin), with my hair up under "my hat without powder, as croppies were the "most of the Rebels. On the day I left Dublin an "express had arrived of the defeat of the Rebels "at I forget the place. On arriving at Drogheda, "when I got to the Inn, before I had alighted "from my horse, numbers asked what was the "news as they saw I came from Dublin, which "I told with a degree of pleasure. After I had "put my horse in, a gentleman followed me, and "asked me when I intended to start. 'Then, sir, "if you are going to stay all night, you must come "to my house, for your life is not safe.' I then "told him I would order my horse to be made up "for the night, and if he would get me the pass- "word, as soon as the sentinels were placed I "would order my horse and proceed on all night, "for did I stay word would be passed and I would "be attacked on the way. This was approved, the

" password was obtained, and about ten o'clock
" I went to see my horse. I told the hostler to
" saddle and I mounted in the yard and rode off,
" none seeing me. I rode all night, and on coming
" to Castle Blaney, after feeding my horse which
" was tired, having rode about 40 Irish miles, I got
" off to walk up a long hill. I fell in with two
" girls. I asked them had I any friends. On this
" question being regarded as a Croppy Rebel from
" my hair being up under my hat, and I lied by
" telling them I had made my escape from the
" battle referred to. They at once urged me to
" come to their father's house, where I would be
" safe; that Lord Blaney was friendly to the Rebels.
" They assured me there was not a house but
" had a pike. This information astonished me,
" and seeing men coming up I told the girls I was
" afraid of my life in being followed, and much
" to their surprise and astonishment I mounted
" quickly and darted off. If the men had come
" up and the girls knew them, my lie, always a bad
" refuge, would have led me into a serious difficulty.
" I had determined to sleep at Mrs. Maxwell's,
" nearly four miles from Monaghan, and while I
" was descending a hill I saw two men, each with
" a long pole for pike handles. With a foolish
" hardihood, I dashed at one of the men, seized
" the pike handle and galloped off. On reaching
" Mrs. Maxwell's I threw down the pike and told
" her my story in the presence of a number of
" persons. On coming from the stable she told

"me I must go away or my life would not be safe.
"Having rode about 60 Irish miles and my fine
"horse tired I told her I would, but the people must
"not know I am going away that night, though I
"anticipated to start in safety; so at a late hour
"my horse was got ready and I proceeded and
"reached Omagh the next morning in safety, and
"made known the glad tidings referred to. Omagh
"was the head-quarters of the Queen's County
"Militia, commanded by Lord Portarlington, who
"had taken from the inhabitants all their arms
"as if they were Rebels, while no community in
"the North was more truly loyal. I remonstrated
"on the consequences, and pressed His Lordship
"to restore the arms to me. At first he refused,
"and stated he would withdraw his sentinels.
"Whereupon I stated I would furnish that night
"60 of the most devoted loyal men who would
"mount guard if he did so. Upon which he
"desisted. The next day I sent for several in-
"fluential men and the Presbyterian clergy, and
"held a meeting and prepared an address to the
"Lord Lieutenant. At this meeting I was enabled
"to state that forthwith in the district 5000 loyal
"men would be enrolled and place themselves
"under the orders of officers appointed by His
"Majesty, and would serve for the preservation
"of the County without pay, so that the regular
"troops might be withdrawn. The next morning
"I proceeded to Dublin with this address to the
"Lord Lieutenant, and it so happened that an

" express the same morning reached the Castle
" of the Rebellion in the North, and that Lord
" O'Neill was killed and the whole North was in
" rebellion. Most opportune my address, coming
" at the same hour. Placards were posted through
" the city of my arrival with the address referred
" to, and it was deemed of great importance, and
" my reception was gratifying. Bringing up this
" address opened to me the doors of the Castle, and
" I was frequently informed of matters to see if I
" could be of any service. Mr. Pelham, afterwards
" Duke of Newcastle, having succeeded Lord
" Castlereagh, was very communicative to me,
" and preferred referring to me than to the usual
" channels of information."

Having thus obtained a certain amount of influence with the Government, he secured for his brother, George Buchanan, the appointment of Hearth and Window Collector of Belfast, and got a distant relation appointed to the Customs.

He thus refers to his connection with the Regium Donum: " About this time (1798) orders had
" come to ascertain the effect of extending the
" Regium Donum to the Presbyterian Clergy, to
" insure their adhesion to the Crown. The North
" of Ireland being the chief place where Pres-
" byterians have influence, Mr. Alexander was
" enquired of to point out some Presbyterians to
" whom the Lord Lieutenant could refer the sub-
" ject, and quite unexpected I was named, though
" a young man, yet would be able to give a fair view

"of the case. The day was appointed for me to
"attend the Lord Lieutenant; only Mr. Secretary
"Pelham was present. I had no specific informa-
"tion of the object (of the meeting), and upon His
"Excellency putting the question to me, what
"would be the effect of the proposed increase of
"the measure, I stated that I was not aware
"fully of the subject, but viewing the proposition
"as a prudent measure no doubt could arise but
"such would ensure the attachment of the Clergy
"to the Crown. 'But your Excellency must
"pardon me viewing the measure as one of policy.
"Why not extend it to the Roman Clergy?'
"His Lordship asked me what were their number.
"This I could not answer. He asked me what
"I would propose. I answered, £100 yearly to
"each. From their great number he would not
"recommend such an expense. My answer was,
"'Not the expense of a regiment of horse, my
"Lord.' At that time the priests would have
"accepted it and thereby placed themselves on
"the same footing as other dissenters. Some
"years afterwards I met Mr. Pelham, then, I
"believe, Duke of Newcastle; he crossed to meet
"me, and after a few observations he stated, 'I
"shall never forget your Regiment of Horse.'"

He now married, and has left an account of the way he met his wife. "A relative of mine, Bever
"Buchanan, a young apothecary, having studied
"in Dublin, determined to set up business. A
"friend of mine advised him to select the city

ELIZABETH BUCHANAN.

" quay, which he did. Mr. Clarke, my wife's
" father, had an establishment there for the accom-
" modation of vessels, and his son John, who had
" regularly worked in the forges for five years,
" chiefly attended at that shop, which being next
" to Buchanan's shop, he frequently went in
" there to rest. There I became acquainted with
" him and then with the family, and from thence
" my marriage with my dear old wife. From
" my intimacy with the Bradys, I introduced
" Bever Buchanan there; the result was he married
" the sister of Mrs. Brady. The son of Mr. Brady
" having married the daughter of Bever Buchanan,
" the apothecary, who was his cousin, the same
" Maziere Brady is now Lord Chancellor of Ireland,
" and Bever Buchanan's daughter is the wife of
" the Lord Chancellor."

All these events, as well as the marriage of James Robinson to his sister Jane, he attributed to a Sunday expedition to Kingston in the year 1791, on which occasion he rowed Mr. and Mrs. Brady and Richard Robinson across the Bay.

His marriage with Elizabeth Clarke took place at the house of her father, Mr. James Clarke, Aston Quay, Dublin, on the 28th of December, 1798; the Reverend Mr. Horner officiated, and Mr. Cheyne Brady, brother of Mr. Brady, was the groomsman. His wife, Elizabeth Clarke, was born at Dublin on the 13th November, 1779. Her father, James Clarke, died at Ringsend, near Dublin, on the 14th March, 1823, in his 86th year.

He was married three times. His first wife, mother of all his children, was Elizabeth Stockdale; his second, Mary Mack; and his third, who survived him, Elizabeth Courtney.

In 1799, a proposition having been made in Parliament to supply Dublin with coals, James Buchanan was appointed to examine and report on coal mines in England, and in pursuance of this he visited several of them. Having approved of the scheme, he was authorized to prepare a dock near the city for that purpose, but the Union having taken place the measure was never realized.

In the year 1800 he gave up his profession, and on the 12th of November of that year bought the estate of "Lisanelly," near Omagh, from Sir John Stewart, Bart., for £4500, and caused the old house to be fitted up and offices built, and in the spring of 1801 caused extensive plantations to be made, so that, he says, " the place which I "called Farm Hill became truly attractive, and "so important did Sir John Stewart deem having "a residence at Omagh, that taking into considera- "tion my improvements he purchased back the "property from me in the year 1802 for £8,000."

He was appointed a Magistrate for the County of Tyrone, previous to his removal to "Woodbrook," near Baron's Court, the Marquis of Abercorn's demesne, two miles from Newton Stewart. He says: "From having nothing to do "at Woodbrook, I felt time very heavy, and ad-

" joining my house was a linen Black Green, oc-
" cupied by a Mr. Lane. In the North of Ireland
" the linen merchants were and are still the most
" respectable class, arising from the nature of the
" trade, all purchased with cash and sold for cash.
" Mr. Lane urged me to take up that business, and
" finding that a situation for Black Mills, etc.,
" had been partly erected at a place called Cam-
" owen about 3 miles from Omagh, without special
" prayer to God for guidance, or even consulting
" with prudent men, I went to Duncannon and
" purchased the farm, including what preparation
" had been made by Mr. Wilcox, for 700 pounds,
" and thus became linen merchant. On purchasing
" the grounds I named them Common Green, and
" then I expended above £2,000 on completing
" the work begun, and the Black yard was fully
" occupied by others as well as myself, and cer-
" tainly afforded me full and interesting employ-
" ment."

From 1804 to 1815 he lived at Common Green, and having sunk about £3000 in these mills, and finding himself unequal to the management, he determined to seek an office under Government. On the 3rd of January, 1815, he let his Green and house, and on the 8th of April auctioned his stock and crop at Common Green.

He was confident that his application for employment would be successful, as he says: " Having rendered service to the present Marquis " of Londonderry, who as the Honorable Mr.

"Stewart succeeded in his election for the County "Derry; with the friendship of Sir John Stewart "and the Duke of Newcastle, I was led to think I "stood a good chance."

On the 1st of May he sailed with his family from Dublin to Liverpool. He first took lodgings for his family at Chester and later removed to London, where, he says, "I met a gentleman who "had resided for some time at Baltimore, and "informed of the Consulate being vacant he "spoke so highly of it as far preferable to New "York, that procuring all my documents and "letters as to my service during the Rebellion in "Ireland, and supporting the Abercorn interest in "Tyrone and Lord Castlereagh's brother in the "County Derry; I was also favoured with a letter "from Sir George Hill, the member for the City "of Derry, and thus armed I proceeded to Paris, "as His Lordship was then at Paris. Mr. ——— "was Private Secretary, who kindly took posses- "sion of the documents and applied for the Con- "sulate of Baltimore. The next day I was honoured "with a letter to the Acting Secretary in London, "that His Lordship had granted my request. "On arrival in London I proceeded to the Foreign "Office and was kindly received, when the gentle- "man asked me why I had not applied for New "York, upon which I entreated his pardon in "asking him if he had any particular friend for "whom he was interested, and that if he had not "I would return direct to Paris. He said he had

" " not, but as Lord Castlereagh was returning then, I
" would not be likely to reach Paris before he left
" it. But I proceeded that night, and never
" slept until I reached Paris and waited on Mr.
" ———. I stated my anxiety as to New York
" which my connections with the County Derry ren-
" dered more desirable, for at the time I was not
" aware of the superiority of New York. In
" two days I was honoured with a letter to the
" Secretary in London, approving of the transfer,
" and away I went to London. This was early
" in September, 1815."

He was granted permission to delay his departure until the spring, and in order that his children might obtain some idea of the French language he removed with his family to Boulogne, where he took a house and remained until the 9th of February, 1816.

In the London Gazette of the 10th February, 1816, his appointment is there gazetted:—

"FOREIGN OFFICE, Feb. 10.

"His Royal Highness the Prince Regent has been pleased, in the name and on the behalf of His Majesty, to appoint James Buchanan, Esq., to be His Majesty's Consul at New York."

On the 3rd of April, 1816, he says; "At ten
" o'clock in the forenoon I embarked with my
" family, all but John Stewart, whom we left at
" Omagh with my father and mother, as also

"having George Buchanan, son of my uncle,
"Patrick Buchanan, Charles Caldwell, 2 servant
"maids, Peggy Forbes, Mary Devlin and Margaret
"Hamilton, in the ship 'Alexander Buchanan,'
"221 tons registered, when after a stormy passage
"it pleased God to land us safe after a passage
"of 46 days at New York," where he landed on
the 21st of May and established himself at Bloomingdale.

James Buchanan has left the following account of his family, written on the 1st October, 1834, in his sixty-third year:—

"Having removed from Ireland to America,
"which is likely to become the country of my
"posterity, the following facts may, at some
"remote period, prove interesting to some of them.
"My father's name was John Buchanan. He
"was the eldest son of John Buchanan, of Dona-
"ghanie, near Omagh, in the County of Tyrone.
"His mother, who was named Nixon, died in 1736,
"while he was young, leaving him her only issue.
"My grandfather married again Elizabeth Orr,
"by whom he had Patrick, William and Andrew
"Buchanan, and Elizabeth, who intermarried with
"John Morris. My father married, first, Jane Long,
"only daughter of a very respectable inhabitant
"of Omagh, who died without issue; secondly,
"my mother, Sarah Sproule, daughter of James
"Sproule, of Granan, near Dromore, in the County
"of Tyrone. All these parties named were gentle-

" men farmers living on their own lands and pos-
" sessing abundance of the good things of this life.
" My father occupied a farm called 'Strathroy,'
" now forming part of the Earl of Blessington's
" demesne, near Cappagh Church, where I was born
" on the 1st day of February, 1772. He afterwards
" removed to Omagh, where he purchased a piece
" of ground and built a tenement in which he lived
" many years, and which now belongs to my
" brother John. My father wished to make me
" an architect, but my mother wished to give me
" a good education, intending me for the law.
" She failed in the former but succeeded in the
" latter. A Mr. Alexander Carlisle, a very eminent
" solicitor residing in Omagh, became a resident
" in my father's family, and being much afflicted
" with gout he could not attend Term in Dublin,
" and had a partner, a Mr. Henry Gower, to whom
" I was articled for five years. In the year 1788,
" by reason of Mr. Carlisle's bad state of health,
" I had to attend to the business, and as soon as I
" was out of my clerkship he relinquished it to me.
" I thus commenced early in full practice, resided
" in Dublin, purchased a house on William Street,
" and on the 24th day of December, 1798, I married
" Elizabeth Clark, eldest daughter of James Clarke,
" of Aston Quay, iron founder. Mr. Clarke had
" two sons and two daughters.

"(1) John, the eldest, married Maria Kenny of
" Ballinrabe, in the County of Mayo. He died

"some years ago, leaving his widow and a numer-
"ous family in good circumstances.

"(2) William, who married a Miss Manders,
"and died, leaving two sons and two daughters.

"(3) Elizabeth, my wife.

"(4) Mary Ann, who married the late John
"Ledbetter, of College Green, Dublin, who died,
"leaving two daughters. She married again the
"Rev. Samuel Simpson, Presbyterian Clergyman,
"and both resided in Dublin, having children.

"At the time of my father's and mother's
"death, who both died full of years, leaving all
"their children in the enjoyment of abundance,
"to wit,—

"(1) Myself, their eldest.

"(2) My brother John, who married Mary
"Jane, daughter of James Blacker, a Sheriff's
"Peer and Police Magistrate of Dublin.

"(3) George, unmarried. He and John both
"residing at Omagh.

"(4) William, married a daughter of the late
"George Haslet of Londonderry, who died several
"years ago in Ireland, leaving only one daughter,
"named Ann, who, in 1834, intermarried with
"Henry McFarlane, of London. My late brother
"William died at Montreal of the cholera in 1834.

"(5) Alexander Carlisle, unmarried, His Majes-
"ty's Agent for Emigrants. residing at Quebec.

"(6) Jane, who intermarried with James
"Robinson, now residing at the City of the Falls,

"having a numerous family, two of her daughters
"having married; one, Sarah Jane, to a Mr. Jay
"of Hereford, in England, an eminent solicitor;
"the other, Helena, married Surgeon Waters,
"residing at Birr, Ireland.

"(7) Sarah, who had intermarried with Joseph
"Orr, who died, leaving her a widow, when in
"1829, she again married Mr. Marks, of New
"Road, Fitzroy Square, where she now resides.

"In the year 1799 I purchased Lisanelly, near
"Omagh, from Sir John Stewart, for which I paid
"4400 pounds, and I built a house there and called
"it 'Farm Hill,' where my daughter, Mary Ann,
"was born in the year 1802. Three years after I
"sold it (with improvements and other lands I
"had purchased) back to Sir John Stewart at
"4000 pounds profit. I then removed to 'Wood-
"brook,' near Baron's Court, the seat of the
"Marquis of Abercorn, and under the late Marquis
"raised and commanded the Baron's Court Corps
"of Yeomanry. During the previous year I
"was appointed a Magistrate of the County of
"Tyrone. In 1803 I purchased ' Common Green '
"from Mr. Wilcox, for which I paid 900 pounds,
"and erected black yard and buildings with other
"improvements on which I expended about 3000
"pounds. In order to aid my brother-in-law,
"James Robinson, I became a sharer in a brewery
"at Londonderry, in which I sunk about 2500
"pounds. My removal to Common and my
"residence there is adverted to in my narrative

"of my 'Religious Views.' The influence I pos-
"sessed in Tyrone with the weight of my family
"connections, as also in Londonderry, enabled me
"to promote the interest of the late Sir John
"Stewart in Tyrone, and the present Marquis of
"Londonderry in the County of Londonderry,
"in their respective elections, by reason whereof,
"and from my services as a Magistrate and
"Yeomanry Officer in Tyrone, the late Marquis of
"Londonderry recommended me to His Majesty as
"Consul for New York, where I arrived in the
"month of May, 1816. From the personal in-
"fluence I had with the Marquis, then Lord Castle-
"reagh, and from my representations of the
"policy of drawing the stream of emigration
"from the United States to Canada, I obtained
"the privilege of forwarding to Canada and grant-
"ing land to such British subjects as were desirous
"of leaving the United States. The first body of
"emigrants I forwarded were chiefly from Mona-
"ghan and Cavan, and through the influence of Dr.
"Baldwin of York, Upper Canada (now the city
"of Toronto), two townships were laid out by the
"Lieutenant-Governor for those I should send,
"and were named Monaghan and Cavan. That
"circumstance first led me to look to Canada.
"From not having made any charge for my services
"in forwarding emigrants I was enabled, through
"the late Sir Francis Burton, brother of the late
"Marquis Conyngham, who was administering the
"Government in Lower Canada, to obtain for
"my sons the grant of the lands in Gore of Locha-

"ber on the Ottawa, and from the same claims
"the grant of 1200 acres free of fees in Adelaide,
"in the London District, which I named Strathroy,
"where my son, John Stewart, resides. My success
"in life rose chiefly from lands, I therefore prefer
"it to all other speculations. I have acted un-
"wisely in many instances by entering into
"businesses which I did not understand, and by
"erecting buildings before my profit arose; to
"all such forth, I therefore warn my children
"against building until the money so expended is
"in no way essential to their support or comfort.

"I need not inform you who are now grown,
"that my daughter Mary Ann married Alexander
"Buchanan, Q.C., whose father was Physician to
"the Forces at Quebec, whose grandfather and
"my father were cousins by the mother's side,
"his father named John, the grandfather Alexan-
"der, and resided at Fintona. My daughter
"Sarah married Robert Blackwell of Holywood,
"son of a very old acquaintance of mine of Belfast,
"arising out of our religious opinions. My daugh-
"ter Elizabeth married William, only surviving
"child of the late George Whitla, of Lisburn,
"County of Down, Ireland; and Isabella married
"William Augustus Baldwin, son of Dr. Baldwin
"of Spadina, near the City of Toronto, Upper
"Canada.

"Thus have I brought down the events which
"bear on my life to the present time, 1st of Octo-
"ber, 1834, leaving it with my beloved children
"to register the events and changes to which they

"may be subject; and on principle I enjoin upon all my posterity, that let the offence or cause be what it may, never shut your hand, your door or your heart against any of the posterity of your common parent. Regard this as the dying injunction of your father and dread to disobey it. My great desire is that my children may be known as a family fearing the Lord, united, and being beloved of one another for their father's sake. If a member of our body becomes diseased, nay corrupt, we do not cut it off; on the contrary, we use all means practicable to restore it to health. Such then, my beloved children, is the course I enjoin you to pursue. No treatment so likely to reform as that which is mild, gentle and affectionate. Relatives, from pride, are too ready to cast off their poor members; be it your glory, my children, to act otherwise, keeping mainly in view their eternal interest as ministering to the soul should be the most powerful motive to endeavour to reclaim and lead from sinful pursuits, so let it ever have your place among you. I will add, and your deservedly reverenced mother will join me in the testimony, that to the good and gracious Providence of God we are beholden for all our blessings and mercies. Never undertake any matter without you find you can ask the Almighty to bless you in the pursuit of it; this will guard you against all improper actions, and do not, I pray you, my children, ever be ashamed to admit your accountability to and dependence upon God for time and eternity."

On the 12th of June, 1837, with his wife and his daughter Amelia, he sailed for England in the packet ship Quebec, and landed at Portsmouth on the 14th of July. He mentions as having seen at Fintona "Mrs. Buchanan, the widow of Dr. Buchanan."

They sailed on their return by the "Westminster" packet ship on the 11th of October, 1837, for New York, where they arrived the 7th of November.

On the 14th of December, 1837, he records the marriage of his son, Robert Stewart Buchanan, to Elizabeth Curzon, daughter of William Jephson, who had married a daughter of Mr. Farquhar, "a " truly respectable inhabitant of New York. Mr. " Jephson is from Mallow, and of the family of " that name there who represent that town in " Parliament."

In September of the following year (1838) he mentions having visited the Honorable James Buchanan,[1] Senator of Pennsylvania, near Lan-

---

[1] James Buchanan (1791-1868), President of the United States from 1857 to 1861. The following letter, which was kindly communicated by Mr. Chauncey K. Buchanan, of Tarrytown, N.Y., was written by Mr. James Buchanan to Charles F. Rockwell, and gives his own account of his origin:—

WHEATLAND, NEAR LANCASTER,
12th April, 1868.

MY DEAR SIR:

I regret that I cannot give a satisfactory answer to your enquiries. My father, James Buchanan, came to this country in the year 1783. He was born in the County Donegal, was brought up by his grandmother Russel at a place called Ramelton or Rachmelton. I am quite confident that none of his family except himself emigrated to the United States. I have known & esteemed many Buchanans, and have counted kindred with them but without satisfactory results. My father had a brother called John of whom he spoke with much affection; but he died in Ireland.

Yours very respectfully,

JAMES BUCHANAN.

"My father, James Buchanan, was a native of the County of Donegal, in the kingdom of Ireland. The family was respectable, but their pecuniary circumstances were limited. He emigrated to the United States before the date of the definite Treaty of Peace with Great Britain, having sailed from —— in the brig Providence, bound for Philadelphia, in 1783. He was then in his twenty-second year."—Life of James Buchanan, by George T. Curtis (1883).

caster, accompanied by his wife, his daughter Amelia and his son Carlisle. "His family, or "rather his father's (family), as he is unmar- "ried, consists of the Rev. Edward Buchanan, "residing at Beckworth, eighteen miles from "Lancaster; Jane, married to T. Elliott, of Morris- "burg, Franklin County; Harriet, married to the "Revd. Robert Huy, Greensburg, Westmoreland; "and Maria, married to Dr. Yates, Meadville, "Crawford County. The family springs from the "same ancestor as my family, their progenitor "having settled at Rathinattor, County Donegal, "my family near Omagh."

James Buchanan speaks of the following as having shown kindness to his daughter Jane during her last illness, her death taking place on the 22nd of September, 1826, in the house of his son-in-law, Alexander Buchanan, in Montreal, in her twenty-third year: the Hon. Michael Henry Percival, Lieut. Col. Jones, Henry Black and Mr. Stacey, Attorney General and Mrs. James Stuart, and Mrs. Fisher at Quebec; Major Goff and Adjutant Routh of the 76th Regt.; Mrs. Grant, wife of Baron Grant; Mrs. Parker, wife of Capt. Parker; Mrs. Ogden, wife of Solicitor General Ogden; Mrs. Griffin, wife of Frederick Griffin; Mrs. Porteous, wife of John Porteous, and Miss Arnoldi, of Montreal.

He says that "On the 2nd of April, 1829, I "proceeded to Baltimore, where I had the honour

" of being introduced to Mr. Carroll; from thence
" I went to Washington, where I was introduced
" to General Jackson." On April 24th, 1829, he
sailed from New York, on the Sylvanus Jenkins,
Capt. Allen, for Liverpool, with his daughters,
Sarah and Elizabeth, Mr. and Mrs. Clarke, Mrs.
Parker, and John Galt, the novelist.

In March, 1843, he retired on a pension, and on
the 3rd of May of that year he moved from New
York to Niagara Falls. On the 24th of August he
took possession of his own house there. In this
connection he enumerates his different residences.
" My first house was No. 44 William Street, Dub-
" lin, which I purchased from Mr. Henry Alexan-
" der, Member for the City of Derry, cousin to
" the first Earl of Caledon. My next residence
" was ' Farm Hill ' (Lisanelly), near Omagh, having
" purchased ' Lisanelly ' from the late Sir John
" Stewart, for which I paid him 4500 pounds. My
" next residence was ' Woodbrook,' near Lord
" Abercorn's demesne, having sold back to Sir
" John Stewart 'Lisanelly' for 8000 pounds, in-
" cluding my improvements. My next residence
" was ' Common Green,' which I purchased from
" Mr. Wilcox of Dungannon for 700 pounds, and
" foolishly expended nearly 3000 pounds. I there
" resided from 1804 to 1815, when I went to
" England with all my family; stopped in Chester;
" went to London, thence to Boulogne-sur-Mer in
" France, thence to Bristol, and from thence, on the
" 22nd May, 1816, to New York, at which place

"I resided at, 1st, Bloomingdale; 2nd, Richmond Hill; 3rd, Manhattan Bank House; 4th, St. John's Park; 5th, Washington Square; 6th, Broadway; 7th, Beach Street; 8th, Barrow Street, and from thence to Canada, as is mentioned; in all eight residences with my family and servants in Europe and eight in the City of New York— thus in all seventeen places of residence."

On the 17th of June, 1844, he left Halifax for Liverpool, reaching there on the 28th of July. He was at Omagh in August, when he attended the funeral of his uncle Patrick's widow, who died in her 92nd year, and visited his uncle William's widow, then 82 years old. He arrived home on the 3rd of December. He caused to be placed in Donaghanie Churchyard a tablet bearing the following inscription:—

"This stone was placed here in memory of John Buchanan, of Omagh, who died in October, 1820, aged 84 years. Also to record the burials here of two children of his eldest son James, viz., Sarah, aged nine years and six months, in March, and John Stewart, aged 4 years and 7 months, in July, 1809. The said James came to reside at Camowen in the year 1804, removed to England in 1815, and from thence to New York in 1816."

For his services in causing the remains of the unfortunate Major André to be exhumed and conveyed to England he was, by order of the Duke of York, honored by the placing under the tablet to André in Westminster Abbey of an inscription to that effect.

In the South Aisle of the Nave of Westminster Abbey is the monument of Major John André by Van Gelder. The monument represents Washington "receiving the petition, in which André vainly implores for a soldier's death, and André is seen on the way to execution." The monument bears the following inscription:—

SACRED TO THE MEMORY
OF
MAJOR JOHN ANDRÉ,
who raised by his Merit at an early period of Life to the rank of Adjutant General
OF
The British Forces in America, and employed in an important and hazardous enterprise, fell a sacrifice to his Zeal for his King and Country
On the 2nd of October, A. D. 1780,
Aged 29,
universally beloved and esteemed by the Army in which he served, and lamented even by his
FOES
His Gracious Sovereign, KING GEORGE THIRD, has caused this Monument to be erected

Under this inscription is the following:—

THE REMAINS OF MAJOR JOHN ANDRÉ
were, on the 10th of August, 1821, removed from Tappan by
JAMES BUCHANAN, ESQR.
His Majesty's Consul at New York,
Under Instructions from His R. Highness
THE DUKE OF YORK,
And with the permission of the Dean and Chapter
Finally deposited in a Grave
contiguous to this Monument,
On the 28th of November, 1821.

The New York Tribune of Thursday, November 5th, 1885, giving an account of the attempted destruction by dynamite of the André monument at Tappan, on Tuesday, the 3rd November, 1885, contains the following:—

"Forty years have passed and the bones of André remained beneath the spot where he so bravely met his death, but his memory was kept green in the hearts of his sisters and loving friends, who believed that sufficient time would elapse to cause the national wounds to heal and national prejudice to cease, applied to the American Government through the representative for permission to remove the remains of André to the Mausoleum already prepared in his native clime. This was freely granted, and on the 15th August, 1821, a British Man of War, having on board His Royal Highness the Duke of York,[1] entered the Hudson River, and being joined by Mr. Buchanan, the British Consul at New York, and Mr. Moore, His Majesty's Agent for Packets, proceeded up the river and anchored off Sweden's Landing, directly opposite Dobb's Ferry. Accompanied by Captain Paul, the party landed and took a carriage to Tappan, some two miles distant. They proceeded first to the old Mabie Tavern, the former place of André's confinement, which was kept at that time by a man named Dupuy; from there they went to the house of the Rev. Mr. Demarest, the owner of the property where lay buried the remains of André. They were received with generous hospitality and afforded every facility for the prosecution of their sacred mission. There was no difficulty in finding the place. The two cedars which had been planted at the foot of the grave forty years previous had grown up to a height of ten feet. These, together with a pile of stones, marked the foot of the grave, while a peach tree (planted by the loving hand of an unknown woman), then in full blossom, marked the head of the grave. On removing the earth it was found that the roots of the peach tree had worked their way through the decayed coffin, and completely surrounded the skull of André like a net work. The bones were carefully removed; nothing of a metallic substance was found to show

---

[1] This is not correct. The Duke of York was not present, but was represented by Mr. Buchanan.

that he was buried in his regimentals, but the leathern string that bound his cue was found in a perfect state of preservation. The sarcophagus containing the remains was taken to the house of Mr. Demarest, where it remained for two or three days, when it was removed to His Majesty's Packet. The remains were then conveyed to London, where they were interred in Westminster Abbey on the 28th of November following.

"The two cedars were taken up and carried to England, where they were made into snuff-boxes and other devices. The Duke of York desiring to show his appreciation of the generous conduct of Rev. Mr. Demarest, ordered a snuff box to be made from one of these cedars and presented to him."

John H. Griffith, David D. Brewer, John H. Outwater and Col. James C. Hading were also present.

The following is an extract from the account given by him of the disinterment of André's remains. Mr. Buchanan represented the Duke of York in the matter, and it took place Aug. 10, 1821:—

. . . "My next step was to proceed to Tappan, distant from this city (New York) twenty-four miles. Thither I went, accompanied by Mr. Moore, His Majesty's Agent for Packets. Upon reaching the village, which does not contain above fifty or sixty houses, the first we enquired at proved to be the very house in which the Major had been confined while a prisoner there, by one Dupuy, who was also Postmaster, who took us to view the room which had been used as a prison. Excited as we were, it would be difficult to describe our feelings on entering this little chamber; it was then used as a milk and store-room —otherwise unaltered from the period of his confinement —about twelve feet by eight, with one window looking into the garden, the view extending to the hill, and directly to the spot on which he suffered—as the landlord pointed out from the window while in the room, the trees growing at the place where he was buried.

"Having enquired for the owner of the field. I waited on the Rev. Mr. Demarest, a minister residing in Tappan, to whom I explained the object of my visit, and who generously expressed his satisfaction at the honour ' which at length,' to use his words, ' was intended the memory of Major André,' and assured me that every facility should be afforded by him. Whereupon we all proceeded to examine the grave, attended by many of the inhabitants, who by this time had become acquainted with the cause of our visit; and it was truly gratifying to us, as it was honourable to them, that all were loud in the expressions of their gratification on this occasion.

" We proceeded up a narrow lane, or broken road, with trees on each side which obscured the place where he suffered, until we came to the opening into the field which at once led to an elevated spot on the hill. On reaching the mount, we found it commanded a view of the surrounding country for miles. General Washington's headquarters and the house in which he resided was distant about a mile and a half or two miles, but fully in view. The army lay encamped chiefly in view of the place, and must necessarily have witnessed the catastrophe.

"The field, as well as I could judge, contained from eight to ten acres, and was cultivated ; but around the grave the plough had not approached nearer than three or four yards, that space being covered with loose stone thrown upon and around the grave, which was only indicated by two cedar trees about ten feet high. A small peach tree had also been planted at the head of the grave, by the kindly feeling of a lady in the neighbourhood.

" Many expressed the belief that the body had been secretly carried to England, but these surmises were set aside by the more general testimony of the community. . . . . Arriving at Tappan by ten o'clock a. m., though I was not expected until the following Tuesday. as I had fixed, yet a number of persons soon assembled, some of whom betrayed symptoms of displeasure at the proceeding, arising from the observations of some of the public journals, which asserted ' That any honour paid Major André was casting imputation on General Washington, and the officers who tried André.'

"As these characters were of the lowest caste, and their observations were condemned by every respectable person in the village, I yet deemed it prudent, while the worthy pastor was preparing his men to open the grave, to resort to a mode of argument, the only one I had time or inclination to bestow upon them, in which I was sure to find the landlord a powerful auxiliary. I therefore stated to these noisy patriots that I wished to follow a custom not unfrequent in Ireland, from whence I came, namely, of taking some spirits before proceeding to a grave. The landlord approved the Irish practice, and accordingly supplied abundance of liquor, so that in a short time General Washington, Major André and the object of my visit there were forgotten by them, and I was left at perfect liberty with the respectable inhabitants of the place to proceed to the exhumation, leaving the landlord to supply the guests, a duty which he faithfully performed to my entire satisfaction.

"At twelve o'clock, quite an unexpected crowd assembled at the grave, as our proceeding up the hill was seen by the inhabitants all around.

"The day was unusually fine; a number of ladies, and many aged matrons who witnessed his fall—who had seen his person—who had mingled tears with his sufferings—attended, and were loud in their praises of the Prince, for thus at length honouring one who still lived in their recollection with unsubdued sympathy. The labours proceeded with diligence, yet caution; surmises about the body having been removed were revived, and it would be difficult to imagine any event which could convey a degree of more intense excitement.

"As soon as the stones were cleared away, and the grave was found, not a tongue moved amongst the multitude,—breathless anxiety was depicted in every countenance.

"When at length, one of the men cried out he had touched the coffin, so great was the enthusiasm at this moment that I found it necessary to call the aid of several of the ladies to form an enlarged circle, so that all could see the operation; which being effected, the men proceeded with the greatest caution, and the clay was removed with the hands, as we soon discovered the lid of the coffin was broken in the centre.

"With great care the broken lid was removed, and there to our view lay the bones of the brave André, in perfect order. I among others, for the first time, discovered that he had been a small man.

"This observation I made from the skeleton, which was confirmed by some then present. The roots of the small peach tree had completely surrounded the skull like a net.

"After allowing all the people to pass around in regular order and view the remains as they lay, which very many did with unfeigned tears and lamentations, the bones were carefully removed and placed in the sarcophagus (the circle having been again formed); after which I descended into the coffin, which was not more than three feet below the surface, and with my own hands raked the dust together, to ascertain whether he had been buried in his regimentals or not, as it was rumoured among the assemblage that he was stripped; for, if buried in his regimentals, I expected to find the buttons of his clothes which would have disproved the rumour. (' It has since been ascertained, from an American officer present at the burial, that the regimentals of Major André were given to his servants, after the execution. This statement has satisfied Mr. Buchanan, and will account for the absence of any vestiges in his tomb.') But I did not find a single button, nor any article save a string of leather which had tied his hair at the time. This string I forwarded to his sisters in England. I examined the dust of the coffin so minutely (as the quantity would not fill a quart) that no mistake could have arisen in the examination. Let no unworthy motive be attributed to me for recording this fact, I state it as one which I was anxious to ascertain for the reason given. Having placed the remains in the sarcophagus, it was borne amidst the silent and unbought regret of the numerous assemblage, and deposited in the worthy pastor's house, with the intention of removing it to His Majesty's Packet, in New York City, on the Tuesday following. As soon as the removal of the sarcophagus to the Packet was known in this city, it was not only honourable to the feelings of the citizens, but cheering to my mind, depressed as it had been, to find the sentiment which prevailed.

"Ladies sent me flowers; others, various emblematic devices, garlands, etc., to decorate the remains of the ' lamented and beloved André.' A beautiful and ornamented myrtle among those sent, I forwarded with the sarcophagus to Halifax, where Lieut. General Sir James Kempt, Governor of Nova Scotia, caused every proper mark of respect to be paid to the remains. From thence they reached London, and were deposited near the monument which had been erected to his memory in Westminster Abbey, and a marble slab placed at the foot of the monument on which is set forth their removal by the order of His Royal Highness, the Duke of York. (On the monument is also recorded the services of Consul Buchanan.)

"Having represented to His Royal Highness the generous conduct of the Rev. Mr. Demarest, I recommended that His Royal Highness should convey to him a snuffbox made from out of one of the trees which grew at the grave, which I sent home. But my suggestion was far outdone by the princely munificence of His Royal Highness, who ordered a box to be made out of the tree, and lined with gold, with an inscription, 'From His Royal Highness the Duke of York, to the Rev. Mr. Demarest.'

"Whilst speaking of this act of liberality, I was unexpectedly honoured with a silver inkstand with the following inscription: 'The surviving sisters of Major André, to James Buchanan, Esq., His Majesty's Consul at New York.' They also sent a silver cup, with a suitable inscription, to Mr. Demarest. I need not add that I cherish this inkstand (which I am now using), and shall bequeath it to my children as a memorial which I prize with no ordinary feeling.

"I omitted to mention that I had the peach tree, which had been planted on the grave (the roots of which had surrounded the skull as set forth), taken up with great care, with as much of the clay as it was possible to preserve around the roots, and brought it to my garden in New York, where my daughters attended it with almost pious solicitude, shading it during the heat of the day, watering it in the cool of the evening, in the hope of preserving it to send it to England. Had it reached his sisters, they would have, no doubt, regarded it as another Minerva; for though it did not spring out of, yet it was nourished by their beloved brother's head.

"I have only to add, that, through the kind interference of my brother Consul at Philadelphia, I obtained Major André's watch, which he had to part with when a prisoner during the early part of the war. This watch I sent to England lately; so that I believe that every vestige connected with the subject of this narrative has been sent to the land of his birth, in the services of which his life was sacrificed."

James Buchanan died at Elmwood, the residence of his son-in-law, Hugh Taylor, advocate, near Montreal, on the 10th October, 1851, in his 80th year, and was buried in the tomb which he had caused to be erected at Drummondville, near the Falls of Niagara. His wife died on the 1st February, 1852, in her 73rd year, at the residence of her daughter, Mrs. Alexander Buchanan, No. 7 Cornwall Terrace, St. Denis Street, Montreal.

He had the honour in the course of his career of meeting many high personages, and in not a few cases the opportunity of becoming intimately acquainted with, among others, the following: Robert Stewart, Lord Castlereagh, the Irish Secretary in 1798, afterwards the Marquis of Londonderry, born in 1769, and died in 1822; Mr. Pelham, the Irish Secretary, afterwards Duke of Newcastle; Sir John Stewart, K.C., and at one time Attorney General of Ireland, who died in 1825; Sir Matthew Wood, three times Lord Mayor of London; M. Asherby, Secretary of the Cis-Alpine Republic; Sir George Hill, Member for Londonderry, and Mr. Joseph Hardcastle, of Hatcham House, near London.

On his retirement from the office of British Consul at New York he received the following letter from Ex-Chancellor James Kent, the distinguished author of the Commentaries on American law:—

"NEW YORK, March 31, 1843.

MY DEAR SIR,—

I signed, with great pleasure, an address to you engrossed on parchment, and which was shown to me at the Custom House. But this is not enough for me, and I cannot deny myself the pleasure of writing a personal and private line to you, to assure you of my great respect and esteem, and of my regret, that this city is soon to lose the pleasure and benefit of your society.

Your conduct, while Consul in this city, has been so full of urbanity and kindness, so conciliatory to the interests and feeling of the two nations, and so distinguished for moderation, integrity, candor and Christian charity, zeal and benevolence, that my attachment and affections have been warmly excited in your favour.

I hope the evening of your life may be serene and happy, and I shall always think of you with the tenderest regard. Mrs. Kent joins me in the sincerest respect and regard to Mrs. Buchanan, and in the strongest wishes for your welfare.

Yours truly and affectionately,
JAMES KENT.

JAMES BUCHANAN, ESQ."

He was a warm advocate of Free Trade, and was in favour of opening the River St. Lawrence to all nations. His advocacy of measures of public interest was untiring, and in prosecuting it the press was freely used. His book, " Sketches of Indian Character," passed through two editions. The full title of the book was:—Sketches of the History, Manners and Customs of the North American Indians, by James Buchanan, Esqre., His Majesty's Consul for the State of New York. London, Printed by Black, Young & Young, Tavistock Street. MDCCCXXIV. London, Printed by W. Clowes, Northumberland Court. This book is dedicated to His Excellency Lieut. Gen. the Earl Dalhousie, G.C.B., and is dated at New York, May, 1, 1821. It was published at 10s. 6d. in boards.

He published a plan for civilizing the Indians of this continent. Among his numerous writings were:—A Tract on the Preservation from Contamination of the Destitute Female Children in London; A Letter to Sir Robert Peel, with a plan as to the destitute female children of London, Dublin and Edinburgh; A Letter to Lord Stanley, with a plan for the removal of the pauper population of the County of Kent; A Report upon the Banking Institutions of the State of New York; A Tract on the Effects of State Prison Discipline in the States of New York and Connecticut. Moreover, he published, in 1836, a recommendation to Sir Francis Bond Head of a railroad from Hamilton to Michigan, pointing out how the funds for its construction might be raised. He was an advocate of the Federal Union of all the North American Provinces, and as early as 1841 he addressed a letter to the Duke of Wellington advocating the free admission of grain from all countries that would receive British manufactures on the same terms. He was through life active and energetic in promoting worthy objects. It is said that Sir John Franklin named one of the rivers which he discovered after him. A similar compliment is also said to have been paid him by Captain Back.

The following extracts are from newspapers in which reference was made to his death:—

"Mr. Buchanan was an Irishman by birth, and was largely endowed with that warmth of heart for which his countrymen are noted all over the world; while he had much of the prudence foresight, perseverance and energy—the *pervidium ingenium*—of his Scottish ancestors. Few men had so extensive a circle of friends and acquaintances, by whom he was loved and respected, and to whom his death will be a source of regret, as the late British Consul in the great commercial emporium of North America."

" His charitable gifts, hospitality, and general urbanity will live long in the memory of those who formed his acquaintance in this country (Canada) as well as in New York."

He had issue:—

I. Sarah, born 25th September, 1799, at Omagh, and died 25th March, 1809, at Common Green, Omagh, Ireland.

II. James Clark, born 25th April, 1801, at Dublin; named after his grandfather, James Clarke. He came to New York with his father, and is mentioned as having, on the 5th January, 1823, "embarked on board His Majesty's sloop of war 'Pheasant,' Captain Clavering, for England, and landed at Portsmouth on the 6th day of February." He was subsequently appointed British Consul at Santa Martha, South America, where he died unmarried, on the 10th December, 1849.

III. Mary Ann, born on 11th June, 1802, at "Farm Hill," near Omagh. She was named after her aunt, Mary Ann Clarke, who was married first, to John Ledbetter, of College Green, Dublin, and 2ndly, to the Rev. Samuel Simpson, a Presbyterian clergyman of Dublin. Mary Ann was married on 2nd March, 1824, to Alexander Buchanan, of Montreal, Advocate. She died at Saco, Maine, on 20th July, 1862, and was buried at Montreal, Canada.

IV. Jane, born on 30th October, 1803, at " Woodbrook," near Baron's Court, Tyrone. She was named after her aunt, Jane Buchanan, who was married to James Robinson. She died unmarried on 22nd September, 1826, at Montreal.

V. John Stewart, born 1st January, 1805, at " Woodbrook," and died 14th July, 1809, at Common Green.

VI. Robert Stewart, born 16th June, 1806, at Common Green, and was named after Lord Castlereagh. He was married at New York, by the Rev. Mr. Hawke, on 14th December, 1837, to Elizabeth Curzon, daughter of William Henry Jephson and Maria Farquhar, and granddaughter of Colonel William Jephson, of Mallow Castle, Cork, Ireland. He died on 18th September, 1861, at New York, and was buried at St. Mark's Church. His widow survived him over thirty years, dying on 18th April, 1893, at New York, They left no issue.

VII. Alexander Carlisle, who was born 25th December, 1808, at Common Green, was named after Alexander Carlisle, an Irish solicitor. He accompanied his father to America, but in 1819 went back to Ireland and was educated at a school in Londonderry. In 1825 he returned to New York, and in the same year went to Montreal, where he was for some years in business with his brother Robert, the firm being known as Buchanan & Co. In 1835 he took charge of the Emigration Office at Quebec, and on the 1st July, 1838, was appointed by the British Government Chief Emigration Agent in succession to his uncle, Alexander Carlisle Buchanan. He married at Quebec, on 3rd November, 1840, Charlotte Louise Caldwell, daughter of the Hon. Edward Bowen, Chief Justice for the District of Quebec. He died on 2nd February, 1868, at Quebec.[1] She died on 20th November, 1894, at same place. They had issue:

1. Carlisle Edward, born 4th May, 1846; entered service of the Bank of Montreal, and died 15th March, 1867, at Port Hope, Ont.

2. Ernest Bowen, of Australia, born 4th April, 1855; married first, 26th November, 1886, Alice Mackenzie, who died 26th December, 1887; 2ndly, Beatrice Elliot and has issue:—

(1) Carlisle LeStrange, born 22nd February, 1900.

---

[1] "His was a fine example of a quiet, useful, unostentatious life. Those who knew him find it difficult to determine which most to admire, his public virtues or his private worth. To his intimates both are a pleasant retrospect; to his friends they are a precious possession; for many a day will pass ere 'Carlisle Buchanan' will be forgotten in those quiet home circles which he made bright and happy by his presence."—"Portraits of British Americans," by Fennings Taylor, 1868.

(2) Arthur Hamilton, born 1st January, 1902.

(1) Orovida Valentine.

3. Arthur Hamilton, born 17th June, 1858; entered service of Bank of Montreal, of which he is now Manager at Spokane, U. S. A. He married 15th April, 1899, at Montreal, Frances (Lily), daughter of Alexander Brock Buchanan, of Montreal.

4. Noel Herbert, born 2nd October, 1860; entered service of Molsons' Bank, and was drowned 31st March, 1883, at Brockville, Ont.

1. Sophia Louise (Winnifred) married 25th September, 1867, George Tudor Pemberton, and has issue:—

(1) Leigh Tudor, born 12th April, 1869; married 27th October, 1897, Georgina Scott.

(2) George Carlisle Tudor, born 12th June, 1870; married 13th September, 1898, Roberta Mary Bayley Bruce.

(1) Helena Tudor, married 10th November, 1903, Percy C. Stevenson.

2. Ida Mary, married 25th April, 1877, John Hamilton, of Quebec, and has issue:—

(1) Constance Naomi, married 20th June, 1900, Arthur Carrington Smith.

(2) Edith Craigie.

(3) Mary Frances Vera.

(4) Jessie Irene.

VIII. Sarah, born on 24th March, 1810, at Common Green, and named after her grandmother,

Sarah Sproule, daughter of James Sproule, of Granan, and second wife of John Buchanan of Omagh. She came to New York with her father, but went back to Ireland in April, 1829. On the 23rd September, 1829, she was married in the church of Cappagh, near Omagh, to Robert Blackwell, son of Alexander Blackwell, of Holywood, near Belfast. She died on 18th February, 1875, at Lower Mount Street, Dublin. They had issue:—

    1. James Buchanan, born 13th October, 1830, and died 22nd July, 1831.

    2. Alexander, born 16th April, 1834; married 2nd February, 1867, Wilhelmina Crofts of Ballamena House, County Cork, and died 20th July, 1888.

    3. James Buchanan, born 3rd August, 1837, and died 1st April, 1841, at New York.

    4. Robert, born 1846, and died 8th November, 1888.

    1. Anna Arthur, married 8th February, 1854, Thomas Studdert of Kilkishen House, County Clare, Ireland.

    2. Elizabeth Buchanan, married James B. Ievers of County Clare, Ireland, and died 1st February, 1898.

    3. Margaret Eleanor Whitla, married Hodder Roberts of Mount Reber, Cork, and died in 1880, in Ireland, leaving issue.

    4. Sarah Caroline, died 4th March, 1860.

IX. Elizabeth, born on 3rd December, 1811, at Common Green, and named after her mother. She was married on the 5th November, 1830, to William Whitla, only son of George Whitla, of Lisburn, Ireland. She died on the 30th May, 1886, at Chepstow Villas, Bayswater, London. They had issue:—

    1. George Whitla, born 31st July, 1832; appointed Assistant Surgeon in 1857, Surgeon in 1872, Surgeon Major in 1873, Brigade Surgeon in 1892, Hon. Deputy Surgeon General in 1893, and retired in 1893. He married 1st, Miss Goodden, by whom he had issue one son, George (died 1885), and one daughter, Susan; 2nd, Catherine Barbara Gould Jackson, by whom he has issue 2 daughters, Helena and Charlotte, both married.

    2. James Buchanan, born 2nd September, 1834; appointed Ensign in the 88th Regt. of Foot, Connaught Rangers, in 1855, and served through the Indian Mutiny with his regiment; Lieutenant in 1859, Captain in 1867, and retired in 1871. He married Elizabeth M. Forbes, who died in March, 1899. He lives in Toronto, Canada.

    3. John, born 1835, and died while young.

    4. William, born 13th March, 1840; entered the army in 1858, and became in 1886 Lieut.-Colonel commanding 2nd Battalion of the Lincolnshire Regiment (the 10th Foot). He

commanded a detachment of the 1st Battalion in the Perak River Expedition in 1875, and commanded the troops when a combined naval and military force attacked and captured two stockades and five guns, and for this was mentioned in the despatches and received Brevet of Major and Medal with clasp. He retired in 1888 and now lives in London, England.

5. Sydney, born 1843, and died while young.

6. Seymour Conway, born 1845, and died while young.

7. Francis, born 1849; married and lives in California, and has issue.

8. Valentine Herbert, born 1853 married and lives in Queensland, and has issue.

1. Elizabeth Clarke, married Capt. Thomas Peter Carr, County Inspector in the Royal Irish Constabulary, and died January, 1871, leaving issue.

2. Eleanor, married Col. Lewis Mansergh Buchanan, C.B., of Edenfel, Omagh, Tyrone, and died 1877, leaving issue.

3. Emma Hardcastle Haldane, married Henry Lucas, of Rathealy, Co. Cork, late Captain in the 25th Regiment and Major S. Cork Militia; died 24th August, 1899, and left issue.

4. Alicia Jane, married Charles C. Bridges, son of John Bridges of Birch, Essex, and has

issue. (1) Sydney; (2) Guy; (3) Oliver; (4) Trevor; (5) Winifred.

5. Ada, married Colonel Theophilus Higginson, C.B., late Commanding 1st Punjab Infantry (Punjab Frontier Force), who died 1903, leaving issue:—

(1) Harold Whitla, Captain Royal Dublin Fusiliers,[1] married 1903 Ivy Letitia Broun, fourth daughter of the late James Broun, of Orchard, Carluke, N.B., and Petit Menage, Jersey, C.I., and has issue:—(1) James, born 1906.

(2) Ada Dorothea.

X. Maria, born on 20th March, 1813, at Common Green, and named after her aunt, Mrs. John Clarke. She died unmarried, on 5th February, 1837, at New York.

XI. John Stewart, born on 3rd January, 1815, and named after Sir John Stewart, Bart. When his father sailed for New York in 1816, John Stewart was left with his grandfather at Omagh. It is probable that he came to America with his father in November, 1820. On the 21st September, 1831, he took possession of a grant from His Majesty of 1200 acres of land in Upper Canada, con-

---

[1] Served in West Africa 1897-8. Took part in the operations on the Niger. With the expedition to Lapia and Argeyal. Medal with 2 clasps. Served in the S. African War 1899-1902. Took part in the operations in Natal '99, including action at Lombard's Kop. At the defence of Ladysmith, including action of 6th January, 1900. In the Transvaal, west of Pretoria, July to 29 November, 1900. Again in the Transvaal 30 November, 1900 to January, 1902. Mentioned in Despatches London Gazette, 10th Sept., 1901. Queen's medal with 4 clasps and King's medal with 2 clasps. Served at Aden 1903, during operations in the Interior. *Hart's Army List* (1910).

ferred on James Buchanan for his services in relation to the Province. John Stewart married at Toronto on the 6th July, 1839, Mabel Ann, second daughter of Dr. Samuel Robinson, formerly of Eccles Street, Dublin, who had come to Canada, and of Elizabeth Smith, who had previously been married to Joseph Hume, of the County of Wicklow. John Stewart afterwards removed to Chicago. He died there on the 21st April, 1875, and his widow died there on the 5th November, 1890. They had issue:—

1. Elizabeth Robinson, born 27th July, 1840; died 27th August, 1840.
2. James R., born 5th October, 1841; died 9th June, 1853.
3. Samuel R., born 29th June, 1843; married 20th November, 1872, Etta Heagel, who died 13th February, 1888, and died 30th April, 1904, at Chicago, leaving issue:—
    (1) Stewart H., born 7th August, 1874.
4. Elizabeth R., born 1st October, 1845; married 11th October, 1874, H. M. Dupee, of Chicago, and has issue:—
    (1) William H., born May, 1877.
    (2) Horace, born 21st November, 1883.
    (1) Mabel.
    (2) Margaret.
5. John R., born 5th September, 1847; married November, 1876, Gertrude Bliss, and died 27th March, 1883, at Chicago, leaving issue:—

(1) Walter, born August, 1878.

(2) Blanche, died January, 1882.

6. Catherine Hume R., born 3rd April, 1849; married 11th April, 1875, Wm. Spencer, of Chicago, and died 31st August, 1880, leaving issue:—

(1) George Buchanan, born 5th February, 1876.

(2) William Archer, born 15th February, 1878.

7. William Hume R., born 3rd April, 1849.

8. Mabel R., born November 12th, 1851; married 20th September, 1877, Robert S. Buchanan, of Chicago.

9. James O. R., born 9th November, 1853.

10. Robert R., born 24th January, 1856; died 27th November, 1905, at Chicago.

XII. Isabella Clarke, born on 10th November, 1815, at Boulogne, France, and was named after her aunt, Mrs. William Clarke. She was married at New York on the 25th September, 1834, by the Rev. Lewis Pintard Bayard, Rector of St. Clements Church, New York, to William Augustus Baldwin, son of the Hon. William Warren Baldwin, and brother of the Hon. Robert Baldwin, Q.C., C.B., and died on the 21st May, 1850. He died on the 14th June, 1883, aged 75 years, at "Masquoteh," Deer Park, Toronto. They had issue:—

1. Henry St. George, of Toronto, born 12th November, 1837; married 9th February, 1869,

Amelia Sarah Pentland, of Cobourg, Ont., and had issue:—

(1) Bertram St. George, born 17th September, 1870; died 25th February, 1893.

(2) Harold Augustus, born 16th November, 1871.

(3) Ethel Isabel.

2. James Buchanan, M.D., of Toronto, born 14th July, 1839; married Elizabeth C. Morrison; died 30th May, 1897, at Toronto, and had issue:—

(1) Kenneth Joseph Morrison, born 15th March, 1874.

(2) James Carlisle Buchanan, born 25th April, 1886.

(1) Florence Emeline, born 28th October, 1875; died 6th December, 1884.

(2) Sybil Isabella.

3. William Augustus, M.D., of Toronto, born 6th December, 1840; married Ella Winnifred Poston, of Quebec, and died 13th July, 1894, and had issue:—

(1) Charles William Augustus, born 22nd April, 1884; Cadet Royal Navy, 1st July, 1899.

(2) St. George Pentland, born 26th February, 1885.

4. Robert Russell, of Toronto, born 20th July, 1842; married 30th September, 1893, Ada Jane Webster, of Guelph, Ont., and died 3rd June, 1906, leaving no issue.

5. Æmelius Warren, of Toronto, born 8th September, 1844; married 13th September, 1883, Susie Cotterell (who died 10th October, 1888), by whom had issue:—

(1) Reginald Æmelius, born 15th July, 1887; died 17th August, 1888.

(1) Alice Muriel.

(2) Emmeline Gladys.

He married secondly, 13th November, 1889, Julia Pringle, of Cobourg.

1. Phoebe Buchanan, born 18th April, 1836; married 20th October, 1857, George Lefroy, of Toronto, formerly of Athy, Ireland, and died 9th January, 1891, at Toronto. Had issue:—

(1) Ernest Baldwin, born 20th February, 1861.

(2) Harold Baldwin, born 14th January, 1863.

(3) Benjamin St. George, born 2nd January, 1865.

(4) William Baldwin, born 14th April, 1869; died 5th July, 1872.

(5) Augustus George, born 25th November, 1874.

(1) Catherine Isabella, born 18th December, 1858; died 25th May, 1905.

(2) Phoebe Isabella Beatrice.

2. Isabella Elizabeth, born 3rd August, 1847; married 4th January, 1877, to William

Ross Baldwin, of Lismore, Ireland, and died 4th November, 1890. Had issue:—

(1) William Augustus, born 3rd February, 1878; died 19th September, 1904.

(2) Godfrey St. George, born 2nd January, 1881; died 13th February, 1910.

(1) Phoebe Isabella Margaret, married 18th September, 1901, John M. Hedley.

(2) Wilhelmine Russell.

XIII. Amelia Hobart, born on 27th July, 1817, at New York; was named after Lady Castlereagh. She was married on the 26th June, 1845, at the residence of her father, near the Falls of Niagara, to Hugh Taylor, of Montreal, advocate, by the Rev. William Leeming, Rector of the Parish. She died on the 19th November, 1876, in Folkestone, and he died on the 30th December, 1893, at Weston Lodge, Upper Norwood, Surrey, aged ninety years. They had issue:—

1. Reid, born 27th November, 1847; admitted to the Bar of the Province of Quebec in 1869; he married first, in February, 1873, Mattie, daughter of Dr. Smallwood of Montreal (who died 25th June, 1892), and had issue:—

(1) Algernon Waldemar Hugh, born 20th October, 1876.

(2) Adrian Aubrey Charles, born 25th September, 1877, Captain Royal Dublin Fusiliers.[1]

---

[1] Served in South Africa War 1899-1902. Employed with Mounted Infantry. Severely wounded. Mentioned in Despatches London Gazette, 10th September, 1901. Queen's Medal with 6 clasps and King's Medal with 2 clasps. Served at Aden 1903 during operations in the Interior. Attached to Egyptian Army. *Hart's Army List* (1910).

He married secondly, on 28th April, 1903, Edith Constance Maud Widdrington, only daughter of Captain Widdrington, and by her has a daughter,

(1) Chrysilla Griselle Widdrington.

2. Horatio Herbert, born 18th August, 1858.

1. Elizabeth Mary.

XIV. George Augustus Frederick, born on 10th February, 1819, at New York, and died there on 7th September, 1819.

XV. William Oliver, born on the 22nd October, 1820, at New York, and named after Oliver Sproule, formerly of Omagh, M.D., brother of his grandmother, and after his uncles, William Buchanan and William Clarke, He was a civil engineer. He married on the 22nd of October, 1845, at Williamsburg, U.C., Mary Ellen Crysler, daughter of Colonel John Crysler, of Crysler's Farm, Dundas Co., U.C. (who was born on the 9th July, 1825, and died 3rd September, 1905), and died on the 15th December, 1904, at Montreal. They had issue:—

1. Joseph Hardcastle, born 6th February, 1847; died 17th February, 1849,

2. Florence Anna, born 29th July, 1848; married 15th June, 1869, to Captain H. Bonham Clay, 13th Hussars, and has issue:—

(1) Bertha Florence, married the late Grant Macintosh, of Montreal.

(2) Cecil Buchanan.

(3) Ethel Agnes, married William Forbes Forbes, of Montreal.
(4) Mabel Elizabeth.
(5) Eveline Ellen.
(6) Constance Josephine.
(7) Harold Bonham.
(8) Gladys Margaret.

3. Bertha Elizabeth, born 29th July, 1848; married 19th September, 1867, to John Henry Pangman, Seigneur of St. Henri de Mascouche, and has issue:—

(1) Florence Bertha, died 10th March, 1892.
(2) Henry Gerald.
(3) Claud Oliver, married Lillian, daughter of A. H. Murphy, and has issue.
(4) Mabel Ella.
(5) Cecil Carlisle married Maud, daughter of Edward L. Sewell, of Quebec, and has issue.
(6) Lionel Buchanan, married 19th February, 1908, Mary Graham, daughter of the late Professor Dawson.
(7) John Henry, married 20th May, 1910, Gladys Arnold, daughter of Mrs. S. C. Stevenson.

4. James Oliver, born 29th November, 1849; married 6th September, 1876, Emmeline, daughter of the Hon. Mr. Justice Morrison, of Toronto, and has issue:—

(1) Earl, died.

(2) Zulu Emmeline, married George Gooderham Mitchell, of Toronto.

(3) Gladys, married Norman Seagram, Toronto.

(4) Roy Beresford.

(5) Oliver.

5. Robert Stewart, born 22nd September, 1852; married 20th September, 1877, Mabel, daughter of John Stewart Buchanan, of Chicago, and has issue:—

(1) Persis Elizabeth, born 24th January, 1881; died 19th February, 1884.

(2) Bertram Oliver, born 7th April, 1883.

6. Reginald Heber, born 5th January, 1855; married 29th October, 1880, Hattie, daughter of Revd. Dr. Bancroft, of Montreal, and has issue:—

(1) Rupert Bancroft, married Miss Winchester.

(2) Dorothy Bancroft.

(3) Olive Bancroft.

(4) Louie.

(5) Heber.

7. Harold Walter, born 12th June, 1857; married Anna Catherine, daughter of the late Michael Conrad Gie, of Ealing, London, who died 23rd December, 1905.

8. Sydenham Percy, born 11th December, 1863; married 15th August, 1891, Helena August Bloor, and has issue:—

(1) Drayton.

(2) Gretchen.

9. Victor Carl, born 26th September, 1869; married 6th June, 1895, Margaret, daughter of M. Erb, of Berlin, Ont., and has issue:—

(1) Kathleen Margaret Lydia.

XVI. Caroline, born on the 2nd March, 1824, at New York, and named after a Miss Black. She was married on the 7th August, 1851, at Drummondville, Niagara Falls, by the Revd. William Leeming, Rector, to Kenneth Mackenzie Moffatt, Captain in the Royal Canadian Rifle Regiment, son of the Hon. George Moffatt, of Montreal. Col. Moffatt, who was born in 1823, entered the army in 1847, and for some years commanded the Royal Canadians, which regiment was ultimately disbanded. He died on the 11th March, 1885, at Toronto, where he was Commissioner of the Canada Loan Co. She died on the 16th December, 1894, at Toronto. They had issue:—

1. George Buchanan, born 13th December, 1854; received his commission of Inspector in the Northwest Mounted Police in 1883; married 3rd September, 1884, Katherine Jane, daughter of Augustus Jukes, M.D., of St. Catharines, Ont., and has issue.

2. William Rowan Hume, born 30th July, 1856.

3. Kenneth Ogilvie, born 7th July, 1861; married 12th March, 1890, at Toronto, Kathleen Monaghan.

1. Sophie, born 15th March, 1852, and died 28th August, 1854.

2. Ida Caroline, now living in England.

XVII. Jane Georgina, born on 13th January, 1829, at New York, and was named after her sister Jane, and Georgina added out of regard to her uncle, George Buchanan, who at the time she was born had come from Ireland on a visit to his brother, James Buchanan. She was married on the 16th September, 1852, at Monkstown, near Dublin, to Joseph Orr Robinson, solicitor, of Inner Temple, London, and died on the 17th November, 1885, at St. Catharines, Ont. Joseph Robinson died on the 13th April, 1898, at Rockferry, England. They had issue:—

1. Edgar Albert, born 1853 and died 1854.

2. James Buchanan, born 1855; married 1892 Helen Nichol, of Milwaukee, Wis., and has issue.

3. Edith, born 1857, and died 1861.

4. Arthur Wells, born 1861; married 1892 Margaret Beatrice, daughter of T. M. Taylor, of Montreal, and has issue.

5. Theodora Josephine, born 1866; married 1889 to Ewald Lowen of Eberfeld, Germany, and died there 5th February, 1900, leaving issue.

The Buchanans of Carbeth.

The Buchanans of Carbeth.[1]

I. Thomas Buchanan, First of Carbeth, is said by Auchmar [2] to have been the second or third son of Sir Walter, third of that name Laird of Buchanan, but Strathendrick says that he was a younger son of Thomas Buchanan, of Gartincaber and Drummikill.[3] He acquired Carbeth, in 1476. He had two sons:

(1) Thomas, his successor; and
(2) John in Easter Ballat.

II. Thomas Buchanan, of Carbeth, succeeded his father about 1493, and on his death, about 1555, was succeeded by his nephew, Thomas Buchanan, son of John Buchanan in Easter Ballat.

III. Thomas Buchanan, of Carbeth, was married twice; first, to a daughter of Douglas of Maines, by whom he had:

(1) Thomas, his successor.

He married, secondly, Janet, daughter of the Laird of Buchanan and by her had five sons and one daughter:

(2) John of Gartincaber, ancestor of the Buchanans of Blairlusk; [4]
(3) Walter of Ballindoran;
(4) William of Blairnabord;

---

(1) The account of this branch of the family is taken almost entirely from Strathendrick.
(2) Auchmar, p. 235 (1820 Edition).
(3) Strathendrick, p. 346.
(4) For an account of the Buchanans of Blairlusk, see p. 189.

(5) Archibald;
(6) Robert; and
(1) Janet, married to Gregor McGregor, of Glengyle.

IV. Thomas Buchanan, of Carbeth, who succeeded about 1605, and died about 1610; married Isobel Leckie and had:
(1) Thomas, his successor;
(2) James of Balfunning;
(3) William of Arnpryor, who married Agnes Rig, and died 1631, leaving two daughters, Margaret and Elizabeth, who sold Arnpryor.

V. Thomas Buchanan, of Carbeth, married, first, a daughter of Adam Colquhoun, merchant in Dumbarton, and had two sons:
(1) John, his successor; and
(2) Walter.

He is said to have married, secondly, Agnes Blair.

VI. John Buchanan, of Carbeth, married about 1632, Janet, daughter of William Buchanan of Ross, and had two sons:
(1) John, his successor.
(2) Moses of Glins, who married Jean Hamilton, daughter of William Hamilton of Auchintoshan, and had Jean who, in 1700, married John Dennistoun of Colgrain.

VII. John Buchanan, of Carbeth, 1633-1710, who married, first, a daughter of Cleland of Wardhead, by whom he had two daughters:

(1) Janet, married to John Callender of Westertoun; and
(2) Margaret, married to Thomas Buchanan of Boquhan.

He married, secondly, Margaret Steven, daughter and heiress of Walter Steven of Easter Catter and Finnick Tennent, by whom he had:
(1) John, his successor;
(2) Moses of Glins; and
(1) Jean, married, in 1696, to William Buchanan of Auchmar.

VIII. John Buchanan, of Carbeth, 1668-1724, married, in 1693, Margaret (died 1746), daughter of Stirling of Kippendavie, and had, among other issue, two sons, William, his successor, and Moses, born 1706, a surgeon in Jamaica, died about 1737.

IX. William Buchanan, of Carbeth, 1695-1737, married in 1717, Margaret, eldest daughter of James Kincaid of Auchinreoch (she died in 1767), by whom he had issue, among others, John, his successor; James, born 1724, went to sea and died 1745; Moses, born 1727, died 1741; Charles, born 1728, died 1752, in Jamaica, where he was a surgeon.

X. John Buchanan, of Carbeth, 1720-1790, married Ann Buchanan (1719-1794), daughter of James Buchanan, of Cremannan, and had issue:
(1) William, born 1747, Captain 35th Regiment, was at battle of Bunker Hill, died at New York 1777;

(2) James;
(3) Ann, 1750-1815;
(4) Margaret, 1751-1769;
(5) Christian;
(6) John, who succeeded his father;
(7) Elizabeth, 1758-1812;
(8) Charles, 1759-1772; and
(9) Jean, 1762-1807.

XI. John Buchanan, of Carbeth, 1755-1825, married, in 1802, Margaret, daughter of James Lock, and had:
  (1) Margaret Lock, born 1804;
  (2) John, his successor;
  (3) James, born 1809, settled in Canada, married there, in 1836, Mary Patrick, daughter of Thomas Chase Patrick, of Bushhill, formerly of Suffolk, England, and had among other issue, Charles Kincaid Buchanan;
  (4) Ann Jane, born 1811, died in Edinburgh.

XII. John Buchanan, of Carbeth, born 1807; died 14th March, 1872. He married, in 1836, Mary Louisa, daughter of Sir Henry Bayley, K.C.B., and had, among other issue, two daughters (who, having succeeded him, sold Carbeth), Ann Jane Buchanan, of Carbeth, married in 1894, Archibald Bell; and Henrietta Charlotte Buchanan married, in 1871, the late Colonel John Stirling Stirling of Gargunnock, late Royal Artillery, and has issue:
  (1) Charles, born 1873;

(2) Anselan John Buchanan, born 1875;
(3) James Hay, born 1882;
(4) Henry Francis Dundas, born 1883;
(1) Louisa Christian.
(2) Kathleen Caroline Anna.
(3) Josephine Marion.

The Buchanans of Ardoch.

The Buchanans of Ardoch.

I. William Buchanan, first of Ardoch, eldest son of Thomas Buchanan, of Over Gartincaber, born 1651, acquired in 1693, the lands of Ardoch from William Cochran of Kilmaronock, and married Grizel Buchanan, and died 1723, having had, Thomas, born 1678, a writer in Dumbarton, a Sheriff Clerk and a Commissioner of Supply. "His attachment to the Jacobite cause brought "him into suspicion during the commotions of ". 1715, and it is said that he was detained in the "Castle of Dumbarton to prevent him joining in "the rising of that year."[1] He married, in 1704, Agnes, daughter of Rev. John Bogle, and died in 1717, leaving issue:

(1) John, who succeeded his grandfather;
(2) Francis, merchant in London, born in 1715 and died in 1773 s. p.

II. John Buchanan, an eminent lawyer in Glasgow, born in 1706 and died 13th January, 1774. He married, first, in 1731, Mary, daughter of William Crawford, merchant in Glasgow, and had issue:

(1) Mary, born in 1732; married in 1764, Rev. James Graham, Minister of Bonhill; died 1814;
(2) Thomas, his successor;

---
(1) Strathendrick, pp. 354-57.

(3) Agnes, born 1734; married 1759, John Buchanan of Ledrishmore, died 1812, s. p.

He married, secondly, in 1747, Elizabeth, daughter of Walter Buchanan, of Teucher Hill, writer in Glasgow, and relict of Alexander Buchanan of Cremannan, and had one daughter,

(4) Frances, born 1751; married in 1770, John Maxwell, of Dargaval; died 1774, leaving issue.

III. Thomas Buchanan, merchant in Glasgow, born 6th November, 1733; died 10th December, 1789. He married, first, in 1759, Margaret, daughter and heiress of Moses Buchanan of Ballochruin, and had a son:

(1) John Buchanan, of Ardoch and Balloch, his successor.

He married, secondly, in 1764, Jean, daughter of John Gray of Dalmarnock, and had among others:

(2) James Gray-Buchanan, of Scotstown.

(3) Elizabeth, born 1772; married 1793, Alexander Gordon, of Glasgow, and died 1849, leaving issue.

He married, thirdly, in 1774, Helen, daughter of William Graham, of Birdstone. and had among others:

(4) William W. S., born 1777; married, in 1803, the Hon. Elizabeth Murray, daughter of Lord Elibank, and died in 1864, leaving issue.

(5) Helen, born in 1779; married in 1810, John Balfour; died 1816, leaving issue;
(6) Marion, born 1782, died 1822;
(7) Robert, born 1786, died 1870; married, first, in 1817, Margaret, daughter of William Dunlop, of Annanhill; secondly, in 1832, Margaret Dickson, by both of whom he had issue;
(8) Thomas Graham, born 1787, died 1871, unmarried;
(9) Archibald, Commander R. N., born 1789; married 1819, Matilda, daughter of James d'Albiac, and died 1822 leaving issue.

IV. John Buchanan, of Ardoch and Balloch, born 8th January, 1761; married in 1785, Elizabeth, daughter of John Parkes, of Netherton, and had by her, who died 4th September, 1807,

(1) Mary, born 1787, married Robert Findlay, of Easter Hill, died 1869;
(2) John, his successor;
(3) Margaret, born 1802 and died 1825;
(4) Elizabeth, born 1807 and died 1867.

In 1794 he was appointed Deputy Lieutenant; in 1820, Vice-Lieutenant of the County of Dumbartonshire; and in 1821 he was elected M.P. for the County. He died 26th June, 1839, having sold Ardoch, in 1836, to his half brother, Robert Buchanan.

V. John Buchanan, of Ardoch, J.P., born 24th March, 1799; married in 1840, Helen, daughter of John MacGregor, of Edinburgh, and died 8th January, 1875, leaving issue,

VI. Thomas John Buchanan, Lieutenant 52nd Light Infantry and Captain Royal Sherwood Foresters Militia; born 8th April, 1843; married 17th September, 1868, Janet d'Albedhyll, daughter of Lieutenant Colonel John Money Carter, late 1st Royal Scots, and grand-daughter of Alexander, 8th Lord Elibank, and died 2nd November, 1878, having by her, who died 8th May, 1890, had issue:

VII. John Parkes Buchanan, born 10th June, 1869; married 21st April, 1896, Hilda, daughter of Colonel Richard I. Crawford, and died 30th July, 1900, leaving issue, Maurice John Parkes, born 6th March, 1897.

Gray-Buchanans of Scotstown.

Gray-Buchanans of Scotstown.

James Gray-Buchanan, of Scotstown, merchant in Glasgow, second son of Thomas Buchanan, 3rd of Ardoch, was born 17th June, 1766; married 9th July, 1798, Anne, youngest daughter of John Parkes, of Netherton, by whom he had, Thomas, his successor. In 1841 he assumed the additional name of Gray on succeeding to his cousin, John Gray of Eastfield and Scotstown, and, in 1847, he acquired the lands of Ardoch from his half brother, John Buchanan. He died in 1855, leaving a son:

Thomas Gray-Buchanan, of Ardoch and Scotstown, merchant in Glasgow, born 8th November, 1804; married 15th October, 1835, Mary, daughter of Michael Rowand (who died in 1888). In 1857, he succeeded to the lands of Ardoch which he sold, in 1863, to John Findlay of Easter Hill and Boturrich, from whom they were subsequently acquired by Sir George Leith-Buchanan. He died 19th June, 1875, leaving issue:

(1) James Ross Gray-Buchanan, of Scotstown, who served for many years in the 26th Regiment of Cameronians, and late Lieutenant-Colonel and Hon. Colonel Commanding 3rd and 4th Bat. Cameronians Scottish Rifles; born 30th

January, 1840; married 26th August, 1863, Kate, daughter of James Farie, of Farme, and by her (who died in 1888), had issue: Thomas Farie, born 1875, died 1899 unmarried; James Morris, born 1877; Malcolm, born 1878, died 1882; Walter Bruce, Lieutenant 3rd Bat. Cameronians Scottish Rifles, born 1885; Cecil Gordon, born 1886; Janet Edith; Mary Rose; Kate Farie; Violet Sybil; Gertrude; and Elizabeth.

(2) Michael Rowand, of Ettrickdale, born 1846; married 1877, Frederica, daughter of Henry Stuart, and has issue, Claude, born 1878; Kenneth, born 1880; Ronald, born 1883; and Frederick, born 1887.

(3) Thomas Gray, born 1849, died 1852.

(4) Alexander Wilson Gray-Buchanan, of Parkhill, County Stirling, born 19th March, 1851; married 3rd August, 1881, Mary Sophie, daughter of Colin R. Dunlop, and died 18th July, 1909, and had issue: Rev. Alastair Gray-Buchanan, B. A., Minister of St. Martin's Episcopal Chapel, Leeds, Eng., born 24th November, 1883; Mary; Annie; and Ellen.

(1) Margaret Rowand, died 1839.

(2) Anne Parkes, married 1859, Henry John MacLean, Captain Rifle Brigade, son

of Sir George MacLean, K. C. D.; died 1871, leaving issue.

(3) Mary Rowand, married 1865, A. R. A. Boyd, Lieutenant 92nd Gordon Highlanders, son of Surgeon General D. Boyd, and died in 1872, leaving issue.

(4) Jane Catharine, married in 1874, George James Dunlop, son of James Dunlop, of Tollcross, and has issue.

The Buchanans of Auchmar.

The Buchanans of Auchmar.

I. William Buchanan, First of Auchmar, was the first son of George Buchanan, 17th Laird of Buchanan, by his second wife, Janet Cunningham. He was granted the lands of Auchmar by his father on the 3rd January, 1547. He married Elizabeth Hamilton, daughter of the Laird of Inchmachan or Eglishmachan, and died before 1588. He had three sons and two daughters:

(1) Patrick;
(2) George, who succeeded his brother Patrick; and
(3) Mr. William, the first cadet of the family, who went to Ireland and became manager and factor for the Estate of the family of Hamilton, then Lords of Clandeboys, and afterwards Earl of Clanbrazil, Co. Down. He married in Ireland and had one son, Major William Buchanan, "a very brave gentleman, "who was major to George, Laird of "Buchanan's Regiment, at the fatal "conflict betwixt the Scots and English "at Ennerkeithing. The Major, upon "defeat of the Scottish army, being "well mounted, made his way through "a party of English horsemen, and

"though pursued for some miles, came "off safe, having killed divers of the "pursuers. He went afterwards to "Ireland and purchased an Estate "there called Scrabohill, near Newtown "Clandeboys, in the County of Down. "He had two sons, the eldest continued "in Ireland and the younger went "abroad."[1] He had also two daughters, both married in that country:

(1) Margaret, married to Cunningham of Blairquhosh, and
(2) A daughter married to James Colquhoun, of Glasgow.

II. Patrick Buchanan, second Laird of Auchmar, married Helen, daughter and heiress of Mr. Thomas Buchanan of Ibert, "nephew to the "great Mr. George Buchanan, which Thomas be-"came lord privy seal by resignation of that office "in his favour by Mr. George his uncle."[2] Mr. Thomas Buchanan was married to the daughter of John, 18th Laird of Buchanan. Patrick died s. p. in 1603 and was succeeded by his brother.

III. George Buchanan, of Auchmar, who married Janet Stewart, daughter of Andrew Stewart, and had,

(1) Patrick, his successor;
(2) John, whose issue became extinct;
(3) Andrew, whose issue became extinct;

---
(1) Auchmar, p. 190.
(2) Auchmar, p. 187.

(4) Mr. Maurice, who was the second cadet of the family of Auchmar. He was a preacher in the County of Tyrone, and had one son, James, who had only one son, Captain Maurice Buchanan, who in 1723 resided near Dublin;

(5) Major William, who was a captain in the Swedish Service in Germany. "He "was upon account of his valour, con- "duct and other laudable qualities, "very much esteemed, having signal- "ized himself upon diverse occasions, "particularly in vanquishing an Italian, "who had acquired very much fame "by his martial achievements, and "dexterity always in performing divers "feats of arms, having carried the prize "in all places he went to, till at the "last he was overcome by this Captain "William, no less to his honour, than "to the Italian's disgrace. Upon ac- "count of this action he obtained a "major's commission, but was within "a few days thereafter killed in the "said service."[1] He married Anna Pennell, an English woman, and his descendants continued in Germany;

(6) Robert, whose issue became extinct; and

(7) George, who had one son William, who married at London and left a son

---

[1] Auchmar, p. 191.

James, who in 1723 was a merchant in London;
(1) Janet, married to Robert Colquhoun, of Camstradden, and
(2) A daughter married to Captain Pettigroe.

George Buchanan died before 1662.

IV. Patrick Buchanan, who married about 1629 Agnes, daughter of William Buchanan of Ross, and had by her one son and five daughters,
(1) John, his successor;
(1) Janet, married to William Buchanan of Cameron;
(2) Mary, married to Thomas Anderson;
(3) Elizabeth, married to Walter McFarlane;
(4) Agnes, married to William Galbraith of Arnfinlay, and
(5) Jean, married to Bartholomew Nairne of Meikle Batturich.

V. John Buchanan, who married, in 1666, Anna, daughter of John Graham of Duchray, and had,
(1) William; and
(2) Colin, who married Anna, daughter of James Hamilton of Aitkenhead.
(1) Margaret, married Robert Graham of Glenny;
(2) Catherine, married, first, George Buchanan, son of Arthur Buchanan of Auchlessie, and afterwards to Andrew Stewart of Drymen;

(3) A daughter married to Robert Stewart of Calliemore, and

(4) Elizabeth, married to George McFarlane of Drymen.

VI. William Buchanan, the historian of the Family of Buchanan, married in 1696, Jean, daughter of John Buchanan, of Carbeth, and died in 1747, and had,

(1) John, who died in 1744;
(2) Bernard, who died between 1721 and 1747;
(3) Alexander, his successor.

VII. Alexander Buchanan, who married Christian Campbell (who died in 1808). He had two sons,

(1) William; and
(2) James.

VIII. William Buchanan sold his lands in 1789 to Andrew Buchanan of Jamaica, merchant. He married, in 1796, Sarah Bartlet, second daughter of Benjamin Bartlet, storekeeper, Edinburgh Castle. He was drowned, in 1797, off the coast of America.

IX. James Buchanan, the 9th Laird of Auchmar, was born about 1758 and died s. p. in 1816. In 1803 he sold his rights of redemption of the lands of Auchmar to Andrew Buchanan, of Jamaica, who sold them the same year to his brother-in-law, Peter Buchanan. Andrew Buchanan had married Jean, and Peter Buchanan had married Margaret, both daughters of Isaac Buchanan (1705-1788), of Gartfarn, son of John

Buchanan, of Little Croy, and of his wife, a daughter of George McPharlan, merchant [1] of high standing in Glasgow, and had among other sons, Peter Buchanan, the younger, who, having succeeded his father, sold Auchmar in 1830, to the Duke of Montrose, and Isaac Buchanan.

The second son, the Honourable Isaac Buchanan of "Auchmar," of Hamilton, Upper Canada, was born at Glasgow on the 21st July, 1810. He entered upon a mercantile career and went, in 1813, to Canada, where he achieved a reputation as merchant and political economist, and having entered Parliament became a member of the Government. He married, in January, 1813, Agnes, daughter of Robert Jarvis, of Glasgow, and had,

(1) Peter Toronto Buchanan, of Hamilton, born 7th May, 1844, at Toronto, Upper Canada; member Buchanan Society, 1861; died at Hamilton, 9th November, 1898, unmarried.

(2) Robert Andrew Washington Buchanan, of Hamilton, born New York City, 29th February, 1848; died at Hamilton in 1852.

(3) Harris Buchanan, of Pittsburgh, Pa., born at Birkenhead, England, 10th April, 1851; member Buchanan Society, 1870; married Victoria Cleghorn and Katherine H. Barker; died at East Liberty, Pittsburgh, on the 1st May, 1903; issue,

---

[1] Strathendrick, pp. 342 and 376.

Isaac Victor Buchanan and George Peter Buchanan, both of Pittsburgh and members of the Buchanan Society, 1903.

(4) Isaac Robert Buchanan, of Denver, Colorado, born Hamilton, 27th May, 1852; died Denver, 21st March, 1884, unmarried.

(5) James Isaac Buchanan, of Pittsburgh, born 3rd August, 1853, near Hamilton; member Buchanan Society, 1870; married 11th July, 1901, Eliza MacFarlane, daughter of Isaiah Graham Macfarlane.

(6) Robert Jarvis Buchanan, of Hamilton, born near Hamilton, 22nd August, 1859; unmarried.

(7) Douglas Buchanan of Pittsburgh, born near Hamilton, 9th December, 1860; member Buchanan Society, 1893; married Sarah Eleanor Grayson; issue, Douglas Grayson Buchanan and Evelyn Eleanor Buchanan.

The Buchanans of Hales Hall.

The Buchanans of Hales Hall.

The Buchanans of Hales Hall, near Market Drayton, Staffordshire, claim descent from the Buchanans of Auchmar. Archibald Buchanan settled in the North of Ireland in 1686. His grandson, John Buchanan, of Donnelly, co. Donegal, married in 1785, Elizabeth, daughter of John Phillips, Wavertree, Lancashire, and died in 1796, leaving issue:—

1. Phillips Buchanan, an officer in the 3rd Light Dragoons, who was killed at the battle of Waterloo.

2. Alexander Henry Buchanan, of whom hereafter.

3. William Theophilus Buchanan, of North Cote, near Westbury, Gloucestershire. He was an officer of the 13th Light Dragoons, and served through the Peninsular war, being engaged almost daily during the march of Lord Hill's division across the Pyrenees, and also frequently on the Toulouse. He married in 1823, Eliza Anne, daughter of Rev. Richard Massey, of Coddrington, Cheshire, and died in 1865.

4. James Buchanan, died young.

1. Eleanor, married Clement Swetenham, of Somerford Booth, Cheshire.

Rev. Alexander Henry Buchanan, J.P., of Hales Hall, which he acquired in 1824, born in 1790;

married in 1819, Susanne, daughter of Nathaniel Maxey Pattison, of West House, co. Chester, and had issue:—

1. Phillips Buchanan, J.P., late of Hales Hall, formerly of the 6th Dragoons, born in 1820; married in 1848, Louisa Lucy, daughter of Robert Townley Parker, M.P., of Cuerdon Hall, Lancashire, and died in 1895, having by her (who died in 1891) had issue:—1. Alexander Phillips, d. s. p. 1862. 1. Louisa Constance, died in 1862. 2. Edith Mary, married in 1874, Edward Maltby Wakeman, of Coton Hill, Bridgnorth, and has issue. 3. Jessie Marion, married in 1884, Francis Bernard Critchley-Salmonson, Rosenau, Devon, and has issue Ronald.

2. James Maxey Buchanan, entered Army in 1844, and became Captain 70th Regiment; married Sophia Matilda, daughter of Arthur Champion Barwell, B.S.C., and had issue:—1. Henry Barwell Maxey Buchanan, now of Hales Hall; 2. Leicester Buchanan, d.s.p.; 3. Percy Maxey Buchanan, married in 1889, Ida Mary, daughter of John Forbes-Robertson; 4. Reginald Buchanan, who left issue, Reginald Barwell, Sydney, Ethel Maud and Mabel. 1. Nina Maxey, married in 1890, John Hinton Campbell, and has issue, Eric who died and Robin Hasluck; 2. Ethel Helen, married in 1889, Major H. D. Wilmot Mitchell, 14th Hussars, and has issue; 3. Mildred Clare, married in 1894 Arthur Knowles, of Alvaston House, Cheshire, and has issue, John Buchanan and Richard.

3. William Buchanan, died at Madeira, in 1862.

4. Alexander Buchanan (Rev.), married in 1872, Ann Alice, daughter of Richard Fort, M.P., Read Hall, Lancashire. He died in 1906, leaving issue:—Dorothy Elsie, who died; Monica, who married Captain Peter Mason, 20th Hussars; and Evelyn, who married Harvey de Montmorency, Royal Artillery.

5. Clement Buchanan, died in 1856.

6. Henry Brian Buchanan, of Newquay, Cornwall, Lieut.-Colonel late Rifle Brigade, born in 1845; entered the army in 1867, and retired in 1884 with the rank of Lieut-Colonel. He married, in 1886, Alice, daughter of Lewis Pratt.

1. Susan, married in 1852, Arthur Brooke, son of Sir Richard Brooke, Bart., of Norton Priory, Cheshire, and died in 1852, leaving issue.

2. Helen Mary.

Henry Barwell Maxey Buchanan, of Hales Hall, B.A., Cambridge, formerly in the Royal Navy, born in 1852, succeeded his uncle in 1895; married first, in 1878, Sabrina Kate, daughter of Col. MacHutchin, and has issue:—Harry Leslie Barwell, born in 1879, and Claud James, born in 1883; secondly, in 1906, Ellen Alice Emma, youngest daughter of the late Stephen Lynch, son of Major Lynch of Partry House, Ballinrobe, co. Mayo, Ireland.

The Buchanans of Spittal.

The Buchanans of Spittal.

The ancestor of the family of Spittal and the first to acquire these lands was:—

I. Walter Buchanan, of Easter Catter, said by Auchmar to have been the son of Patrick, second of that name, 16th Laird of Buchanan, but by others to have been the son of Walter Buchanan of Buchanan. This Walter Buchanan, First Laird of Spittal, married Isabel Cunningham, daughter of the 1st Earl of Glencairn. He acquired the lands of Spittal in 1519, those of Arrochymore in 1530, and those of Blairvockie (Blairwoky or Blairvoky[1]) in 1535.

II. Edward Buchanan, of Spittal, succeeded his father,[2] and married Christian Galbraith, daughter of the Laird of Culcruich. He had two sons: (1) Robert, his successor, and (2) George, first cadet of Spittal, and the ancestor of the Buchanans in Arrachybeg, who had one son, William, who obtained part of the lands of Arrachybeg in Buchanan parish. William had one son, Donald, who had four sons: William, Duncan, Robert and Walter. Of these, William had one son, Donald of Arrachybeg, who had issue. Duncan had one son, John, who had also

---
1 Auchmar, p. 194.
2 Auchmar says that Walter Buchanan was succeeded by his son John, but the account given in Strathendrick appears more satisfactory.

one son, Duncan, who, in 1723, was in the Foot Guards. Robert, who was killed in 1645, had no male issue. Walter, who lived in Cashill in Buchanan parish, had two sons, John and William, who had issue.

III. Robert Buchanan, of Spittal, married Margaret Galbraith and had two sons: (1) Walter, his successor, and (2) Andrew, the second cadet of Spittal. "This Andrew," says Auchmar, "seems to have been a man of education, and "was factor to part of the Earl of Mar's estate "for some time. He bought Blairvocky from "Spittel, and having never married, disponed "that interest to Walter Buchanan, his nephew, "ancestor to the Buchanans of Blairvocky."[1]

IV. Walter Buchanan, of Spittal, married, first, in 1593, Jean, daughter of John Stirling of Craigbarnet, and, secondly, Margaret Lawson, and had two sons: (1) Edward, his successor, and (2) Walter Buchanan, the third cadet of Spittal and the first Laird of Blairvockie.[2]

V. Edward Buchanan, of Spittal, married, first, about 1630, Helen, daughter of Edmondstone of Balleun, and had two sons: (1) James, who married in 1648, Janet Buchanan, daughter of John Buchanan of Cashlie, and had five sons: Edward, who succeeded his grandfather; Captain John, who "was captain in the Dutch and Eng- "lish service, during the whole time of the wars

---
[1] Auchmar, p. 197.
[2] See page 301.

"betwixt the French, English and Dutch, with "their other confederates, from the year 1690, "till the last peace; and was also an officer in "the service of the Dutch, and some other states "of Europe, a good many years before the com- "mencement of these wars"; Captain Archibald, "who for divers years before his death was "one of the captains of the King's horseguards, "being a gentleman inferior to none of his "age and station in all valuable qualities";[1] Andrew and Walter, both of whom died unmarried. James Buchanan died before his father between the years 1659 and 1664, and in 1666 his widow married Walter Buchanan, fiar of Blairvockie;[2] and (2) Captain John Buchanan, of Sir George Buchanan's Regiment, "who was "killed at the fatal conflict betwixt the Scots "and the English at Ennerkeithing."[3]

Edward, 5th Laird of Spittal, married, secondly, in 1646, Margaret Buchanan, daughter of John Buchanan of Ross, and had: (3) Robert, Dean of the bakers in Glasgow, whose son Robert, writer in Glasgow, married Jean Buchanan, daughter of Archibald Buchanan, Laird of Drumhead, who died in 1729; and (4) Edward, "who "was a man of great learning, and died while "at the study of divinity in the College of "Edinburgh."[4]

---
[1] Auchmar, p. 199.
[2] Strathendrick. p. 369.
[3] Auchmar, p. 195.
[4] Auchmar, p. 196.

Edward Buchanan died in 1669.

VI. Edward Buchanan, of Spittal, who succeeded his grandfather, married in 1673, Christian Mitchell, daughter of Mr. Thomas Mitchell, minister at Kilmarnock, and had two sons: (1) John, his successor; and (2) Thomas, chirurgeon in Glasgow, who married a daughter of Napier of Ballachairn, and by her had a daughter Christina, married Thomas Napier, of Glasgow; and a son, John Buchanan, M.D., who married the daughter of Sir Archibald Primrose, Bart., and had a daughter, Susan.

VII. John Buchanan, of Spittal, married in 1707, Margaret Muirhead, daughter of Patrick Muirhead of Rashie Hill, and relict of Robert Buchanan of Arnpryor, and had three sons and one daughter: (1) Robert, who succeeded his father; (2) Peter, afterwards of Spittal; (3) Thomas, also afterwards of Spittal; and (1) Christian, who married, as his second wife, Robert Buchanan of Leny.

VIII. Robert Buchanan, of Spittal, succeeded his father before 1733. He entered the Dutch service, and became Colonel Commandant of Dundas's Regiment of Scots Dutch. In 1735, he sold the lands of Gartachorran to Thomas Buchanan, surgeon in Glasgow, and in the same year he sold the lands of Spittal to his brother, Peter Buchanan. He died after 1770, s.p.

IX. Peter Buchanan sold Spittal in 1755 to his brother, Thomas Buchanan. Peter Buchanan married Agnes, second daughter of James Hamilton of Hutcheson, but died s.p. "He, (Peter "Buchanan of Spittal) as well as the memorialist "(Thomas Buchanan afterwards of Spittal, Leny "and Bardowie) were apprehended in 1746 at "the same time with Arnprior, and carried "prisoners first to Stirling Castle, and after- "wards to Carlisle, in which last place they were "confined for many months in irons, and in a "loathsome dungeon with a crowd of other "prisoners of all ranks, and though he and the "memorialist were afterwards acquitted and "liberated, yet Peter Buchanan's constitution, "in consequence of what he suffered, was quite "broken, and even his memory affected."[1]

X. Thomas Buchanan, who was an officer in the Dutch service, married, first, Katherine, youngest daughter of Henry Buchanan of Leny, who died s.p., and secondly, Elizabeth, daughter of John Hamilton of Bardowie, by which marriage the Buchanans of Spittal succeeded to Bardowie. They also succeeded to Leny as heir of entail on the death of Margaret Buchanan, last survivor of the family of Henry Buchanan of Leny. By Elizabeth Hamilton he had issue: (1) Henry, died unmarried; (2) John Buchanan, who succeeded to the estates of Spittal and Bardowie and took the name of Hamilton, born in 1758, married 1790, Margaret, daughter of Sir Hew Crawford of

---

[1] Strathendrick, p. 370 and seq.

Jordanhill, and died s.p. in 1818; (3) Robert Hamilton Buchanan, Lieutenant R.N. British Fusiliers, born in 1760, married Cornelia Tinker, and died leaving a son, Robert Hamilton Buchanan, Captain 24th Regiment Bengal Native Infantry, who died unmarried before his uncle, John Buchanan-Hamilton; (4) Francis Buchanan, who succeeded his brother John, and assumed the name of Hamilton; (5) Peter Buchanan, Captain in the 23rd Regiment of Fusiliers, born in 1767, died unmarried; (1) Elizabeth Buchanan married, first, Robert Grahame of Gartmore; secondly, Robert Fairfoul, of Strowie, and (2) Marion Buchanan, born 1766, married J. H. S. Crawford of Cowdonhill.

XI. Francis Buchanan-Hamilton, M.D., of Spittal, Bardowie and Leny, succeeded his brother, John Buchanan-Hamilton.[1] " In 1828 " he was served heir male to his great-great-great- " great - great - great - great - grandfather, Walter " Buchanan of Spittal, and established his claim, " in absence of other competitors, as Chief of " the Clan of Buchanan."[2]

" Francis Buchanan was born at Branziet, " Stirlingshire, 15th February, 1762. He studied " for the medical profession at the University " of Edinburgh, and received his degree in 1783;

---

[1] A few years ago the Government of India published a Sketch of his life edited by Colonel David Prain, I.M.S., C.I.E., F.R.S., Director of the Royal Botanic Gardens, Kew.

[2] Strathendrick, p. 371. In 1828 Dr. Francis Buchanan published his "Claim of the Head of the Family of Buchanan of Spittal as Chief of the Family of Buchanan."

" after travelling for some years he was, in 1794,
" appointed surgeon in the Honourable East
" India Company's service on the Bengal estab-
" lishment. On his arrival in India, he was
" sent with Captain Symes on his mission to the
" Court of Ava in a civilian capacity. In 1800
" he was chosen to examine the state of the
" country which the Company's forces had lately
" conquered from Tippoo Saib, together with the
" Province of Malabar; and in 1802 he accom-
' panied Captain Knox on his embassy to Nepal.
" On his return, he was appointed to the staff of
' the Marquis Wellesley, then Governor-General.
" In 1805 he went with the Marquis to England,
" and in the following year was again sent out by
" the Court of Directors for the purpose of making
" a statistical survey of the territory under the
" Presidency of Fort-William, which comprehends
" Bengal proper, and several of the adjoining
" districts. In 1814, on the death of Dr. Rox-
" burgh, he succeeded him as superintendent of
" the Botanical Garden. He returned to Scot-
" land in 1815, and spent the latter years of his
" life at Leney, in Perthshire, an estate to which
" his father had succeeded as heir of entail, and
" which, on the death of his elder brother, Colonel
" Hamilton, without children, came into his
" possession, with the other family estates, when
" he assumed his mother's name of Hamilton.
" He was the author of ' Travels in the Mysore,'
" then published, under the patronage of the

"Court of Directors, in 1807; 'The History of "Nepal,' 1818; 'A Genealogy of the Hindoo "Gods,' 1819; and 'An Account of the Fishes "of the Ganges,' with plates, 1822. He also "contributed largely to various literary and "scientific journals; was a member of several "societies, and a Fellow of the Royal Societies "of London and Edinburgh.'"[1] He married Anne Brock, daughter of Andrew Brock, and died at Leny on the 15th June, 1829, having had issue (with a daughter, Catherine, who died unmarried in 1839) an only son;

XII. John Buchanan-Hamilton, F.R.S., of Spittal, Leny and Bardowie, born 1822; married 1845, Margaret Seton, daughter of George Seton, Commander, H.E.I.C.S., of the family of Cariston, co. Fife, and by her (who died in 1892) had issue: (1) Francis Wellesley, born 1853, died unmarried in 1893; (2) George Buchanan, born 1856, died unmarried in 1886; (3) John Hamilton; (1) Margaret Seton, married in 1867, Robert Jardine of Castle Milk, M.P., afterwards Sir Robert Jardine, Bart., and died in 1868, leaving issue a son, Robert William Buchanan Jardine, born in 1868, who married in 1894, Ethel Mary, daughter of Mr. Benjamin Piercy of Marchwiel Hall, Denbighshire, by whom he has issue. He succeeded his father in 1905. (2) Anne Helen, died in 1851; (3) Katherine Elizabeth died in 1905.

---

[1] Anderson's Scottish Biographical Dictionary.

John Buchanan-Hamilton died on the 16th May, 1903, and was succeeded by his son,

XIII. John Hamilton-Buchanan, born in 1861; married in 1884, Phoebe Elizabeth, daughter of John Clark Brodie, C.B., of Idvies, Forfarshire.

The Buchanans of Blairvockie.

The Buchanans of Blairvockie.

I. Walter Buchanan, first Laird of Blairvockie, 1614, (in Blairvockie 1603), was the first cadet of Spittal, being the second son of Walter Buchanan of Spittal. He married, first, Margaret McCalpen (McAlpine), who died in 1619, by whom he had Alexander, his successor, and other issue; secondly, about 1624, Giles or Geiles Buchanan.[1]

II. Alexander Buchanan, of Blairvockie, 1632, married Agnes Buchanan, and died in 1672. He had, (1) Walter Buchanan, of Blairvockie, married 1666, Janet Buchanan, and died 1675; (2) Alexander, alive in 1673, probably died before 1675, and (3) William.

III. William Buchanan, of Blairvockie, 1691, who succeeded his brother in the estate. " William the third brother," says Auchmar, " having obtained the interest of Blairvocky, sold " the same to John Buchanan, younger of Spittel. " William Buchanan, the last of Blairvocky, " resided mostly in Ireland. He had four sons, " Alexander, William, Walter and Henry. Alex-

---

[1] From notes kindly furnished by the late Mr. A. W. Gray Buchanan, Laird of Parkhill, Polmont, who took a great interest in antiquarian and genealogical studies.

" ander, the eldest, resides in Glendermon, within
" two miles of Derry, being in very good repute
" and circumstances. William, Walter and Henry
" reside near Omagh, in the county of Tyrone,
" in the kingdom of Ireland."[1]

[1] Auchmar, p. 198.

The Buchanans of Montreal.

The Buchanans of Montreal.

Doctor John Buchanan, of the 49th Regiment of Foot, was the son of Alexander Buchanan, of Fintona, co. Tyrone, Ireland, and was descended from William Buchanan, last Laird of Blairvockie, who sold his estates about 1695, and went to Ireland. John Buchanan was born at Eccles Green, near Fintona, in 1769; became an Army Surgeon and was at the attack of Copenhagen in 1801; went to Canada, in 1802, on the medical staff of the 49th Regiment, and died in 1815, at Quebec. He married, first, Lucy Richardson, who died, in 1803, at Three Rivers, and had issue:—

I. Alexander Buchanan, Q.C., of Montreal, born 1798; admitted to the Bar of Lower Canada in 1819; appointed King's Counsel in 1835; appointed, in 1835, a Commissioner to treat with the Commissioners of Upper Canada respecting the boundary line between Upper and Lower Canada; Chairman of the Commission appointed, in 1838, to enquire into the cases of the State Prisoners confined in the Montreal Gaol; Commissioner of the Court of Requests for the District of Montreal in 1839; Crown Prosecutor for Montreal from 1840 to 1845; President of the Commission appointed, in 1842, to enquire into the State of the Feudal Tenure in Lower Canada; member of the Commission appointed, in 1842, to revise the Acts and Ordinances of Lower Canada; in 1851 Member of the Council of the Montreal Bar; married in 1824, Mary Ann Buchanan, daughter of James Buchanan, H.B.M. Consul at New York (who died in 1862), and died in 1851, at Montreal, having had issue:

1. Hon. George Carlo Vidua Buchanan, of Sweetsburgh, and later of Montreal, born 1825; admitted to the Bar of Lower Canada, 1846; appointed a Queen's Counsel in 1873; a Commissioner for Consolidating the General Statutes of the Province of Quebec in 1877, and a Judge of the Superior Court for the District of Bedford in 1881; married in 1863, Abbie Louisa Snow, and died in 1901. He had issue:

(1) Charles Ernest Buchanan, born 1871.

(1) Mary Maud, married 1896, George G. Foster, K.C., of Montreal, and has issue, George Buchanan, born 1897, and Ruth Elizabeth.

(2) Florence Geraldine, died 1885.

2. Elizabeth Jane Buchanan, born in 1827; married in 1851, Captain George Blicke Champion de Crespigny, XXth Regt., after-

---

1. The report of this Commission is printed *in extenso* in Dr. W. B. Munro's Documents, relating to the Seigniorial Tenure in Canada at page 303. Also see Appendix to this book at page 2.

wards Lieut.-Col. commanding School of Musketry at Hythe, second son of Charles Fox Crespigny, of Harefield House, Uxbridge, Middlesex; and died in 1897, at Folkestone, England, and having had issue:

(1) George Harrison Champion de Crespigny, Hon. Lieut.-Colonel, 3rd Batt. Northamptonshire Regt., of Burton Latimer Hall, Kettering, Northants, born in 1863; married, in 1890, Gwendoline Blanche, daughter of W. C. Clark-Thornhill, of Rushton Hall, Northants, Fixby, Yorkshire, and Swakeleys, Middlesex; and has issue: George Arthur Oscar, born in 1894; Mildred Frances and Gwendoline Sibyl.

(1) Julia Constantia, born in 1852, died in 1876.

(2) Georgiana Elizabeth, unmarried.

3. Wentworth James Buchanan, of Montreal, late General Manager of the Bank of Montreal, born in 1828; married, in 1859, Agatha, daughter of Major Arnold R. Burrowes, 3rd Foot Guards, and died in 1905, leaving issue:

(1) Claude Wentworth Buchanan, of Montreal, born in 1872.

(2) Fitzherbert Price Buchanan, of Montreal, born in 1874.

(3) Richard Trevor Buchanan, of Woodlands, Que., born in 1876; married in 1905,

Frances Eliza Cecilia, daughter of Edward C. Hale, of Lennoxville, P.Q., and has issue.

(1) Mary Ada (Minda), married on 23rd August, 1910, Oleg Tripet-Skrypitzine.

(2) Alice Agatha, married in 1902, Frank H. Weir, of Montreal, and has issue.

4. William Robert Buchanan, of Honolulu, S.I., born in 1830, and died in 1902, at Honolulu. He married, first, Miss Muselwhite and had issue: Charles A.; William; Gertrude, died unmarried; Amy, married to Mr. Hope; and Helen, married to Mr. Brundage. He married, secondly, Emma C. Fitzsimmons, née Brickwood, and had issue: Wentworth M., married, 1907, Gertrude M. Regan; Alexander; Irene Martha, married to William H. Cornwell, Jr.; Grace, married to Allen Dunn; Mary, married to Henry N. Almy, and Agnes Judd.

5. Alexander Brock Buchanan, of Montreal, late Secretary and Inspector of Branch Returns of the Bank of Montreal, born in 1832; married, in 1857, Elizabeth Ann, daughter of Francis Best and Emily Atkinson (born in 1834) and has issue:

(1) George Reid Buchanan, born in 1858, and died in 1861.

(2) Alexander Buchanan, of Montreal, late in the service of the Bank of Montreal, born in 1861; married in 1903, Anna

Mary, daughter of the Hon. James O'Brien, Senator, of Montreal.

(3) Rupert Charles Buchanan, late of Montreal, and now of Vernon, B.C., born in 1867; married, in 1896, Mary Jane, daughter of William McLimont, of Quebec, and has issue: Alexander Ronald, born in 1901; William Henry Keith, born in 1903, and Nancy Greaves.

(4) Arthur William Patrick Buchanan, K.C.,[1] of Montreal, born in 1870; LL.B. Laval University, Montreal, 1893; admitted to the Bar of the Province of Quebec in 1894; appointed a King's Counsel in 1908; married, in 1897, Berthe Louise, daughter of William Quirin, of Boston, and has issue: Erskine Brock Quirin, born in 1898, and Audrey Isabel Patricia.

(5) Albert Edward Clarence Buchanan, of Montreal, born 1870.

(1) Elizabeth Emily (Lemmy) died in 1880.

(2) Frances (Lily) married in 1899, Arthur Hamilton Buchanan, now manager of the Bank of Montreal, Spokane, U.S.A., son of the late Alexander Carlisle Buchanan, of Quebec.

(3) Ethel (Cherry), died in 1898.

(4) Gwendoline, died in 1896.

---

[1] Member of the Buchanan Society in 1900.

6. Margaret Lucy Buchanan, born in 1834 and died in 1837.

7. Frederick Albert Buchanan, born in 1836, and died in 1842.

8. Mary Alexandrina Buchanan, born 1841, and died in 1841.

9. Mary Buchanan, born in 1842, married in 1876, the late Rev. R. Mainwaring Williams, M.A., of Harnhill Rectory, Cirencester, Gloucestershire, and died in 1901, leaving issue:

(1) Herbert Mainwaring Williams, Lieut. Army Veterinary Department, born in 1879, married.

(1) Gladys Louisa, married in 1910, Hugh Edward Whittaker Cantrell.

(2) Marjorie Mary.

II. John Buchanan, of L'Orignal, Upper Canada, born in 1800; married in 1829, Catherine, daughter of the Hon. Alexander Grant, of Duldregan House, L'Orignal, U.C., and died in 1837. He had issue:

1. Lucy, died in 1847.

2. Jane Louisa, born in 1830, died in 1907, unmarried.

3. Alexander Grant Buchanan, born in 1833; married, in 1878, Anna Field (who died without issue).

III. Jane Mary Buchanan, born in 1801; married in 1820, Captain William Hall, and died in 1872, leaving issue.

Doctor Buchanan had another son, George Buchanan, who died at Liverpool, in 1870, leaving issue.

Doctor Buchanan married, secondly, in 1809, Ursule, daughter of the Hon. Joseph Francois Perrault, Prothonotary of the Court of King's Bench for the District of Quebec, who died in 1809, aged 23 years.

Family of Dr. George Buchanan of Fintona, Co. Tyrone.

Family of Dr. George Buchanan of Fintona, Co. Tyrone.

Beaver Buchanan, of Fintona, born in 1710, was descended from William Buchanan, last of Blairvockie, who settled in Ireland. According to Mr. Thomas Hardinge Buchanan, of Dublin, who has made extensive researches as to the family of Buchanan in Tyrone, Beaver Buchanan was the son of William Buchanan of Fintona, who died in 1764. This William Buchanan married, in 1733, Margaret Creery, and had four sons, John, who had a son William; Andrew, William and Beaver, and three daughters, Anne, wife of Andrew Anthony; Margaret and Alice. This William Buchanan appears to have had two brothers, Eccles Buchanan of Fintona, who died in 1762, and John Buchanan of Mullamenagh, living in 1764. Eccles Buchanan, of Fintona, was married three times: first, in 1724, to Mary Pitkern; secondly, in 1748, to Margaret Johnston; and thirdly to Elizabeth ———. He had four sons, Thomas, John, Robert and George, and a daughter, Margaret.

Beaver Buchanan, who was living in 1780, but dead before 1804, had at least three sons: (1) Dr. George Buchanan, of Fintona; (2) Thomas Buchanan, of Fintona, living in 1804; and (3)

Eccles Alexander Buchanan, of Fintona, living in 1826.

Dr. George Buchanan, of Fintona, was born in 1740, and married, 11th March, 1774, Ann Mullan (who died in 1838 aged 81 years), and died in 1818. They had issue:—

I. Bever Buchanan, of Dublin, born in 1775, was the first President of the Apothecaries' Hall of Ireland; married, in 1795, Elinor Hodgson, and died on the 1st January, 1813, having had issue:—

1. Elizabeth Ann, married Maziere Brady, son of Francis Tempest Brady, of Dublin, born in 1796, who became Lord Chancellor of Ireland, was created a Baronet and died in 1871, his wife having predeceased him in 1858. Their son was the late Sir Francis William Brady, K.C., County Court Judge of Tyrone, who was born in 1824; called to the Irish Bar in 1846, appointed Queen's Counsel in 1860 and County Court Judge to Tyrone in 1872. He was twice married: first, to Emily, daughter of the Right Rev. Samuel Kyle, Bishop of Cork; and, secondly, to Geraldine, daughter of the late George Hatchell, M.D., Physician to the Lord Lieutenant of Ireland. Sir Francis Brady died on the 26th August, 1909.

2. Dr. George Buchanan, of Downpatrick, co. Down, Surgeon to the Royal Infirmary, co. Down; married Ann, daughter of Dr. Richard Wright, of Dublin (who died about 1845), and ied on the 19th October, 1841. He had issue:—

(1) Francis Robert Buchanan, born 1827, and went to America.

(2) Richard Wright Buchanan, Solicitor, of Sion House, Kingstown, and of the Court of Chancery, Dublin, born in 1829, and died in 1882; he married Martha, daughter of Thomas Perrott, of Uplands, Fermoy, co. Cork (who died in 1908), and had,—

(1) George, born in 1856; Lieutenant, R.A.; died 1879, unmarried.

(2) Rev. Charles Henry Leslie Buchanan, Rector of Kilnaughter, co. Antrim, born 1864, married Florence, daughter of Rev. William Moore, Rector of St. Patrick's, Newry, and has issue:—(1) Richard Moore, (2) George Henry Perrott, and (3) Florence Mary.

(1) Elizabeth, died 1880, unmarried.

(2) Emily, unmarried.

(3) Louisa, died 1879, unmarried.

(3) Rev. Charles Todd Buchanan, of Dublin, afterwards rector of Mullafad, co. Fermanagh, and of Ballynoe, co. Cork, born 30th November, 1831, married Arabella Hardinge, daughter of William Going, of "Altavilla," Cahir, co. Tipperary (who died 24th December, 1903), and died 1st March, 1907, having had issue:—

(1) Dr. George Charles Buchanan, of "Woodside," Beamsville, Ont., Canada, born 11th July, 1862; married 6th August, 1888, Florence Mary, daughter of W. O. Thompson,

of Minnesota, and has issue:—(1) Charles Richard, born 13th July, 1892; (1) Mary Alice Lucille; (2) Theresa Marjory Kathleen.

(2) Rev. William Alexander Going Buchanan, Rector of Marble Bar, West Australia, born 24th August, 1867; died 28th May, 1906, unmarried.

(3) Thomas Hardinge Buchanan, of Dublin, born 13th July, 1869; married, 1889, Anna, daughter of Parker Dunscombe, of Dublin, and has issue:—(1) Charles Hardinge, born 27th June, 1900; (2) Parker Dunscombe Gordon, born 29th June, 1905; (1) Nanette Emily; (2) Margery Norreys.

(1) Matilda (Sissy), died in infancy.
(2) Anne, died in infancy.
(3) Arabella Caroline, unmarried.

(1) Elinor, died in infancy.
(2) Jane, died in infancy.
(3) Georgiana Buchanan, died in 1898.

3. William Buchanan, married in Dublin, 1822, Mary Hutchinson, and had issue:—

(1) Stanley Buchanan, who was a doctor in Newport, Monmouthshire, and died there leaving a daughter, Elinor, married to Mr. Allen, who had a daughter Elizabeth.

(2) Francis Buchanan, went to Australia.

(3) Beaver (Beverly) Buchanan, who went to New Zealand and died on the 29th July, 1870, at Lyttleton.

(4) William Pollock Buchanan, died in infancy.

(5) William Frederick Buchanan, went to Australia.

(1) Henrietta.

4. Beaver Buchanan, died in infancy.

5. Elinor Buchanan, married to Charles Magrath, of Dublin, and died about 1876.

II. Eliza Buchanan, born in 1776, married to Hans Denniston, and died in 1796.

III. John Buchanan, born in 1777, and died in 1785.

IV. William Buchanan, born in 1779, went to Australia, and died in 1834.

V. Jane Buchanan, born in 1780, married to John Pollock, and died in 1830.

VI. Ann Buchanan, born in 1782, married to James Greer, of Omagh, and died in 1805, leaving a daughter married to Robert Hamilton, of Omagh.

VII. Margaret Buchanan, born in 1784, married to James Wilson, Clerk of the Crown, Omagh, and died in 1861.

VIII. George Buchanan, born in 1786, and died in 1790.

IX. Dr. Robert Buchanan, born in 1787, married Eliza Fraser, and died in 1872, at London. He was a Surgeon in the Scotch Greys and resided in Pontefract Castle, Yorkshire. He had a son William and two daughters, Louise, married to a French gentleman, and Emily, married to

Colonel Morris, Army Pay Department, who had a son Captain Godfrey Morris, and a daughter, Louisa Morris.

X. John Buchanan, born in 1789, who became an Army Surgeon, and was killed in 1814 during the Peninsular War, and whose descendants are in Yorkshire, England.

XI. James Buchanan, of Fintona, born 29th September, 1793; appointed Coroner at Fintona; married 1st February, 1819, Amelia Blakely, and died 5th August, 1862, at Castle Lodge, Fintona. His wife died on the 10th June, 1848, aged 53 years. They had issue:—

1. George Buchanan, born in 1820, and died 13th August, 1846.

2. Alexander Eccles Buchanan, born in 1822, and died 21st January, 1848.

3. John Buchanan, who died abroad, unmarried.

4. Robert Buchanan, born at Fintona, 22nd November, 1833; became Coroner at Fintona; married 1st November, 1860, Mary Thompson, and died on 14th March, 1873. They had issue:—

(1) Walter James Thompson Buchanan, born 12th November, 1861; I. M. S. Inspector-General of Jails, Calcutta; served with China-Lushai Expeditionary Force in 1899-1900, for which he received medal with clasps; married on 30th March, 1892, Lilian Edith Byrne, daughter of E. Simpson

Byrne, C.S., Accountant-General, Bengal; and has issue:—Maurice Beaver, born 7th December, 1893.

(2) Charles Alexander Buchanan, of " Deroran ", Stirling, and stockbroker in Glasgow, born at Fintona on 20th March, 1863; married 4th June, 1891, Mary Catherine Kay, daughter of R. Murray Kay, Ayr; and has issue:—Edmund Pullar, born 18th July, 1893; Marjory Murray, and Elizabeth Esther.

(3) Robert Eccles Buchanan, Civil Engineer, Londonderry, born at Fintona, 10th June, 1864; married 1st April, 1891, Ethel Maud Williams, daughter of Thomas Richard Williams, of Sellars Hall, Finchley, London; and has issue:—Edgar James Bernard, born 16th February, 1892; Richard Brendan, born 6th May, 1894; and Ethel Elizabeth.

(4) Harry William Buchanan, born 9th May, 1869; married, first, 28th June, 1897, Isa Mabel Bracey (who died 11th January, 1900), daughter of Captain Bracey, of Durban, by whom he had issue a son, John Trevor, born 1898; died 1898; secondly, 15th July, 1902, Isabel Frances Muriel Bell, elder daughter of Lieut.-Col. Bell, late 56th Regiment and A. P. D., and has issue:—Charles William Edmund, born 27th January, 1904.

(5) Rev. Louis George Buchanan, M.A., Vicar of St. Luke's Wimbledon, Surrey, born 5th March, 1871; married 18th December, 1907, Violet Theodora, only daughter of Major Loftus Corbett Singleton, 92nd Gordon Highlanders.

    1. Emily Buchanan, unmarried.

    2. Helen Mary Buchanan, married 7th April, 1891, Herbert Williams, and has issue:—Evelyn Mary and Emily Phyllis.

    3. Annie Gamble Buchanan, died in infancy.

5. James A. Buchanan, died abroad, unmarried.

1. Anna Maria Buchanan, born 15th July, 1823; married in 1841, Thomas Wood, of Enniskillen; died 2nd October, 1850, and had issue:—

    (1) Isabella Wood, unmarried, of Dublin.

    (2) John Wood, married Eleanor Bradford, of Dundalk, and died in 1887, leaving issue:—Maud, Arthur and Edwin.

2. Emily Buchanan, born 23rd April, 1825; married 15th June, 1852, John Eccles Hamilton, Surgeon, R.N., and died in 1895, leaving issue:—

    (1) John Robert Hamilton, M.D., born 24th August, 1857; died 4th April, 1883.

    (2) Alfred James Hamilton, Surgeon,

Tasmania, born 1st January, 1861; married 31st March, 1898, Alice Geoghegan.

(3) Alexander Hamilton, Colonel Indian Army, born 27th February, 1862; married 22nd January, 1903, Mary Agnes Cunliffê, and has issue:—Cicely and George Frederick.

(4) George Hamilton, solicitor, born 8th April, 1863; died 7th May, 1893.

(5) Claude Hamilton, Major Indian Army, born 2nd September, 1864; married 26th March, 1898, Ethel Dodgson.

(6) Emily Hariette Hamilton, married 6th October, 1897, James Gaisford, late Captain Indian Army, and has issue:— Emily, born 16th September, 1899; died 14th March, 1900; Thomas, born 11th November, 1902, died July, 1907, and George, born November, 1906.

3. Margaret Georgina Buchanan, born 17th January, 1830; married 16th September, 1851, John Nelis, of Omagh, and had issue:—

(1) James Alexander Nelis, born 22nd May, 1854; became M.B., Dublin University; in 1901 he retired as Lieut.-Colonel in I. M. S.; in 1901 married Anna Thornhill, daughter of Cudbert B. Thornhill, C. S. I., India Civil Service.

(2) Captain George Nelis, born 20th February, 1856, L.R.C.S., I. R. Army Medical Corps; died 9th June, 1895, at Bombay, unmarried.

(1) Emma Laura Nelis, married 18th March, 1873, Dr. John R. H. Sutton (he died 15th December, 1907), and had issue:—Marguerite Eveline, married 3rd September, 1907, Captain Hugh St. George Hamersley, R.A.; Matilda, and Frederick Sutton, born 4th July, 1878, Captain, R.A.

(2) Edith Harriette Nelis, unmarried.

4. Harriet Buchanan, born 22nd December, 1831; married in 1859, William Young, of Londonderry; died 31st January, 1876, and had issue:—

> (1) James Buchanan Young.
> (2) William George Young.
> (1) Amelia Harriet Young, married T. Minnice, of Londonderry, and had issue:—Louis and Violet.
> (2) Charlotte Young, married B. Robertson, I.C.S., C.I.E., and had issue, Kathleen Beatrice.
> (3) Louise Margaret Young, died 1897.
> (4) Sophie Margaret Young, B.A.
> (5) Maud Emmeline Young.

XII. George Buchanan, of Dublin, born in 1796, married Rebecca Harpur, and died in 1850, leaving a son George, who had a daughter, Anne.

XIII. Hans Buchanan, born in 1797, and died in 1799.

XIV. Eliza Buchanan, died an infant.

The Buchanans of Arnpryor.

The Buchanans of Arnpryor.

I. John Buchanan, First Laird of Arnpryor, was the second son of Walter, fourth of that name, Laird of Buchanan. He had also the lands of Gartartan and Brachern. "This John Buchanan was termed," says Auchmar,[1] "King of Kippen" upon the following account:

"King James V., a very sociable debonair prince, residing at Stirling, in Buchanan of Arnpryor's time, carriers were frequently passing along the common road, being near Arnpryor's house, with necessaries for the use of the king's family, and he having on some extraordinary occasion, ordered one of these carriers to leave his load at his house, and he would pay him for it, which the carrier refused to do, telling him he was the king's carrier, and his load for his majesty's use, to which Arnpryor seemed to have small regard, compelling the carrier in the end to leave his load, telling him if king James was king of Scotland, he was king of Kippen, so that it was reasonable he should share with his neighbour king in some of these loads, so frequently carried that road. The carrier representing this usage, and telling the story as Arnpryor spoke it, to some of the king's servants, it came at length to his majesty's ears, who shortly thereafter with a few

[1] Auchmar, p. 203.

attendants came to visit his neighbour king, who was in the meantime at dinner. King James having sent a servant to demand access, was denied the same by a tall fellow, with a battle-ax, who stood porter at the gate, telling, there could be no access till dinner was over. This answer not satisfying the king, he sent to demand access a second time; upon which he was desired by the porter to desist, otherwise he would find cause to repent his rudeness. His majesty finding this method would not do, desired the porter to tell his master, that the Good Man of Ballageich desired to speak with the king of Kippen. The porter telling Arnpryor so much, he in all humble manner came and received the king, and having entertained him with much sumptuousness and jollity, became so agreeable to king James, that he allowed him to take so much of any provision he found carrying that road, as he had occasion for; and seeing he made the first visit, desired Arnpryor in a few days to return him a second at Stirling, which he performed, and continued in very much favour with the king always thereafter, being termed king of Kippen while he lived."

He married Dorothea Levingstoun and had two sons:—(1) Andrew, his successor, and (2) Duncan. "This brave gentleman," says Auchmar, "with "divers others of his name being killed at the "battle of Pinkie in Queen Mary's minority he "was succeeded by Andrew his eldest son."[2]

---
[2] Auchmar, p. 205.

II. Andrew Buchanan, of Arnpryor, married Eupham Stirling, and had two sons,—(1) John, his successor, and (2) Walter, of Hilltoun, or Milntoun, of Bochlyvie, who married his cousin, Margaret, daughter and heiress of Duncan Buchanan of Brachern. He was killed at the "bloody conflict" of Glenfroon, which took place in 1603 between the Clan Gregor and the ancient family of Colquhon of Luss, and left two sons, John and Andrew. John Buchanan, of Brachern, Cashlie and Gartinstarrie, sold the lands of Brachern, in 1621. He married first Jonet Buchanan, by whom he had, (1) Duncan, his successor; secondly, Isobel Leckie, by whom he had, (2) Jonet, married James Buchanan, fiar of Spittal; thirdly, Helen Forgie, by whom he had, (3) Andrew Buchanan, of Ballochneck, and (4) Elizabeth, married to Duncan Buchanan, of Harperstoun. Duncan Buchanan, of Cashlie and Gartinstarrie, who sold Cashlie in 1658, married Katharine Napier, and had two sons: (1) John, and (2) Andrew, who acquired the lands of Nenbolg and Provanstoun. John Buchanan, of Gartinstarrie, had two sons: (1) James Buchanan, who succeeded his father, and (2) John Buchanan, maltman, in Glasgow.

III. John Buchanan, of Arnpryor, married Isabella Shaw, and died in 1598. He had: (1) John, his successor; (2) Andrew; (3) Mr. David Buchanan, "a gentleman of great learning: he "flourished in the latter part of the reign of king

"James VI., and beginning of the reign of king "Charles I. He wrote a large Natural History, "which was not completed at the author's death, "and therefore never printed, to the great "loss of the learned and curious. He wrote "also a large etymologicon of all the shires, "cities, rivers and mountains in Scotland, which "was printed, though not in many hands;"[1] and (4) Mr. William Buchanan.

IV. John Buchanan, of Arnpryor, who sold his estate Arnpryor in 1624 to William Buchanan, third son of Thomas Buchanan of Carbeth, and went to Ireland, where he was killed by the Irish in 1641. He married Margaret Levingstoune, and had: (1) Captain William Buchanan, "a "gentleman of very much courage, and of the "greatest art and dexterity in managing a sword "of any of his time. He killed an Italian in "Dublin, in the presence of the lord lieutenant, "and other nobility of that kingdom; the same "Italian having gone through most nations in "Europe, always having had the victory of all "he encountered with. Captain William, being "one of Buchanan's captains at Ennerkeithing, "a certain English officer, when the two armies "advanced near to one another, stept forth, and "challenged any of the Scottish army to ex- "change a few blows with him. The challenge "was accepted by captain William, who, though "a very little man of person, did in a trice kill

---
[1] Auchmar, page 310.

"that English champion. This captain William resided mostly in Ireland, in which kingdom his progeny continued;"[1] and (2) David Buchanan; (1) Dorothy Buchanan, who was twice married, firstly, to Robert Buchanan, sergeant of the King's wine cellar, and had two daughters, Jean and Mary, both married in Ireland; secondly to Captain Hublethorn, Governor of Waterford, by whom she had a son, Captain Hublethorn, and some daughters; (2) Alice, married to William Buchanan, of Drumbeg, and had issue; and (3) Anna, married to Edward Cunningham, of Finnick Drummond.

---

[1] Auchmar, page 206.

the Buchanans of Lenny.

The Buchanans of Lenny.

I. John Buchanan, First Laird of Lenny, son of Sir Walter Buchanan, who married, about 1392, Janet de Lenny and had two sons: (1) Andrew, his successor; (2) William, ancestor of the Buchanans of Auchineden.

II. Andrew Buchanan, of Lenny, 1458, married Marion, daughter of Lockhart of Barr, and had issue: (1) John, his successor; (2) Archibald; (3) Walter, ancestor of the Buchanans of Bochastel, from whom was descended John Buchanan, merchant in Glasgow;[1] (4) Walter; (5) George, ancestor of the Buchanans in Campsie and Baldernock;[2] (6) Gilbert, vicar of Lenny and Canon of Inchmahome.

III. John Buchanan, of Lenny, married Marion, daughter of the laird of Mushet, and had (1) Robert, his successor; and (2) John.

IV. Robert Buchanan, of Lenny, married a daughter of the laird of Gleneagles, and had (1) Patrick, his successor; (2) John, killed at Flodden, 1513; (3) Robert, married Marion Graham, daughter of the Earl of Menteith (about 1520) and had two sons, John, who succeeded his uncle Patrick, fifth laird; and Robert, who succeeded his brother John as seventh laird.

[1] See page 347.
[2] See page 385.

V. Patrick Buchanan, of Lenny (1505), married a daughter of Semple of Fulwood and left no male issue. He was succeeded by his nephew,

VI. John Buchanan, of Lenny, who was killed at the battle of Pinkie, 1547, leaving no issue, and was succeeded by his brother,

VII. Robert Buchanan, of Lenny, married, first, Janet Graham, daughter of Patrick Graham of Inchbrakie; secondly, Barbara, daughter of the laird of Mushet, and had issue: (1) John, who died young; (2) Robert, his successor; (3) Sir John Buchanan of Scotscraig, married Margaret Hartysyde, but left no male issue, his estate going with a daughter of his to a son of the Earl of Marr; (4) James Buchanan, of Shirrahall, Orkney, who had a son Thomas, who sold Shirrahall, and had three sons, Arthur, John and William, and a daughter, Margaret, married to John Buchanan, of Ballacondochie.

VIII. Robert Buchanan, of Lenny, married Elizabeth, daughter of Stirling of Ardoch, died in 1615, and had: (1) Robert, his successor; (2) John, married Agnes, daughter of Barclay of Towie, and had John, who became the eleventh laird, and Katherine; (3) George, murdered by the Drummonds near the Kirk of Buchanan in 1638.

IX. Robert Buchanan, of Lenny, married Katharine Campbell, daughter of the laird of Lawers, by whom he had a son Robert. His widow married, secondly, John Buchanan, first of Arnpryor, of the second line.[1]

X. Robert Buchanan, of Lenny, died without male issue and was succeeded by his cousin, John Buchanan, son of John Buchanan, second son of Robert Buchanan, eighth laird of Lenny by Elizabeth Stirling.

XI. John Buchanan, of Lenny, married, 1666, Jean, daughter of John Macfarlane of that Ilk, and had: (1) John, married, about 1690, Mary, daughter of John Lennox, of Woodhead, died s.p. before his father; (2) Henry, who succeeded his father; (3) Robert, died young, and a daughter Mary.

XII. Henry Buchanan, of Lenny, married, first, about 1696, Janet, daughter of John Buchanan of that Ilk; secondly, Katherine, daughter of Campbell of Lawers, and died in 1723. By his first wife he had: (1) John, died unmarried; (2) Colin, died unmarried 1734; (3) James died s.p.; (4) Robert, succeeded his brother, married, first, a daughter of Archibald McAulay, Provost of Edinburgh; secondly, Christian, daughter of Buchanan of Spittal, and died s.p. 1739; (5) Elizabeth, married Francis Buchanan of Arnpryor, succeeded her brother Robert, and died s.p. 1776; (6) Margaret Buchanan, of Lenny, having succeeded her sister Elizabeth, died unmarried. By his second wife, he had: (1) Henry, died s.p.; (2) John, died s. p.; (3) Lilias, died s.p.; (4)

---
[1] See the Buchanans of Arnprior (second family), page 347.

Jean, married Patrick Drummond, of Drummond; (5) Katherine, married Thomas Buchanan, afterwards of Spittal and died s.p. On the death of Margaret Buchanan of Lenny, Thomas Buchanan of Spittal succeeded to Lenny. He had married, secondly, Elizabeth, daughter of John Hamilton of Bardowie, and by her had among other children, Francis Buchanan-Hamilton, who succeeded to Spittal, Lenny and Bardowie. He was descended on his mother's side from Andrew Buchanan, second laird of Lenny. Francis Buchanan-Hamilton married Anne Brock, by whom he left, on his decease in 1829, one son John Buchanan-Hamilton, who died in 1903.[1]

---

[1] See the Buchanans of Spittal, page 289.

The Buchanans of Auchineden.

The Buchanans of Auchineden.

From William Buchanan, First Laird of Auchineven or Auchineden, second son of John Buchanan, first Laird of Lenny, living in 1463, was descended,

John Buchanan, 7th Laird of Auchineven, who succeeded his father in 1580, and had three sons: (1) Walter, his successor; (2) Dugald, who went to Ireland; (3) John, deacon of the baxters of Glasgow, who had a son who married Marion Watson, and had Katharine, married to William Anderson, Glasgow; Elizabeth, married to George Dalziell, Glasgow, and Mariota, married to Robert Buchanan of Arnpryor.

Walter Buchanan, 8th Laird of Auchineden, married a daughter of Edmonstone of Ballewan and had:—(1) John, his successor; (2) Walter, who had among other issue, Walter Buchanan, maltman of Glasgow, whose son, Andrew Buchanan, had two sons, Reverend Walter Buchanan, D.D., of Edinburgh, born 1755, died 1832; and Andrew Buchanan, merchant in Glasgow, who married Margaret, daughter of James Cockburn, W. S., Edinburgh. This Andrew Buchanan had a son, Walter Buchanan, of Shandon, born 1797, M.P. for Glasgow from 1857 to 1865, and died in 1883; married in 1824, first,

Mary, daughter of John Hamilton of Middleton, by whom he had a daughter, Ellen, first wife of Charles Wilsone Broun of Castle Wemyss, afterwards of Swinfen Hall, Staffordshire; secondly, in 1851, Christina Laura, daughter of James Smith of Jordanhill, by whom he had a daughter, Christina Laura, who married her cousin, James George Smith, youngest son of William Smith, of Carbeth-Guthrie, and has issue.

John Buchanan, 9th Laird of Auchineden, (1668) married Elizabeth Crawford, daughter of James Crawford, of Partick, and had: (1) John, and (2) Walter Buchanan, writer in Glasgow, who acquired the lands of Teucerhill in Govan parish, and married about 1710, Janet, daughter of John Leckie of Mye, by whom he had a son, John Buchanan of Teucherhill, who died s.p., and a daughter Elizabeth, who succeeded her brother and married, first, in 1736, Alexander Buchanan of Cremannan, by whom she had Walter, Alexander and Janet; secondly, in 1747, as his second wife, John Buchanan of Ardoch, and had a daughter Frances, married to John Maxwell of Dargaval.

John Buchanan, 10th Laird of Auchineden, married a daughter of Graham of Killearn, and had a son John, his successor.

John Buchanan, 11th Laird of Auchineden, married Katrine, daughter of Graham of Killearn, and had John and Margaret. " He "was a subscriber to Auchmar's book in 1723, "and was present at the meeting, on the 5th "March, 1725, when the Buchanan Society of "Glasgow was founded."[1]

John Buchanan, 12th Laird of Auchineden, was a merchant in Jamaica. He was admitted, in 1761, a member of the Buchanan Society. He died s.p., and was succeeded, in 1769, by his sister, Margaret Buchanan, who sold the estate in 1771.

---

[1] Strathendrick, page 298.

The Buchanans of Arnprior.
(SECOND FAMILY.)

The Buchanans of Arnprior.

(Second Family.)

The Estate of Arnprior was held by two families of Buchanan at different times. The last Laird of the first line was John Buchanan, who sold Arnprior, in 1624, to William Buchanan, third son of Thomas Buchanan of Carbeth.

Walter Buchanan, who acquired Arnprior, was a writer in Edinburgh. He married Agnes Rig and died in 1631. He had besides a son William, who probably died in infancy, two daughters, Margaret and Elizabeth, who sold Arnprior in 1637 to John Buchanan, eldest son of Walter Buchanan of Auchlessie and Bochastel, who thus became the first of the second family of Arnprior.

John Buchanan, of Arnprior, married first, a daughter of Halden of Enterkine, by whom he had a son, Robert, his successor; secondly, Katherine Campbell, widow of Robert Buchanan of Lenny. He was living in 1688.

Robert Buchanan, of Arnprior, advocate, was married twice; first, to Mariota, daughter of John Buchanan of Glasgow; secondly, to Margaret Muirhead, by whom he had a son, Francis, his successor; and a daughter Jean, who married John McNab of McNab, who had a son Archibald

McNab. This Archibald McNab,[1] who was an extraordinary character, was born in 1781, went to Upper Canada in 1823, and obtained from the Government the grant of a township (afterwards called Township of McNab) on the Ottawa River, for the purpose of establishing a settlement of his clansmen and others from the Highlands of Scotland. In 1831, the Chief met two young men in Montreal, George and Andrew Buchanan, whom he induced to settle in the township and build mills. As the Chief's grandfather on his mother's side was Buchanan of Arnprior, and he claimed his two new friends as kinsmen, he suggested that the new town be called Arnprior, which it was, and on the site then chosen, the flourishing town of Arnprior stands to-day. After many vicissitudes, "The McNab" left Canada, and settled in the village of Lanion, in France, where he died in 1860.

Francis Buchanan, of Arnprior, married Elizabeth, daughter and heiress of Henry Buchanan of Lenny. He was attainted and executed at Carlisle, 18th October, 1746, for his participation in the Rebellion of " '45."

---

[1] From the report of a lecture on "The McNab," delivered by Mr. James Craig, barrister of Renfrew, Ontario, before the Montreal Caledonian Society in 1897.

The Buchanans of Powis.

The Buchanans of Powis.

The family of Buchanan of Powis, near Stirling, was descended from Sir Arthur Buchanan, of Auchlessie, second son of Walter Buchanan, of Bochastel, and brother of John Buchanan, of Arnpryor.

Sir Arthur Buchanan, of Auchlessie, married Margaret Drummond, and had among others:—James Buchanan, his successor, who married Elizabeth Stewart, and had:—(1) Arthur; (2) James, died unmarried, and (3) Duncan Buchanan, his successor.

Duncan Buchanan, of Auchlessie, married Grizel Robertson, and had three sons:—(1) Alexander, his successor, who was taken prisoner at Culloden and tried, but acquitted on account of his extreme youth; died unmarried; (2) Walter, died unmarried, and (3) John, of Arnpryor.

John Buchanan, of Auchlessie and Arnpryor, succeeded his brother Alexander, and in 1758, when the forfeited estates were restored, received Strathyre, which was a part of the estate of his cousin, Buchanan of Arnpryor, and had been forfeited on his attainder in 1746, he being the heir male of the family of Arnpryor, since which time this branch has been designated of Arnpryor. He married about 1771-2, Murray Kynynmound, daughter of Patrick Edmondstone, of Newton, and died in 1817, leaving three sons:—(1) Alexander Buchanan, of Arnpryor, Captain in the 39th Regiment, his successor, who died in 1845, leaving an only son, Alexander Buchanan, who died in 1848, whose daughter, Catherine Elizabeth Grace, married, in 1869, John Baillie Baillie-Hamilton, who assumed the surname of Buchanan before Baillie-Hamilton. John Buchanan-Baillie-Hamilton of Arnpryor, Perthshire, J.P., D.L., and Commissioner of Supply for Perthshire, who was the second son of Gerard Baillie Hamilton by Augusta, daughter of the late Col. Henry Anderson Morshead of Widey Court, Devon, was born in 1837 and died in 1908, at Cambusmore, Callander, Perthshire, having had issue: Alexander Walter, born and died in 1872; John Edmondstone, born 1874; Arthur, Captain Seaforth Highlanders, born 1876, married in 1906, Ina Erskine, daughter of Sir Malcolm McNeill of Edinburgh; Morshead, Lieut. R.N., born 1878; Neil Alexander, Lieut. Black Watch, born 1880; Elizabeth; Nannie Katherine and Grizel Baillie; (2) Thomas, and (3) James Edmondstone Buchanan, Captain 3rd Foot Guards, killed in action at Talavera, in 1809.

Thomas Buchanan, H.E.I.C.S., who purchased Powis, was born in 1774; married, in 1811, Catherine, daughter of Lieut.-General Sir Ralph Abercrombie, K.B., and died in 1842, leaving issue:—(1) John, of Powis, and of Newton, co.

Perth, to which estate he succeeded in 1857; (2) Ralph Abercrombie, Lieut. R.N., died unmarried in 1855; (3) James John Abercrombie, died in 1837; and (4) Alexander, Lieut. 79th Highlanders, who married, in 1850, Lady Grierson, and d.s.p., in 1855.

John Buchanan, of Powis, born 13th October, 1812; married 17th July, 1837, Harriet, eldest daughter of Joseph Nimmo, H.E.I.C.S., Bombay, and died 18th March, 1891, having had issue:— (1) Thomas Alexander Buchanan, of Powis; (2) Ralph Edmondstone, late Capt. 59th Regiment, born 1st August, 1846; (3) James Kynynmound Edmondstone, born 25th March, 1849; (4) John, born 19th July, 1851; (5) Francis Charles, born 8th December, 1852; (1) Catherine Aimee, died young; (2) Elizabeth Grace, and (3) Annie Harriet.

Thomas Alexander Buchanan, of Powis, late Captain H.M. Indian Army, was born 26th March, 1842; married 3rd May, 1873, Mary Anne, daughter of the late W. Griffiths, and has issue:—(1) Ralph Alexander Edmondstone, born 26th July, 1875; (2) Archibald, born 16th December, 1882, and (1) Olivia Evelyn.

The Buchanans of Gartacharne.

The Buchanans of Gartacharne.

I. Alexander Buchanan, First Laird of Gartacharne (or Gartocharn), had two sons: (1) Andrew Buchanan, his successor; and (2) George Buchanan, who had three sons, John, who went abroad, Alexander, and William, who settled in Edinburgh.

"The small Estate, a portion of the five-pound "lands of Gartacharne, in the Barony of Eden-"bellie," says Strathendrick, "has been held in "property for more than two hundred years by "a family of Buchanans, whose ancestor was "Walter Buchanan, of Glenny, a cadet of Bu-"chanan of Leny, one of the oldest branches of "Buchanans of that Ilk." (*Strathendrick*, page 803.)

II. Andrew Buchanan, of Gartacharne, the eldest son of Alexander Buchanan, 1st Laird of Gartacharne, who is mentioned in a Charter from Archibald, Lord Napier, in 1673, had two sons:— (1) Alexander Buchanan, his successor; and (2) George Buchanan, of Buchanan House, ancestor of the Buchanans of Auchintorlie, Drumpellier and Craigend.

III. Alexander Buchanan, of Gartacharne, who married, in 1676, Margaret, eldest daughter of Walter Buchanan, of Meikle Balquhane, and died in 1695. He had three sons:—(1) Walter

Buchanan, who died before 1712, and was succeeded by his brother; (2) George Buchanan; and (3) Thomas Buchanan, living in 1712.

IV. George Buchanan, of Gartacharne, who married before 1725, Elizabeth Buchanan, and died before 1740. He had issue:—(1) Alexander Buchanan, his successor; (2) George Buchanan, born in 1727; (3) George Buchanan, born in 1730, who married, in 1755, Janet, daughter of George Buchanan, of Gartincaber; (4) Agnes Buchanan, born in 1723, married in 1750, Robert Buchanan, of Ballintone; (5) Mary Buchanan, born in 1733, married, in 1760, Duncan McGrigor, of Dukehouse.

V. Alexander Buchanan, of Gartacharne, succeeded to that Estate before 1740, and was living in 1779. He married, first, Elizabeth McAlister, and by her had issue:—(1) George Buchanan, born in 1740; (2) James Buchanan, born in 1742; (3) Alexander Buchanan, who succeeded to the Estate; (4) Thomas Buchanan, born in 1756; (1) Janet, born in 1748, married, in 1767, to John Miller, of Hillhead, Kilmarnock; (2) Elizabeth, born in 1750, married, in 1770, to John Livingstone of Baldearnock, co. Stirling; and (3) Mary, born in 1759.

Alexander Buchanan, of Gartacharne, married, secondly, in 1763, Janet, widow of William Buchanan, of Douchlage, Drymen, who was living in 1770, and by her had issue:—(5) Walter Buchanan, of whom hereafter, and two daughters, Mary, born in 1764, and Margaret, born in 1767.

VI. Alexander Buchanan, of Gartacharne, born in 1744, married in 1771, Elizabeth, daughter of Gilbert Ware, of Barachan, New Kilpatrick, and died in 1810, being succeeded by his son,

VII. Thomas Buchanan, of Gartacharne, who married Agnes Buchanan, of Ballindore, and had a son,

VIII. Alexander Buchanan, of Gartacharne, born in 1817, married Mary, daughter of Hugh McCallum, of Douchlage, and died in 1893, having had issue:—Alexander Buchanan, now of Gartacharne; John Buchanan, Thomas Buchanan, and three daughters.

Walter Buchanan, of Southend, co. Argyle, fifth son of Alexander Buchanan, 5th Laird of Gartacharne, was born in 1770, married in 1798, Elizabeth Speir, of Bridge of Weir, co. Renfrew (who died in 1827), and died on the 27th February, 1855, having had among other issue:—

(I.) Patrick (or Peter) Buchanan, of Dundee, in the Province of Quebec, Canada; born 1st May, 1803; went to Canada, in 1818, and settled at Dundee. He married, on the 11th August, 1825, Lucy Baker (who died in 1856), and died on the 9th March, 1873, at Dundee, having had issue:—

1. Elizabeth Spiers Buchanan, born 1828, married about 1853, Thomas Caverhill, of Montreal, and died 1904, having had issue:—(1) Frank Caverhill, of Montreal, married Charlotte Rosalind Harrison,

and died in 1899, leaving issue:—Rosalind Florence, married to Geoffrey L. Mander, of Wolverhampton, England; Jessie Beatrice Harrison and Frances Buchanan; (2) Jane Caverhill, died unmarried; (3) Walter Caverhill, died in youth; (4) George Caverhill, of Montreal, born in 1858, married Emily Margaret Caverhill, and has issue, Marjorie and George Rutherfurd; (5) John Buchanan Caverhill, of Montreal, married Jenny B. Irving, and has issue, Thomas and Jessy Irving; (6) Jessy Caverhill, married J. Alexander Hutchison, M.D., of Montreal, and died in 1899, leaving issue.

2. Margaret Buchanan, born 1830, died 1847.

3. Walter Buchanan, born 1832.

4. James John Buchanan, born 1835, and died 1888. He married twice, and had issue:—(1) Spiers, born 1862; (2) John, born 1867; (3) James George, born 1871, died 1872; (1) Etta; (2) Anna, married Alexander G. Cross, K.C., of Montreal, now puisne judge of the Court of King's Bench for the Province of Quebec, and died 1899; (3) Elizabeth; (4) Elsie; (5) Margaret, died 1889; (6) Jessie; (7) Ethel Cote, died 1895; (8) Jane Sema.

5. Janet Buchanan, born 1836, and died unmarried, 1908.

6. Lucy Anna Buchanan, born 1838, and died 1856.

7. Patrick (Peter) Buchanan, of Dundee, born in 1839, and died in 1909, at Dundee, without issue.

(II.) Walter Buchanan, of Lower Bebington, co. Chester; born 22nd October, 1811; married 22nd August, 1854, Mary, eldest daughter of John Lewthwaite, of Broadgate, Milton, co. Cumberland, and by her (who died in 1890) had issue:—

1. MacIver Buchanan, of Bedford Gardens, Kensington, London, born 14th April, 1863, unmarried.
2. Marian, unmarried.
3. Edith Elizabeth, unmarried.
4. Eleanor Tory, unmarried.

Carrick-Buchanans of Drumpellier.

Carrick-Buchanans of Drumpellier.[1]

The family of Carrick-Buchanan, of Drumpellier, is a branch, descended from Alexander Buchanan, 5th in descent from John of Lenny, 3rd son of John Buchanan, Laird of Buchanan. This Alexander Buchanan had two sons, John, his successor, and Walter Buchanan, first Laird of Glenny, whose grandson, Captain James Buchanan, succeeded to the Estate, but dying in France without issue, he was succeeded by his uncle, Alexander Buchanan, of Gartacharne, the second son of Walter Buchanan, of Glenny.

Alexander Buchanan, of Gartacharne,[2] had two sons, Andrew Buchanan, of Gartacharne, and George Buchanan.

Andrew Buchanan, of Gartacharne, had two sons, Alexander Buchanan of Gartacharne, and George Buchanan.

George Buchanan, of Buchanan House, Glasgow, J.P., the second son of Andrew Buchanan, of Gartacharne, was a Magistrate and Merchant in that City, Treasurer of Glasgow, 1690, and bore arms at Bothwell Bridge, for which he was outlawed. He married, in 1685, Mary, daughter

---

[1] Burke's Landed Gentry.
[2] See Buchanans of Gartacharne, page 357.

of Gabriel Maxwell, and by her had four sons and one daughter.

George Buchanan, born 1686, who became Treasurer of Glasgow in 1726, and Baillie in 1732, and with his brothers Andrew, Neil and Archibald, were the original promoters of the Buchanan Society in that city. He was three times married. His third wife was the daughter of Sir John Forbes, Bart., of Foveran, and had four sons and two daughters. He died in 1773, and was succeeded by his eldest son,

Andrew Buchanan, of Buchanan House, Glasgow, born 1725; married, first, 1755, Agnes, daughter of Arthur Robertson, by whom (who died 1769) he had, among others, issue:—

(1) George, born 1758; married, 1795, at Content, St. Georges, Jamaica, Jane Gorvie, and died 1826, having by her (who died 1815) had issue, among others:—

George, born 1801; married Anne, daughter of H. Lorimore, R.M., and had a son, Arthur, born 1835, married 1859, Anne Elizabeth, daughter of Rev. Dr. Martin, and died 1870, leaving Claud Alexander Francis John Buchanan, born 1860; Andrew James, died 1834; George Alexander, d.s.p., 1840; and Mary Robertson.

Andrew, born 1807, died 1878, in Jamaica, leaving a daughter, Edith, who married, in 1857, Alexander Clerk, son of Sir G. Clerk, Bart.

Robertson, born 1810, d.s.p.

Elizabeth Sheriffe, married Robert Russell.

Catherine, died 1813.

Agnes Jane, married Rev. T. Hugo.

(2) Andrew, born 1765.

(3) William, born 1766, died s.p.

(4) Robertson, born 1769, died 1816.

Andrew Buchanan married, secondly, Janet, daughter of Hugh Niven, and by her (who died 1772) had issue, Hugh, born 1771.

Andrew Buchanan married, thirdly, Frances, daughter of Alexander Innes, Surgeon of the Island of St. Christopher, and died 1783, having by her had issue:—John Oswald, born 1780, Frances, Janet, Mary and Ann.

II. Andrew Buchanan, of Drumpellier.

III. Neil Buchanan, of Hillington, co. Renfrew, M.P. for the Glasgow District of burghs, whose male line is now extinct.

IV. Archibald Buchanan, of Auchintorlie,[1] co. Dumbarton.

I. Mary, married George Buchanan, of Moss and Auchintoshan, co. Dumbarton.

Andrew Buchanan, of Drumpellier,[2] co. Lanark, second son of George Buchanan, born 1690; Dean

---

[1] See Buchanans of Auchintorlie, page 375.

[2] His name appears in McUre's list of the "First Merchant Adventurers at Sea" (*View of the City of Glasgow, p. 209*), and by his trade with Virginia, where he had a tobacco plantation, he became one of the wealthiest citizens of his day. In 1735 he purchased the estate of Drumpellier, Lanarkshire, and the older portion of Drum-

of Guild, 1728-9; married, first, 1723, Marion Montgomerie, of Boutrehill, and, secondly, Elizabeth Binning. He died 1759, having, by his first wife, had issue (with five daughters) two sons:—

> 1. James Buchanan, married Margaret, daughter of the Hon. John Hamilton, son of Thomas, Earl of Haddington, and by her had a son, who died unmarried, and several daughters, of whom Helen married Admiral Sir George Hume, Bart.
>
> 2. George Buchanan, of Mount Vernon, co. Lanark (which he purchased in 1758), born 1728; married 1750, Lillias, daughter of James Dunlop, of Gaukirk, and died 1762, having had issue. He was succeeded by his eldest son, Andrew Buchanan, of Mount

---

pellier house was built by him in 1736. Adjoining Glasgow he purchased three small properties in what was then known as the "Long Croft," the first purchase being made in 1719, the second in 1732, and the third in 1740 (*Glasgow, Past and Present, 11. 196.*) Through his grounds he opened an avenue for gentlemen's houses, which he named Virginia Street, and he planned a town house for himself called Virginia Mansion, which he did not live to complete. Along with his three brothers he founded in 1725 the Buchanan Society for the assistance of apprentices and support of widows of the name of Buchanan. He was also one of the original partners of the Ship Bank, founded in 1750. He was elected dean of guild in 1728, and lord provost in 1740. When after the battle of Prestonpans, John Hay, quartermaster of the Pretender, arrived at Glasgow with a letter demanding the loan of £15,000, Buchanan and five others were chosen commissioners to treat with him and succeeded in obtaining a reduction to £5,500. (*Memorabilia of Glasgow, p. 361.*) On account of his zeal in raising new levies on behalf of the government, Buchanan made himself so obnoxious to the rebels that in December, 1745, a special levy of £500 was made on him under threats of plundering his house, to which he replied "they might plunder his house if they pleased, but he would not pay one farthing." (*Scots Mag., VIII, 30.*) DICTIONARY OF NATIONAL BIOGRAPHY.

Vernon, born 1755, and d.s.p. 1795, when he was succeeded by his brother:

David Buchanan, of Drumpellier and Mount Vernon, who took the additional surname of Carrick on being left property by Robert Carrick, banker of Glasgow, and purchased back Drumpellier from his cousin, Robert Sterling. He was born in 1760; married 1788, Marion, daughter of James Gilliam, of Mount Alta, Virginia, and died 1827, leaving issue by her (who died in 1800):—

1. Robert Carrick-Buchanan.
2. Andrew Buchanan, of Greenfield, co. Lanark, J.P. and D.L., born 1799; married 1826, Bethia Hamilton, daughter of William Ramsay, of Gogar, and died 1879, having had:—

(1) David William Ramsay Carrick-Buchanan, of Drumpellier and Mount Vernon.

(2) Hamilton Ramsay Carrick-Buchanan, born 1840; married 1869, Isabella Brown, daughter of Robert Bell, of Stowe, Queensland (who died 1904), and died 1901, having had issue:—Andrew Robert Hamilton, born 1869; David George, born 1872; Francis Henry Theodore, born 1873; James Gilliam, born 1880; Wallis Vernon, born 1881; and Bethia Isabel.

(1) Bethia Hamilton, married 1853, Sir John Don Wauchope, of Edmondstone,

Bart., and died on 20th February, 1911, at Edinburgh, having had issue.

(2) Elizabeth Mary, married 1850, Andrew Blackburn, of Killearn, who died 1885, leaving issue.

(3) Sarah Mary Clothilde, married 1870, Thomas Dunlop Findlay, of Easterhill.

(4) Frances Susan Cecile, died 1895, unmarried.

1. Elizabeth Belsches, married 1817, Robert Graham, M.D.

2. Marion, married 1818, John Hay, R.N., of Morton.

Robert Carrick-Buchanan, of Drumpellier, born 1797; married 1824, Sarah Maria Clothilde, eldest daughter of Sir Joseph Wallis Hoare, Bart., of Annabelle, co. Cork, by Lady Harriett O'Bryen, and died 1844, having had issue:—(1) David Carrick Robert, late of Drumpellier; (2) Wallis O'Bryen Hastings, 92nd Highlanders, born 1826, married in 1853, Anna Henrietta, daughter of Albany Savile, of Oakhampton Park, North Devon, and d.s.p., 1855, at Alexandria; (3) George, born 1827, Captain Scots Greys, died 1863, unmarried.

Sir David Carrick Robert Carrick-Buchanan, K.C.B., J.P. and D.L., Lieut.-Col. 3rd and 4th Battalions Scottish Rifles, late Royal Regiment of Lanark Militia, born 1825; married 1849, Frances Jane, daughter of Anthony Lefroy, M.P., of Carrickglass, co. Longford (who died 2nd June,

1911); died s.p., 1904, and was succeeded by his cousin,

David William Ramsay Carrick-Buchanan, of Drumpellier and Corsewall, D. L. of Wigton, formerly Captain 2nd Royal Lanark Regiment, born 1834; married, 1863, Lady Kathleen Alicia, daughter of the Earl of Donoughmore, and by her (who died 1892) had issue:—(1) Arthur Louis Hamilton, of Mount Vernon, Glasgow, Lieut.-Col. 3rd Battalion Gordon Highlanders, born 1866, married 1903, Adeline Musgrave, daughter of Richard Musgrave Harvey, and has issue; (2) Nigel Francis William (Rev.), M.A., born 1870, died 1904; (1) Kathleen Mary; and (2) Bethia Charlotte.

The Buchanans of Auchintorlie.

The Buchanans of Auchintorlie.[1]

Archibald Buchanan, of Auchintorlie,[2] co. Dumbarton, and of Hillington, co. Renfrew, purchased Auchintorlie from his brother Andrew, and succeeded to Hillington on the death of his brother Neil. He married Martha, daughter of Peter Murdoch, of Rosehill, Renfrew, Provost of Glasgow, and by her had issue:—

1. Peter Buchanan, of Auchintorlie, married Catherine Maxwell, and died without issue.

2. George Buchanan, who succeeded to Auchintorlie, and d.s.p.

---

[1] Burke's Landed Gentry.

[2] "Auchintorlie, or, as it was formerly called, Silverbanks, was in early times part of the barony of Erskine; but having been acquired by the Luss family, it was feued out in 1685 by Sir Humphrey Colquhon to John Colquhon, whose daughter Elizabeth, wife of Captain James Colquhon, sold it, in 1709, to Mungo Buchanan, W.S. From him it passed by purchase, in 1737, to Andrew Buchanan, of Drumpellier, who acquired at the same time Connalton, Chapelton, and Dunerbuck. These lands, with the exception of the last mentioned, Andrew Buchanan subsequently sold to his brother Archibald, whose grandson Archibald acquired Dunerbuck. This Archibald, by his wife Mary, second daughter of Richard Dennistoun, of Kelvingrove, had, besides other issue, Andrew, now of Auchintorlie, who has erected a fine new mansion on the property. Within the grounds of Auchintorlie are the remains of a building known as Tresmass Castle, occupying most probably the site of some encampment intended to overlook the line of defences established by the Romans between Kilpatrick, the reputed termination of the wall, and the fortress of Dumbarton."—Irving's History of Dumbartonshire, p. 479.

3. Andrew Buchanan, First of Ardinconnal.[1]

1. Mary, married Alexander Speirs, of Elderslie, co. Renfrew.

Andrew Buchanan, of Ardinconnal, co. Dumbarton, and Auchingray, co. Lanark, J.P. and D.L., born 1745; married 1769, Jane, daughter of James Dennistoun, of Colgrain and Dennistoun, and died, 1833, having had issue:—

1. Archibald Buchanan, of Auchintorlie and Hillington, J.P. and D.L., born 1773; married 1816, Mary, daughter of Richard Dennistoun, of Kelvin Grove, co. Lanark (who died 1868), and died 1832, having had, among other issue:—

Andrew Buchanan, of Auchintorlie, J.P. and D.L., born 1817; married 1845, Mary Jemima Dundas Adamina, daughter of Sir James Fergusson, Bart., of Kilkerran, and d.s.p., 1886.

Richard Dennistoun Buchanan, Captain 72nd Highlanders, born 1830, died unmarried.

Christian Alston, married Robert Meiklam, and d.s.p., 1849.

---

[1] "Laggarie and Ardinconnal were, in 1464, in the possession of Patrick McGregor, whose descendants, known as Stewarts, sold them in 1617 to the McAulays of Ardincaple. At the breaking up of their estates, about the middle of last century, they fell into the hands of different proprietors, but were soon after re-united by Andrew Buchanan, who built a mansion house at Ardinconnal."—Irving's History of Dumbartonshire, p. 416.

Jane Dennistoun.

Mary Dennistoun, died unmarried, 1870.

Isabella Dennistoun.

Georgina Grace, married, 1857, General George Hermand Fergusson, son of Sir James Fergusson, Bart., and died 1862. Their only son, George James Ferguson-Buchanan of Auchintorlie, J.P. and D.L., assumed, in 1890, the additional name of Buchanan on succeeding to Auchintorlie. He was born in 1862: was A.D.C. to the Governor of Bombay, 1882-1885: served in the 2nd Battalion Scottish Fusiliers in the South African War: was Major Reserve of Officers, and Lieut.-Col. 3rd Scots Fusiliers. He married in 1886, Grace, daughter of Claude B. Hamilton, J.P., of Barnes, co. Dumbarton, and has issue, two daughters, Noel Grace and Avril Nora.

2. James Buchanan, of Blairvadock, who acquired Ardinconnal from his father in 1811, and from whom it was purchased, in 1827, by Sir James Colquhon, of Luss.

1. Jessie, married, 1800, James Menteith, of Craighead, and died 1801.

2. Martha, married, 1801, George Murdock Yuille, of Cardross Park, co. Dumbarton.

James Buchanan, of Blairvadock, Ardinconnal, J.P. and D.L., co. Caithness, born 1776; married 1805, Lady Janet Sinclair, daughter of the Earl of Caithness, and died 1860, having had issue:—

1. Andrew Buchanan (Sir), 1st Baronet.
1. Helen John Sinclair, married 1828, William Woolton Abney, D.L., of Measham Hall, co. Derby, and d.s.p., 1893.
2. Jane Dennistoun, married, 1826, William Tritton, of Wington, Somerset, and died 1851, leaving issue.
3. Cammilla Campbell, married, 1829, Richard Fox, of Awbawn, co. Cavan.
4. Charlotte MacGregor Murray, married 1834, Charles Henry Forbes, Kingairlock, co. Argyle.
5. Mathilda Frances Harriett, married 1844, Patrick Maitland, of Freugh, and died 1894, leaving issue.

The Rt. Hon. Sir Andrew Buchanan, 1st Bart., of Dunburgh, co. Stirling, G.C.B., P.C., D.L., co. Stirling, born 1807; married, first, 1839, Frances Katherine, daughter of the Very Rev. Edward Mellish, Dean of Hereford, and by her (who died 1854) had issue:—

1. James (Sir), 2nd Baronet.
2. Edward, born 1844, died 1870, unmarried.
3. Eric Alexander (Sir), 3rd Baronet.
4. Andrew Archibald, born 1850; married 1882, Ellen Maria, daughter of Phillip Edward Blakeway, and has issue:—Andrew

Sinclair, born 1882, and Alexander Wellesley Grant, born 1890, died young.

5. George William Buchanan (Sir), G.C.V.O., K.C.M.G., C.B., P.C., His Majesty's Ambassador at St. Petersburg. " Sir George William Buchanan, who has been Minister-Plenipotentiary at The Hague since May, is the son of Sir Andrew Buchanan, and was born in 1854. He entered the Diplomatic Service in 1875. After serving in Vienna, Rome and Tokyo he was sent to Berne, where he acted as Chargé d'Affaires on various occasions. In 1893 he was promoted to be a Secretary of Legation with the additional character of Chargé d'Affaires at Darmstadt and Carlsruhe. In 1898 he was appointed British Agent to attend the Tribunal of Arbitration in the Venezuelan Boundary dispute, and in the following year became Secretary of Embassy. After a period at Rome and Berlin he was appointed Agent and Consul-General in Bulgaria, with the rank of Minister-Plenipotentiary. While at Sofia, Sir George Buchanan displayed conspicuous tact and firmness in dealing with the delicate situation created by the declaration of Bulgarian independence, and his departure for The Hague caused universal regret among the Bulgarians, who deeply appreciated his services. Sir George Buchanan married, in 1885, Lady Georgiana Bathurst, daughter

of the late Lord Bathurst,"[1] and has issue, Meriel.

1. Florence Jane, married, 1865, Captain Maxwell Fox, R.N. (retired), of Annaghmore, King's co., and died 1882.
2. Frances Matilda, married, 1873, John Willis Clark, of Scrope House, Cambridge, and has issue.
3. Louisa, married 1871, Sir George Francis Bonham, Bart., and has issue.
4. Janet Sinclair.

Sir Andrew Buchanan married, secondly, 1857, Hon. Georgiana Elizabeth Stuart, daughter of Lord Blantyre (who died in 1904). Sir Andrew was Minister in Switzerland, 1852; Envoy at Copenhagen, 1853; Madrid, 1858; and at The Hague, 1860; Ambassador to Prussia, 1862; to Russia, 1864; and to Austria, 1871; and he retired in 1877. He was made K.C.B. in 1860, and G.C.B. in 1866; Privy Councillor in 1863; and created a Baronet in 1878. He died in 1882, and was succeeded by his eldest son,

Sir James Buchanan, 2nd Baronet, Commander, R.N. (retired), J.P. and D.L., born 1840; married 1873, Arabella Catherine, daughter of Captain G. C. Colquitt-Craven, of Brockhampton Park, co. Gloucester, and d.s.p., 1901, when he was succeeded by his brother,

---
[1] The Times, 5th August, 1910.

Sir Eric Alexander Buchanan, 3rd Baronet, of Dunburgh, and Craigend Castle, Milngavie, Stirlingshire, born 1848; married 1898, Constance Augusta, daughter of Commander Charles Edmund Tennant, R.N., of Needwood House, Burton-on-Trent, and has issue:—Charles James, born 1899, and Mary Constance Victoria.

The Buchanans in Campsie and Baldernock.

The Buchanans in Campsie and Baldernock.[1]

John Buchanan, a merchant in America, where he had considerable possessions, most of which he lost in consequence of taking the loyalist side on the breaking out of the War of Independence, was the son of John Buchanan, a merchant in London in 1759, and grandson of Gilbert Buchanan of Bankell, Dean of Guild of Glasgow, 1721, who was descended from George Buchanan, fifth son of Andrew Buchanan of Lenny. Gilbert Buchanan was born in 1653, and married Dorothea, daughter of William Napier. He died in 1730, having had issue: (1) William of Bankell, died unmarried, 1733; (2) Gilbert, Writer in Edinburgh, afterwards merchant in London, who succeeded his brother William in Bankell; (3) John; (1) Jane, married, in 1720, Archibald Buchanan of Drumhead, and died in 1735; and (2) Mary, married, in 1731, James Rowan of Heathriehall.

John Buchanan, the son of John Buchanan, and grandson of Gilbert Buchanan, married Elizabeth Wilson, and had (1) Elizabeth Buchanan who married James Dunlop, of Househill, and died in 1820; (2) Rev. Gilbert Buchanan, D.D.,

[1] Strathendrick, page 307.

of whom afterwards; (3) Frances Buchanan, born 1758, died 1828, married Edward John Burrow of the Life Guards and was the mother of Edward John Burrow, Archdeacon of Gibraltar, whose daughter, Frances Maria, was the second wife of the late Robert Buchanan-Dunlop of Drumhead; and (4) Sarah Buchanan, married a Mr. Sparrow.

The Rev. Gilbert Buchanan, D.D., Rector of Woodmanstow, Surrey, and Vicar of Northfleet, Kent, was born in 1750, and died in 1835. He was not intended at first for orders, but his father having lost all his American possessions, the young man was sent to Cambridge and Mr. Pitt gave him the two livings, which he held till his death. He married Frances Reed and by her (who died in 1800) had three sons and two daughters: (1) Gilbert, of whom afterwards; (2) George, R.N., died unmarried: (3) John, went to America, married and had issue; (1) Frances, born 1786, died 1827, was second wife of Henry S. Hyde Wollaston, and had a son, George Buchanan Wollaston, who married his cousin, Julia Adye Buchanan; and (2) Mary, married 1818, the Right Hon. Sir John Taylor Coleridge, and had issue (with others) John Duke, Lord Coleridge, late Lord Chief Justice of England.

General Gilbert Buchanan, of the Royal Engineers, was born 1785, and married Harriet Wilkes Smith, by whom he had two sons and several daughters:—

(1) General Gilbert John Lane Buchanan, of the Royal Artillery, born 1812, married Julia Hammersley Wallace (who died at Hampton Court Palace on the 21st December, 1900) and died 1875, leaving issue; (2) John Buchanan, an officer in the Army. A daughter Julia Adye Buchanan, married her cousin, George Buchanan Wollaston, of Bishop's Well, Kent, and died on the 25th June, 1910, aged 94, at Chislehurst, leaving issue.

The Buchanans of Drummikill.

The Buchanans of Drummikill.

I. Thomas Buchanan, first of Drummikill, was the third son of Sir Walter Buchanan of that Ilk (1461), and had three sons: (1) Robert; (2) Thomas, of Carbeth; and (3) William.

II. Robert Buchanan, (in 1495) of Drummikill and Moss, who married, about 1472, Margaret Hay and died about 1518, had two sons: (1) Thomas; and (2) John, ancestor of the Buchanans of Cameron.

III. Thomas Buchanan, of Drummikill and Moss, married Agnes Heriot, daughter of James Heriot, of Trabrown and had five sons: (1) Robert; (2) Thomas, who succeeded to Drummikill; (3) Alexander Buchanan of Ibert, died 1574, who had two sons, Mr. Thomas Buchanan, who became Keeper of the Privy Seal, married Janet, daughter of George Buchanan, son of George Buchanan of that Ilk; and John[1] ancestor to the Buchanans of Ballochruin; (4) Patrick; and (5) Mr. George Buchanan, the author, poet and historian, born 1506.[2]

IV. Robert Buchanan, of Drummikill, born about 1495, married 1520, Catherine Napier and

---

[1] James Buchanan, sixth of Ballochruin, merchant in Glasgow, died in 1758, and was succeeeded by his sister, Margaret Buchanan, who married in 1759, Thomas Buchanan of Ardoch. Strathendrick, page 326.

[2] See pages 419 and 423.

had an only son who died young and was succeeded by his uncle.

V. Thomas Buchanan, of Drummikill, married Geils (or Giles) Cunningham, and had: (1) Robert; (2) Walter; (3) John, from whom was descended George Buchanan, of Moss and Auchintoshan, born 1697, married in 1731, Mary, daughter of George Buchanan, of Glasgow, ancestor of the family of Auchintorlie, Craigend and Drumpellier, and had issue, among others, Neil Buchanan of Auchintoshan, who married Anne Bolleyn, daughter of Thomas Murray, of Virginia, and died in 1777, leaving a daughter, Anne Buchanan, of Auchintoshan, born 1774, married 1793, William Cross, of Glasgow, and died in 1810, having had issue, with others:—John Cross-Buchanan, of Auchintoshan, who succeeded to the Estate in 1813, married, in 1824, Jean, daughter of Andrew Wardrop, and died in 1839, leaving issue. (4) William; (5) Mr. Thomas, regent in St. Salvator's College, St. Andrews.

VI. Robert Buchanan, of Drummikill, who died s. p. and was succeeded by his brother.

VII. Walter Buchanan, of Drummikill and Moss, married, first, Janet, daughter of Walter Buchanan, of Spittal, by whom he had: (1) Thomas, his successor; secondly Agnes, daughter of John Kinross, of Kippendavie, by whom he had: (2) William, ancestor of the Buchanans of Ross and Drummikill; (3) James; and (4) Mr. Robert.

THE BUCHANANS OF DRUMMIKILL

VIII. Thomas Buchanan, of Drummikill and Moss, married, first, Logan of Balvie's daughter; secondly, Stirling of Glorat's daughter; and had: (1) William, his successor; (2) John; (3) Walter, who married Margaret Buchanan; (1) Janet, who married John Buchanan; and (2) Agnes, married Thomas Buchanan, younger of Ibert and Ballochruin.

IX. William Buchanan, married a daughter of Temple of Fulwood, and had: (1) Walter, his successor; (2) Thomas, and (3) George, who both went to Ireland; (4) James; (1) Agnes, married John Kincaid, of Auchinreoch; and (2) Margaret, married Walter Buchanan, of Cameron.

X. Walter Buchanan, who sold Moss in 1625 to John Buchanan. He married Jean Hamilton, and died about 1663 having had (1) William, and (2) Dugald, of Gartincaber.

XI. William Buchanan, 11th of Drummikill and 1st of Craigievairn, sold Drummikill to William Buchanan, second son of William Buchanan, first of Ross, in 1669, and bought Craigievairn. He married the daughter of Cunningham of Boquhan and had among others:—John, Commissioner of Supply, 1695, married Dorothy Cunningham, and had a son William, who succeeded, and a daughter married to James Hamilton. William Buchanan, third of Craigievairn, in 1711, married Elizabeth Hamilton, daughter of John Hamilton of Bardowie. William Buchanan, of Bardowie, had among others, John, who succeeded him.

John Buchanan, fourth of Craigievairn, held a commission in 1737 in the Royal Regiment of North British Dragoons. In 1741, he sold Craigievairn to John Buchanan, of Gartincaber, writer in Edinburgh, who died in 1753 and was succeeded by his son Dugald. Dugald Buchanan married Margaret Buchanan and died in 1774. His widow died in 1807 and left her estates to David Snodgrass, advocate.[1]

---

[1] Strathendrick, page 319.

The Buchanans of Drumhead.

The Buchanans of Drumhead.

I. From William Buchanan, who was either a brother or son of Robert Buchanan, second of Drummikill, was descended Archibald Buchanan,[1] of Drumhead, or Blairhennechan, as it was formerly called, born 1723, died unmarried 1789, who entailed the property upon the second sons of his two eldest sisters, Dorothy and Janet, successively, and their heirs male, on the condition that they should bear the name and arms of Buchanan of Drumhead. His elder sister, Dorothy Buchanan (1724-1789), married Robert Shannon, of Blairvadick, and had, among others, Archibald

---

[1] Archibald Buchanan, of Drumhead, was the eldest son of Archibald Buchanan, of Drumhead, who married in 1720 Janet, daughter of Gilbert Buchanan, of Bankell. This Archibald Buchanan, who was the eldest son of Archibald Buchanan, of Drumhead, had issue three sons and six daughters: Gilbert, born 1729, died young; James, born 1733, married in Virginia, but died s.p.; John, born 1735, curate of Weston, Underwood, Bucks., died s.p.; Dorothy, born 1724, mother of Archibald Shannon Buchanan, of Drumhead; and Janet, born 1726, mother of Robert Buchanan-Dunlop, of Drumhead; Jean, born 1727, married Mungo Buchanan, merchant in Glasgow, and had a son, John Buchanan, a clergyman of the Church of England. James Buchanan, his father's brother, became an eminent merchant in London, and left an only daughter, who married Sir Walter Riddell of Riddell, Roxburghshire. Her son, Sir John, on succeeding to the estate of Sundon, in Bedfordshire, added the name of Buchanan to his own, as required by his grandfather's deed of entail. This branch of the family of Drumhead is represented by the present Sir Walter Buchanan-Riddell, Bart., Recorder of Maidstone. (Irving's History of Dumbartonshire, note to page 428.) Major-General Charles James Buchanan-Riddell, C.B., late of the Royal Artillery, a member of this family, died in 1903, in his 86th year. Sir John Walter Buchanan-Riddell, who was born in 1849, succeeded his uncle in 1892. He married in 1874, Sarah Isabella, daughter of Robert Wharton, and has, with other issue, a son Walter Robert, born in 1879.

Shannon Buchanan, who succeeded his uncle in 1789 and assumed the name of Buchanan, and died s.p. in 1791, when he was succeeded by his cousin.

II. Robert Dunlop Buchanan, son of Robert Dunlop, of Househill, and of his wife, Janet Buchanan (1726-1812), second sister of Archibald Buchanan, of Drumhead, was born in 1756 and assumed the name and arms of Buchanan. He married in 1805, Frances, daughter of Samuel Beachcroft, of Wickham Court, Kent, a director of the Bank of England, and died, in 1837, leaving issue:—

    1. Robert.

    2. James, born 1809, died unmarried in 1859.

    3. Charles (Rev.), Vicar of Henfield, Sussex, born 1812, married Fanny, daughter of William Borrer, of Henfield, and died in 1851, leaving issue:—

        (1) Charles Seward (Rev.), Vicar of Henfield, born 1840, married Alice Barbara, daughter of Rev. D. Robertson, and died in 1907.

        (2) Henry Beachcroft (Rev.), of Redoaks, Henfield, Sussex, born 1842, married Mary, daughter of Rev. A. A. Aylward, and has issue, John Henry Graham and Lillian Mary, married to Leopold Stern, and has issue, Graham.

(3) William Buchanan (Rev.), Vicar of Sayer's Common, Sussex, born 1851, married Gertrude, daughter of E. Carlton Homes.

(1) Fanny Elizabeth, married Rev. Prebendary Teulon, Canon of Chichester.

III. Robert Buchanan Dunlop, of Drumhead, born 1807, who died 10th August, 1882. He married, first, in 1837, Emma Smith and had by her (who died in 1851):

1. Robert Buchanan Dunlop, of Drumhead.

2. James, born 1840, late of the Rifle Brigade, married Mary Scott.

3. Charles George, born 1843, married 1889, Blanche Emily, daughter of Francis Trench, and died 1897, leaving issue Phyllis Evelyn, died 1897; Doris and Lois Olga.

4. Henry Donald, Lieutenant-Colonel R.A., born 1845; married in 1869, first, Charlotte Fanny, daughter of Brigadier-General Gilbert Buchanan, R. A. (who died in 1869, without surviving issue); secondly, in 1873, Sabina, daughter of William Woolston, and has issue:

(1) Archibald Henry, Captain Leicestershire Regiment, born 1874, married 1900, Mary Agnes, daughter of Arthur Herbert Kennedy of Upton Park, Slough, and has issue, Robert Arthur, born 1904; and Ian; (2) Colin Napier, Captain and Brevet Major, R.A., born 1877; (3) William Robert (Rev.), Curate

of Christ Church, Eastbourne, born 1881; (4) Henry Donald, Lieut. West Kent Regiment. (1) Sabina, married 1905, Alfred Castle Warner, M.R.C.S., L.R.C.P.; (2) Emma Dorothea, married Rev. F. Eddison, Vicar of Duffield, Derby; (3) Jean Hamilton, married 1905, Rev. Reginald Callander, M.A., Rector of St. Leonard's, Exeter; (4) Rhoda.

5. Francis Campbell, born 1847, died 1885.

1. Elizabeth, died young.
2. Caroline Annabella, died unmarried in 1898.
3. Frances Harriet, died young.
4. Emma, married in 1883, Percy Pollexfen Vere Turner, barrister-at-law, and has issue, Francis, Ruth, Janet, and Vera.

Robert Buchanan Dunlop married, secondly, Frances Maria, daughter of Edward John Burrow, Archdeacon of Gibraltar, who d. s. p. 1882.

IV. Robert Buchanan Dunlop, who succeeded his father in 1882, was born in 1838 and married Harriet Klyne, daughter of Emanuel Baker, M.D., and died in 1892, leaving issue a son,

V. Robert Buchanan Dunlop (Rev.), of Drumhead, Curate of Bexhill-on-Sea, born in 1877, and succeeded his father in 1892.

The Buchanans of Finnick-Drummond.

The Buchanans of Finnick-Drummond.

George Buchanan, in Finnick-Drummond, was the sixth son of John Buchanan, of Little Croy, second son of John Buchanan, of Middle Balfunning, of the family of Drummikill. He was born in 1713, married Margaret, daughter of George Buchanan, of Blairlusk, and died in 1778. He had issue, among others:—John Buchanan; George Buchanan in Finnick-Drummond; Archibald Buchanan, died, in 1772, in Virginia; and James Buchanan, of Dowanhill.

I. John Buchanan, born 1742, married Agnes Steven, and had a son, George Buchanan, of Glasgow; admitted Member of the Buchanan Society, 1807; married Isabella Stevenson, and had issue, among other sons:—William, married Janet Marshall, and was father of George Stevenson Buchanan, Treasurer of the Buchanan Society; and Moses Steven Buchanan, M.D., who married Agnes Leechman, and had three sons—(1) James Buchanan; (2) George Buchanan, M.A., M.D., LL.D., Professor of Clinical Surgery in the University of Glasgow, born 1827, died 19th April, 1905, at Balanton, Stirling. " In the Crimean War " he served as a civil surgeon in the British Army, " and he afterwards published a book entitled

"'Camp Life in the Crimea.' Much of his career
"was associated with the medical and educational
"institutions of Glasgow. He had filled the
"posts of surgeon to the Royal Infirmary and
"the Western Infirmary in that city, and he
"was Professor of Clinical Surgery at Glasgow
"University, a position which he relinquished in
"1900. In 1888 he presided over the surgical
"section of the British Medical Association.
"In addition to acting as one of the editors of the
"Glasgow Medical Journal, he was the author
"of several publications dealing with particular
"questions in surgery, and edited the 10th edition
"of the 'Anatomists' Vade Mecum.' Mr. Buch-
"anan travelled considerably, and was an ardent
"Alpine climber, one of his notable ascents being
"that of Monte Rosa." *The Times*, 20th April,
1905. (3) William Buchanan.

II. George Buchanan, in Finnick-Drummond, born 1744, and died 1832. He married Annabella Downie and had:—(1) George, d. s. p. 1832; (2) Benjamin, married Mary Cameron and died about 1863, leaving issue settled in London; (3) John, in Finnick-Drummond, married Helen Bow, and had—George, went to Valparaiso and died there leaving issue; William, went to Dunedin, New Zealand, married; Benjamin, at Arbuthnot, Kincardineshire, married; Robert, of Glasgow, married Catherine Ewing, and has issue; John, went to Valparaiso and died unmarried; (1) Janet, married, in 1808, Walter Buchanan, of Killearn, and died in 1856.

III. James Buchanan, of Dowanhill, born in 1756, acquired Dowanhill about 1811, and died in 1844. He married Ellison McCallum, and had issue:—

(1) George, born 1802, died unmarried, 1848.

(2) Thomas, born 1803, died unmarried.

(3) James, born 1805, went abroad, married Williamina Linbeg, and died 1878, leaving issue.

(4) John Buchanan, of Dowanhill, born 1807, married in 1839, Jane Young, and died in 1876, having had issue:—(1) James George, born 1840, died 1870; (2) John Young Buchanan, M.A., F. R. S., educated at Glasgow High School and University, Universities of Marburg, Leipsic and Bonn, and Ecole de Médicine, Paris, Chemist and Physicist of the "Challenger" Expedition, born 1844, decorated with the insignia of Commander of the Order of St. Charles by the Prince of Monaco in 1910; (3) Rt. Hon. Thomas Ryburn Buchanan,[1] P.C., born 1846, educated at Sherborne and Oxford and called to the Bar of the Inner Temple, elected a fellow of All Souls in 1870, and was some years in charge of the Codrington Library.

---

[1] The Right Honourable Thomas Ryburn Buchanan died at Bournemouth on the 7th April, 1911, aged 65. For a more detailed account of his career see Appendix, page 2.

M.P. Edinburgh 1882-1885, West Edinburgh 1885-1892, East Aberdeenshire 1892-1900, East Division of Perthshire 1903-1910; Financial Secretary War Office 1906-1908, and Under-Secretary of State, India Office 1908-1909; married in 1888, Emily, daughter of T. S. Bolitho, M.P. (4) Francis Christian, of Clarinish, Row, D.L. of the county of Dumbarton, born 1853, married, 1878, Margaret Gourlie, and has issue—Marsali, Cathlinne, John, born 1884, and Anselan Dennistoun, born 1885, who at the time of his death, on the 26th February, 1901, was a naval cadet on H.M.S. Britannia training ship at Dartmouth. Mr. Buchanan, who is a Fellow of the Society of Antiquaries, Scotland, has devoted much of his life to antiquarian research, in recognition of which the late King Edward appointed him a member of the Royal Commission on Ancient Monuments in Scotland. (1) Agnes Tennent, married R. M. Pollock, of Middleton; (2) Ellison Janet, married R. Jameson Torrie; (3) Jane Mary, married J. O. Fairlie; and (4) Caroline Wilhelmina, married Captain Stuart Rickman, R.N.

(5) Janet, born 1809, married William Pollock-Morris, M.D., of Craig, near Kilmarnock, and died 1882, leaving issue.

The Leith-Buchanans of Ross Priory.

The Leith-Buchanans of Ross Priory.

Sir George Leith-Buchanan, Bart., of Ross Priory, Balloch, co. Dumbarton, was the eldest son of Sir Alexander Wellesley William Leith, 3rd Bart., who married, in 1832, Jemima (who died 1877), second daughter of Hector Macdonald Buchanan, of Ross, co. Dumbarton, and of Jean Buchanan, daughter of Robert Buchanan of Ross and Drummikill.[1] He was a Captain 17th Light Dragoons, born 1833; married, first, in 1856, Ella Maria, daughter of David Barclay Chapman, of Roehampton, Surrey (who died 1857); he married secondly, 1861, Eliza Caroline, daughter of Thomas Tod, of Drygrange, N.B., and by her (who died 1899) had issue:[2]

    1. Sir Alexander Wellesley George Thomas Leith-Buchanan, Bart., born 1866, married 1888, Maude Mary, daughter of the late Alexander Grant, of Glasgow and succeeded his father in 1903.

    2. George Hector, born 1871, married 1904, Matilda Mary Charlotte, daughter of Isadore McWilliam Bourke, late of Rahasane, co. Galway, and Curragh Leigh, co. Mayo.

---
(1) Strathendrick, p. 321.
(2) Burke's Landed Gentry.

3. James Macdonald Buchanan, born 1872, served in South African War 1901-2 (medal with five clasps), married 1905, Katie Isabel, second daughter of George E. Porter, of Hartsperry, St. Kilda, Melbourne, Australia.

4. Charles John (Deerspring, Ancaster, Ontario, Canada), born 1875, married 1905, Mary Eleanor, daughter of William Farmer, of Ancaster, Canada, and has issue: George William Hector, born 1905, and Thomas Wellesley Macdonald, born 1907.

5. Thomas Tod, born 1877.

1. Flora Macdonald, died unmarried 1904.

2. Caroline Elizabeth, married 1885, John Galbraith Horn, Advocate, Edinburgh, and has issue.

3. Margaret Georgina Jemima, married 1897, William McNish Porter, and has issue.

4. Edith Maud, died unmarried, 1904.

5. Kathleen Nora, married, 1904, Captain James M. McLaren, Gordon Highlanders.

6. Jemima Jean.

After the death of his mother, Lady Leith, Sir George Leith took the additional name of Buchanan. He died 29th September, 1903.

The Buchannans late of Miltoun.

The Buchannans late of Miltoun.

Duncan Buchannan, of Miltoun, in Glen Urquhart, county Inverness, had a son Patrick Buchannan, whose arms as matriculated in the Lyon College in 1672, are the arms of Buchanan, within a border gules charged with eight crescents argent. Crest, a rose slipped gules. Motto, Ducitur hinc honos.

Auchmar, referring to the descent of the family of Miltoun, says:—

"All I can offer concerning this family is founded upon a traditional account I had from a certain gentleman, who was an officer in the Laird of Buchanan's regiment, in the year 1645, at which time, that regiment being in garrison at Inverness, one Colin Buchanan, of Miltoun of Peatty, a gentleman of good repute, and whose interests lay within a few miles of the town of Inverness, kept very much correspondence with Buchanan and his officers, while in garrison in that town. He was descended, by anything can be collected from any account given then out, of Maurice Buchanan's son, who was treasurer to the dauphiness of France in the reign of King James I."[1]

Patrick Buchannan had a son, Norman, who had a son, Archibald Buchannan, who left Glen

---

[1] Auchmar, page 266.

Urquhart and settled at Dunscaith, in Skye. He married Katherine, daughter of Ranald McDonald, of Scalpa, and had four sons, Norman, Malcolm, Duncan, and Peter, and a daughter.

Peter Buchannan left Skye and settled near Whitby, county York, England. He married a Miss Richardson and had, besides a daughter, a son,

John Buchannan, who married Sarah, daughter of Alexander Arr, of Renfrew, and had issue:—

John Buchannan, of Whitby, solicitor, Coroner, Registrar of the County Court, Seneschal of the Liberty of Whitby Strand, who married first, Sarah Margaret, daughter of John Holt, of Whitby, by whom he had a daughter, Sarah Margaret, living unmarried. He married, secondly, Ann, daughter of George Langborne, of Whitby, and died in 1891, leaving issue:—

1. George Buchannan, of Whitby, solicitor, who succeeded his father in his various offices, married Marianne, daughter of George Croft, of Richmond, county York and had issue:— (1) Lilias Mary, living in Whitby; (2) Archibald John, solicitor in Whitby; (3) Margaret Hilda, living in Whitby.

2. Charles Buchannan, of Whitby, married Sarah Ellen, daughter of George Wetherill, of Whitby, and had issue:—(1) Alexander Buchannan, solicitor of Thirsk, county York; (2) Malcolm Buchannan, a clergyman in Canada; (3) Charles Buchannan, of Hull.

3. Hugh Cholmley Buchannan, died s.p.

4. Arthur Buchannan, who was married twice; first, to Katherine Elizabeth, daughter of Thomas Wetherill, of Guisborough, by whom he had issue:—(1) Averil Mary, married William Richardson, and has issue; (2) Margaret Isobel, married Thomas Duncan Henlock Stubbs, and has issue; (3) George Herbert Buchannan, solicitor of Scarborough, county York, who married Lilian, daughter of John Chapman Walker, and has issue, James Arthur and Neil. Arthur Buchannan married, secondly, Margaret Elizabeth Richardson, and died in 1895.

The arms of George Buchannan, of Whitby, as matriculated in the Lyon Office in 1872, are Or a lion rampant sable armed and langued gules within a double tressure flowered and counterflowered of fleurs-de-lis of the second, a bordure invecked parted per pale of the third and argent, charged with eight crescents countercharged. Above the shield is placed a helmet befitting his degree with a mantling gules doubled argent and issuing from a wreath of the liveries is set for crest a dexter hand proper holding a ducal cap purpure turned up ermine and tufted on the top with a rose gules, all within two branches of laurel disposed orleways, also proper and in an escroll over the same the motto, Audaces Juvo.

A Genealogical Note.
THE QUATER-CENTENARY OF GEORGE BUCHANAN.

A Genealogical Note.[1]

George Buchanan, while stating that he was descended from a family rather ancient than opulent, gives us but little information. He does not name his father, but tells us that he was cut off in the prime of life before his grandfather; that his mother, Agnes Heriot, was left with five sons and three daughters, and that he himself was befriended, when aged about fourteen, by his maternal uncle, James Heriot, who, however, died within two years (about 1522). Of his brothers, he only names Patrick.

From other sources we learn that the first of this branch of the Buchanan family was Thomas Buchanan, youngest son of Sir Walter Buchanan of that Ilk (died before 1452). Sir Walter married a daughter of Murdoch, Duke of Albany, but it seems probable that his sons were by a previous union, although there is some reason for believing that the marriage took place as early as 1427.

I. Thomas Buchanan is first mentioned in 1461, when he had a charter from his brother Patrick Buchanan of that Ilk of the lands of Gartincaber. He was possessor of the Hospital of Letter in 1461. He had charters of the Temple lands of Letter in 1462, Croftewyr (part of the lands of Drummickill) in 1466, Balwill and Camo-

---

[1] The above was written by the late Mr. A. W. Gray-Buchanan, and is taken from "George Buchanan, Glasgow Quater-Centenary Studies," published by James MacLehose & Sons, Glasgow, in 1907.

quhill in 1472, Kepdowry, Carbeth, Balwill, the Temple lands of Ballikinrain in 1477, was of Bultoun (or Balantoun) in 1484, had a charter of Middle Ledlowan (now the Moss) in 1484, and by 1495 was of Drummiekill, which became the designation of the family. Thomas Buchanan, of Drummiekill, was still alive in 1496. He is stated to have married the heiress of Drummiekill, but it does not appear whether she was the wife mentioned in 1472, whose name is variously read as "Donote," "Dorote," or possibly "Jonote." He left several sons, amongst whom he seems to have divided his lands in his lifetime.

II. Robert Buchanan, the eldest son, succeeded to Drummiekill and other lands. He married, about 1472, Margaret Hay of Dullievairdis, in the Barony of Glenbervie, Forfarshire. She was still alive in 1515. Robert Buchanan died about 1518.

III. Thomas Buchanan, younger of Drummiekill, born probably about 1473, is mentioned in the charter of Middle Ledlowan in 1509. He married, probably about 1493, Agnes Heriot, daughter of James Heriot of Trabrown in East Lothian. Agnes Heriot was probably sister of Andrew Heriot of Trabrown (died 1531) and James Heriot, official of St. Andrews, within the Archdeaconry of Lothian (1516-1522). Thomas Buchanan and Agnes Heriot had five sons and three daughters.

(1) Robert, probably born before 1495, married, about 1520, Katherine, daughter of Archibald Napier of Merchistoun (great-great-grandfather of the inventor of logarithms), by whom he had a son, who died young. He succeeded his grandfather about 1518, and died before August 29, 1525.

(2) Thomas, probably born about 1495, married, about 1515, Giles (alive 1576), daughter of Andrew Cuninghame of Drumquhassle. He succeeded his brother or nephew in Drummiekill shortly after 1525, and was dead before 1544.

Representatives of this Thomas in the direct male line can still be traced. One of his younger sons was Mr. Thomas Buchanan, Provost of Kirkheuch and Minister of Ceres, who was born about 1520. The latter was therefore nephew of George Buchanan, though James Melville calls him "his cusing."

(3) Alexander, who possessed the lands of Ibert, was probably next in order, though he is sometimes named after Patrick. He married Janet Wawer, and died in November, 1574. His eldest son, Mr. Thomas Buchanan, succeeded his uncle in 1578, as Keeper of the Privy Seal, and died about 1582. From his second son, John, were descended the Buchanans of Ballochruin, who have still a Buchanan representative,

but in the female line. The arms on Alexander Buchanan's seal (used by his second son, John, 9th November, 1557) are: A fess between three boars' (?) heads erased.

(4) Patrick was probably born about 1505. His name is in the lease to Agnes Heriot of the Offeron of Gartladdirnack in 1513. He matriculated at St. Andrews in 1525, at the same time as George. He is also mentioned in the renewed lease to Agnes Heriot in 1531, but is not described as "Mr." although his brother is so designated. As "Mr." Patrick Buchanan he was appointed, in 1542 Preceptor of the Hospital of St. Leonards, near Peebles, and about the same time he had a gift of the Deanery of Dunbar. In 1547, at the invitation of his brother George, he accompanied the latter to Coimbra. He seems to have been in Scotland in 1558, as we find a Mr. Patrick Buchanan witness to a tack granted by the Commendator of Arbroath in January 1557-8.

(5) George.

According to the old Buchanan Genealogical Tree, compiled in 1602, the three sisters of George Buchanan were: (1) "the Lady Bonull" (Lindsay), (2) "the Lady Ballikinrain" (Napier), and (3) "the Lady Knokdory." John Napier, 5th of Ballikinrain, married Agnes Buchanan, but she cannot have been a sister of George Buchanan, as the marriage took place before

January, 1491-2. The three sisters were still alive in 1550.

According to Joseph Scaliger, Alexander Morison, sister's son to George Buchanan, published an edition of his uncle's Latin psalms; and McUre calls Marion Buchanan, wife of Andrew Strang, sister-german of George Buchanan, but as she was married only about 1600, she must have belonged to a much later generation.

The Quatercentenary of George Buchanan.

If Robert Burns is second to none as a lyric poet; if Sir Walter is, in Robert Louis Stevenson's words, " out and away the first of the Romantics;" not less surely is George Buchanan "the greatest of the Humanists" —of that band of scholars and men of letters who, not a decade too soon, caught up and preserved all that was most vital in the bequest of classical antiquity, and prepared the post-Renaissance world for its absorption and assimilation. Scotland has every reason to be proud of having produced such a triad, though her pride be somewhat tempered by the thought that to the first-named and to the last-named she has been what Dr. John Brown (after Horace) called an *arida nutrix*—a cross between the *severa mater* and the *injusta noverca*.

Four hundred years ago to-day, " or thereby " (" circa calendas Februarias "), Buchanan, as he tells us in his Autobiography, was born in the Lennox country, on the banks of the Blane, an affluent of the Clyde. " With the few strokes of a master " (in Hallam's phrase), he introduces us to the farmhouse of his nativity and to his parentage, " of more antiquity than wealth "—his father prematurely dead, his grandfather still alive, but a spendthrift, and his mother, Agnes Heriot, "eident," and intelligent, who, in face of every difficulty, proved the guardian angel of the household. One of five sons and three daughters, George, by his proficiency at school, induced his uncle, James Heriot, to send him to Paris, then the most attractive among seats of learning, and there the boy remained for two years, distinguishing himself in the Latin verse composition of which he was to become, in all Europe, the acknowledged master. But, when barely seventeen, he had to come home, his funds having given out with his uncle's death; and, after a twelvemonth's illness, he joined as a recruit the military force with which the Duke of Albany attempted a raid upon England. The expedition was a failure, and in the retreat through snowy weather he fell ill again. From his sick bed he rose to matriculate in 1524 at St. Andrews as a pauper student, and next year graduated B.A. In 1526 he returned to Paris—" the Lutetia of the ancients and the Lætitia of the moderns "—and at the Scottish College proceeded to the degree of M.A. There the impecuniosity which was his portion through life was hardly relieved by an under-mastership at the College of Ste. Barbe, which, accordingly, he threw up to become tutor to the Earl of Cassillis's son, then in Paris. Returning about 1535 with his pupil to Scotland, he was appointed by James V. as tutor to one of his illegitimate sons. The King, becoming aware of his poetical gifts, particularly in satire, employed him to wreak the Royal vengeance on the Franciscan Order, and this he did so trenchantly that he incurred the implacable enmity of Cardinal Beaton, who imprisoned him in the Castle at St. Andrews, whence, escaping to England, he continued his flight to Paris, only to find his arch-persecutor there. Again he shifted his quarters, this time (1539) to Bordeaux, and on the invitation of the head of its College, Gouvéa, accepted a professorship, which he held for three years, winning the attachment of pupils like Montaigne and the applause of the academic world by his Latin plays. In 1542 the plague forced him to leave the Garonne for the Seine, and, once more at Paris, he filled a chair in Cardinal le Moine's College. In 1547 Gouvéa induced him to join the professorial staff of the newly-founded University of Coimbra, where, however, the Portuguese Inquisition, on Gouvéa's death, took over the University and imprisoned Buchanan on a trumped-up charge of heresy. Released from prison, he remained for some time under surveillance in a monastery, where he began his translation of the Psalms into Latin verse. Finally set at liberty, he embarked on board a Cretan vessel at Lisbon, and landing in England, found the country in such turmoil that he returned to his beloved France, where we next hear of him, in 1555, as tutor to the famous Maréchal de Brissac's son, whom he accompanied, in the Maréchal's train, to Italy, where the French were in military occupation of Piedmont and Liguria. In this situation, perhaps the pleasantest of his life, he remained five years, after which he returned to Scotland to act as classical tutor to Queen Mary, to whom he dedicated his now completed translation of the Psalms. In 1566 he became, at the instance of the Regent Murray, Principal of St. Leonard's College, St. Andrews, where for three years in succession he was one of the four office-bearers empowered to choose the Rector. By this time he had joined the Reformed Church, and after the murder of Darnley, he sided with the Lords against Queen Mary. Chosen Moderator of the General Assembly—the only layman ever elected to the post—he, in 1568, accompanied the Regent to the Conference held at York to lay before Queen Elizabeth's Commissioners, Mary's complicity in the murder of Darnley. The case against her had already been drawn up by himself in his famous "Detectio," the trenchant vigour of which has been alternately applauded and censured. He afterwards became tutor to the boy-King, James VI., who in after life spoke with pride of his teaching, though he could never forgive him for his treatise against "divine right," entitled "De Jure Regni apud Scotos." In 1570 we find him Keeper of the Privy Seal, and entitled to sit in Parliament. This post he held for eight years, after which he resumed his "History of Scotland," which he completed and published just thirty days before his death in Edinburgh, 28th September, 1582.[1]

---

[1] In 1788 a monument in the form of an obelisk was erected to the memory of George Buchanan at Killearn, two miles from Moss, where he was born in 1506. This monument, which is 19 feet square at the base and 103 feet high, has affixed to it a marble tablet bearing the following inscription by Professor Ramsay of Glasgow University, which was placed on it in 1850:—

<pre>
              Memoriae Aeternae
              GEORGII BUCHANANI
                Vir Fortes Fortis
               inter doctos Docti
            inter sapientes sapientissimi
              qui tenax propositi
         imperiorum sacerdotum minas ridens
         Tyrannorum saevorum minas spernens
               Purum mininis cultum
                     atque
               Jura humani generis
    A pessima superstitione atque ab infima servitute
               Imperterritus vindicavit
                 Hoc monumentum
       Domum paternam est natalia rura prospectans
           Sumptibus et pietatae popularium
                 Olim exstructum
                  Aetas—postera
                Reficiendum curavit
                 Anno Christi D.N.
                      MDCCCL
</pre>

George Buchanan died on the 28th September, 1582, "in his house in a close in the High Street of Edinburgh, now removed, "which stood on the side of the West side of Hunter Square, called "Kennedy's Close," and was buried in Greyfriars Churchyard Edinburgh.

From this bare outline of his career we can form some notion of the "romance" that clung to him, as to so many other compatriots only less distinguished than he in severe study and in literary production. It was his boyish love of soldiering, as he himself tells us, that enrolled him in the Duke of Albany's abortive raid upon England, and in this as in every other experience of his chequered life, no opportunity of observation was wasted on him. Sir Walter himself is not more responsive to "the delight of battle" than Buchanan, whose history, equal in many ways to those of Livy and Tacitus, has none of that weakness in military detail which Mommsen finds in both. Love of romance in great measure explains the inordinate length at which he dwells on the purely mythical Scottish foretime, and Livy himself gives no richer colour to early legend than Buchanan to the lives of the successors of "Fergus the First." When he treads on surer ground we find him meriting Archbishop Usher's commendation for honest research, and, significantly enough, his attributing to the Emperor Severus the wall between the Forth and Clyde has, in spite of generations of adverse critics, been proved to be correct as against Bede's view that that Emperor's wall connected the Tyne and the Solway. In the age immediately preceding his own, his account of the clandestine dealings with the Courts of France and England, so full of influence in Scotland, has been vindicated against the carping of Pinkerton, Tytler, and others by no less an authority on that period than the late Professor Brewer of King's College, London. As to his treatment of Queen Mary, it may safely be said that he remained her friend so long as she made it possible. This is not the place to enter into that embittered controversy; but it would be well for the idolators of the Queen and the detractors of Buchanan to ponder this, to wit, the view officially taken of her life by the Congregation of Rites in the Roman Curia. Nothing would have been more gratifying to the Vatican than to have enrolled among the saints such a sufferer in its cause —a sufferer who divides with Helen of Troy and Cleopatra of Egypt the claim to be the most interesting tragedy-queen of history. All Catholic Europe—ay, and many who stand without its pale—would have welcomed her accession to so august a fellowship; indeed, enthusiastic divines of her own faith had already, in published volumes, styled her "beata." That with all these inducements the Congregation of Rites has refrained from committing itself to so momentous an act can only be explained by its having found the evidence against her too cogent—evidence not only accessible to the outsider, but such as is contained in the archives of the Vatican, open to the Congregation of Rites alone. Buchanan's "Detectio," in fact, can claim the tacit acquiescence of the Roman Curia.

But it is as a poet, working in the language and on the lines of the Augustan age of Rome, that Buchanan's merits are most generally admitted. His genius had much that savoured of Lucretius and still more of Virgil; while, in addition, he had not a little in common with Horace, both in his lyric and in his satiric vein. He is at his best in the metre of the two first-named poets, and, in many of the Psalms, he charms the sympathetic reader with "the long lilt" of the Lucretian, as with "the sonorous break" of the Virgilian, hexameter. Of the Ovidian distich he was a master, and in that same metre he can rival Martial in pregnant, or pungent, epigram. He is seldom at his best in the Alcaic stanza, often defective in the third line, the most telling of the quatrain; but where he does succeed, he is superb, as witness his noble version of the 77th Psalm:—

> " Videre fluctus te tumidi, Deus,
> Videre fluctus, et trepido gradu
> Fugere: turbavit profundas
> Horror aquae vitreae lacunas."

He is nearly always felicitous in Sapphics; indeed such delicious odes as that to the College of Bordeaux, beginning:—

> " Vasconis tellus, genetrix virorum
> Fortium, blandi genetrix Lyaei,
> Cui Parens frugum favet et relictis
> Pallas Athenis,"

might have been inspired by Horace himself.

As a man of affairs, what the French call a " Publiciste," he was one of the greatest of his century; with his wide horizons, his Catholic sympathies, his enlightened and " perfervid " patriotism, making his " humanistic " gifts and accomplishments the means of at once elevating, refining, and invigorating his countrymen. He could satirise as scathingly as Juvenal, the corruption and degeneracy of the Church, but only after he had eulogised in noble verse its early purity and the virtues of its first Pontiffs. For Anglicans like Bishop Jewell and Roger Ascham he had affection as well as veneration. He was equally consistent with himself in celebrating the life and work of John Calvin and of the Roman Catholic Archbishop of Glasgow, Gavin Dunbar. Narrow sectarianism and the intolerance it inspires were sheer impossibilities to his rich, kindly humour and his all-embracing philanthropy; and he had his reward in a consensu of appreciation from men of the most diverse genius and sympathy—from the semi-pagan Scaliger to the sceptic Gibbon; from the Romanist Dryden to the Tory High Churchman Johnson; from the Evangelical Cowper to the Anglo-Catholic Keble.—*The Scotsman*, Edinburgh, 1st February, 1906.

Some Distinguished Buchanans.

Some Distinguished Buchanans.

CLAUDIUS BUCHANAN, D.D.[1] (1766-1815).

Claudius Buchanan, D.D., a distinguished missionary in India, the son of a schoolmaster,[2] who was afterwards rector of the Grammar School of Falkirk, was born at Cambuslang, in Lanarkshire, March 12, 1766. While yet very young, he became tutor to the sons of Campbell of Dunstaffnage, and was afterwards employed in the same capacity in two other Highland families. In 1782 he went to the University of Glasgow, where he only remained for two sessions. In 1786 he attended one session in the Divinity class. Having indulged the romantic idea of making the tour of Europe on foot, in imitation of Oliver Goldsmith, he left the University and found his way to London, where he arrived September 2, 1787. After suffering much distress, he succeeded in obtaining a situation as clerk, and was next employed by a solicitor for three years. Becoming acquainted with the Rev. John Newton, of St. Mary's Woolnoth, London, the friend of the poet Cowper, he was introduced by him to Henry Thornton, Esq., who, in 1791, generously sent him to Queen's College, Cambridge, where he was senior Wrangler of his year. He afterwards repaid Mr. Thornton. In September, 1795, he was ordained deacon of

---

[1] Anderson's Scottish Biographical Dictionary.
[2] His father was Alexander Buchanan, a schoolmaster at Inverary, where Claudius began his education. Dr. Buchanan was twice married and left two daughters by his first wife.

the Church of England, and admitted curate to Mr. Newton. On 30th March, 1796, by the influence of Mr. Charles Grant, he was appointed one of the chaplains to the Honourable East India Company; and, having received priest's orders, he left Portsmouth for Bengal, August 11, 1796.

In 1800, on the institution of the College of Fort-William, he was appointed Professor of the Greek, Latin, and English Classics, and Vice-Provost of that establishment. Deeply versed in the oriental languages, he conceived he should best promote the honour of God and the happiness of mankind, by enabling every one to read the Scriptures in his own tongue; and he proposed prizes to be competed for by the Universities of England and Scotland, for Essays on the diffusion of Christianity in India. One of the productions which his proposals called forth was a poem " on the Restoration of Learning in the East," by Mr. Charles Grant, now Lord Glenelg. In 1805 he wrote an account of the College of Fort-William. The same year the University of Glasgow conferred upon him the degree of D.D. In March, 1808, he returned to Europe, and offered second prizes, of £500 each, to the Universities of Oxford and Cambridge. In the succeeding September he went to Scotland, and preached in the Episcopal Chapel at Glasgow. In the spring of 1809 he spent some days at Oxford, collating oriental versions of the Bible. He next proceeded to Cambridge, where he deposited some valuable biblical manuscripts collected by himself in India; and the University of which conferred on him the degree of D.D. After preaching for some time in Welbeck Chapel, London, he retired to Kirby Hall, Yorkshire, the seat of his father-in-law, Henry Thompson, Esq. He subsequently went to reside at Cheshunt, Hertfordshire, where, at the time of his death, he was engaged in superintending an edition of the New Testament for the use of the Syriac Christians residing on the coast of Malabar. He died there, February 9, 1815, at the early age of 48. Besides some Jubilee and other sermons, he published the following works:—"Christian Researches in India;" "Sketch of an Ecclesiastical Establishment for British India;" and "Colonial Ecclesiastical Establishment."

David Buchanan [1] (1745-1812).

David Buchanan, an enterprising publisher and printer, was born in Montrose in 1745, and studied at the University of Aberdeen, where he obtained the usual degree of A.M. When he commenced the printing in his native town, that art had made comparatively little progress in Scotland, and indeed, was practically unknown in most of the provincial towns. At an early period, he republished several standard works in a style equal, if not superior, to anything previously attempted in Scotland; among these were the Dictionaries of Johnson, Boyer, and

---

[1] Anderson's Scottish Biographical Dictionary.

Ainsworth; the first of which was then accounted a most enterprising and successful undertaking. He also printed the first of the small or pocket editions of Johnson's Dictionary, which was abridged and prepared by himself; to which may be added a great variety of the English Classics in a miniature form. Being a man of considerable classical acquirements, he uniformly revised the press himself, correcting the errors of previous editions, besides supplying many important emendations and additions to the Dictionaries. Thus the Montrose Press of that day acquired a high reputation, and its productions were extensively circulated throughout the empire. Mr. Buchanan died in 1812. David Buchanan had three sons David, William and George, who all became distinguished.

The eldest son, David Buchanan, journalist and author, was born in 1779 at Montrose. He became a contributor to the "Edinburgh Review" shortly after its commencement. In 1807 he published a pamphlet on the volunteer system originated by Pitt, which attracted considerable attention. He was the editor of the "Caledonian Mercury" from 1810 to 1827, when he accepted the editorship of the "Edinburgh Courant." In 1841 he brought out an edition of Adam Smith's works, with life, notes, and a volume of additional matter, and in 1844 he published "Inquiry into the Taxation and Commercial Policy of Great Britain, with Observations on the Principles of

Currency and of Exchangeable Value." He also brought out an edition of the "Edinburgh Gazetteer," and contributed numerous articles to the "Encyclopædia Britannica." He died on the 13th August, 1848, at Glasgow.

William Buchanan, a Scotch advocate, born in 1781 at Montrose, was educated at Edinburgh University, and called to the Bar in 1806. In 1813 he published "Reports of certain Remarkable Cases in the Court of Session and Trials in the High Court of Justiciary." These reports are marked by purity of diction and methodical arrangement. In 1856 he was appointed queen's advocate and solicitor of teinds and tithes, on the death of Sir William Hamilton. He was now the oldest member of the Scottish Bar, and peculiarly fitted for his office by his antiquarian bent. He published in November, 1862, a "Treatise on the Law of Scotland on the subject of Teinds," immediately recognized by the whole profession as the standard authority on the subject. He married Elizabeth, daughter of the Rev. James Gregory, minister of the parish of Banchory, by whom he had numerous children. He died on the 18th December, 1863.

George Buchanan, civil engineer of Edinburgh, was born about 1790. He was educated at Edinburgh University, and adopted the profession of a civil engineer, in which he became eminent. He was the author of several scientific treatises, a Fellow of the Royal Society of Edinburgh, and

President of the Royal Scottish Society of Arts. He died on the 30th October, 1852. *Dictionary of National Biography.*

DUGALD BUCHANAN [1] (1716-1768).

Dugald Buchanan, an eminent Gaelic poet, was born in the early part of the eighteenth century, in the parish of Balquhidder, Perthshire. Of his early life little is known. He first attracted attention by the sacred songs which he wrote and recited; and on some respectable individual inquiring about his history, they found that he was the teacher of a small school in a hamlet in his native county. Feeling an interest in his fate, these friends procured for him the situation of Schoolmaster and Catechist at Kinloch-Rannoch on the establishment of the Society for Propagating Christian Knowledge. He rendered essential service to the Rev. James Stewart of Killin, in translating the New Testament into the Gaelic language; and accompanied him into Edinburgh, for the purpose of aiding in correcting the press. While there, he availed himself of the opportunity to attend the university, where he heard lectures on anatomy, and the various departments of natural philosophy. Some gentlemen, struck by his talents, endeavored, unknown to him, to procure him a license to preach the Gospel; but without success. He died July 2, 1768.[2] His poems are

---

[1] Anderson's Scottish Biographical Dictionary.
[2] He was buried at Little Lenny in the parish of Callandar.

allowed to be equal to any in the Gaelic language for style, matter, and the harmony of their versification. The two most celebrated of them are read with perfect enthusiasm by all Highlanders.

Lieut.-General Henry James Buchanan, C.B.

Lieut.-General Henry James Buchanan, C.B., late Colonel Norfolk Regiment, was born on 1st November, 1839, at Dursley, Gloucestershire. He was educated at Marlborough, and in 1850 obtained a commission as ensign in the 47th Foot. He served in the Eastern campaign of 1854-55 as adjutant of the 47th Regiment, including the battles of Alma and Inkerman, sortie of 26th October, siege and fall of Sebastopol, and was appointed Town Major of Sebastopol, and received medal with three clasps, Sardinian and Turkish medals, Fifth Class of the Medjidie. He commanded a Column of the Field Force under Brig.-General Ross against the Afreedees on the North-West Frontier in 1877-8, for which he was mentioned in despatches, and in 1880 received the Companionship of the Bath. He became a major-general in 1886, and subsequently held the command of a brigade at Aldershot. In 1892 he became a Lieut.-General. He married Mary Louise, daughter of the Rev. Frederick Mayne, and died on the 7th October, 1903.

Sir John Buchanan of Clarinch, Claremont, Cape Town.

Sir John Ebenezer Buchanan, Knight, of Claremont, Cape Town, is a grandson of James Buchanan, who, about the beginning of the last century, started the infant school system in Scotland. He began with collecting the children of the work people employed in the mills of the well known Robert Owen, at New Lanark, on the banks of the Clyde. Mr. (afterwards Lord) Brougham interested several philanthropists in his work, and induced him to remove to London, where he opened his first infant school at Brener's Green, Westminster. Mr. Benjamin Leigh Smith, many years M.P. for Norwich (father of Madame Bodichon, one of the founders of Girton College, Cambridge) became interested in the venture, and built for James Buchanan a new school and residence near Vincent Square, Westminster, the present playground of the Westminster scholars. The work developed into the training of teachers. Later on, at Mr. Smith's instance, James Buchanan visited Derbyshire and opened a school at Lea, near the residence of the immortal Florence Nightingale, of Crimean fame, who was a relation of Mr. Smith's. Years later, after the younger members of the family had emigrated to South Africa, James Buchanan joined his daughter Annie, who had started a mission school at Mowbray, near Cape Town. Afterwards, he and his daughter removed to the adjoining Colony of

Natal, where James Buchanan died at the age of about 76. His daughter, who remained unmarried, carried on her school and philanthropic labours in Pietermaritzburg for many years and died universally respected and beloved.

James Buchanan's eldest son, William, who had been trained as a teacher, was first engaged in several private families in England, but about the year 1830 he left with his youngest brother, David Dale Buchanan, for Australia. Their vessel called at Table Bay, and while at Cape Town William Buchanan happened to stroll into the Commercial Exchange at a time when a public meeting was there being held for the purpose of promoting education and establishing schools in the Colony. He asked and obtained leave to address the meeting and so interested the promoters that they induced the two brothers to give up their voyage and to remain at the Cape. They afterwards established a private school of their own, in which venture they were joined by their brother, Ebenezer Buchanan, the second son of James Buchanan. The school proved a success, but was subsequently broken up on the separation of the brothers.

William Buchanan took up reporting and started the Commercial Advertiser newspaper, which ran for a number of years after he had retired from active life. He became official shorthand writer to the Legislative Council and died in Cape Town. He had several children, none of whom survive, but his eldest grandson, William Porter Buchanan, is now a successful barrister, practising in the Supreme Court of the Colony.

In 1838, the well-known South Sea Missionary, the Rev. John Williams, visited Cape Town, and induced Ebenezer Buchanan and his newly wedded wife to accompany him for a period of five years, for the purpose of starting schools in the distant mission field. Ebenezer Buchanan remained in the South Sea Islands for eleven instead of five years, engaged in most useful and successful work under the auspices of the London Missionary Society. He returned to England in 1850 and shortly afterwards started with his young family for Natal, where his younger brother, David Dale Buchanan, had preceded him. He became a Solicitor of the Supreme Court and filled many positions of trust, being Town Clerk and City Treasurer of Pietermaritzburg, the Capital of the Colony, for upwards of twenty years. He died at the age of 85, nearly completing the jubilee of his diamond wedding. His wife survived him about three years and attained the same age, near the end of the last century. The worthy old couple had lived in the reigns of four British sovereigns. Their eldest surviving son, now Sir John Buchanan, also adopted the profession of the law, and after being called to the Bar at the Inner Temple, practised in the Supreme Court of Cape Colony. He became a Judge of that Court in 1880, and has repeatedly acted as Chief Justice of the Colony and President of the Legislative Council. He has had a very full and varied public career and is still on the Bench. His younger surviving brothers and sisters are resident in Natal or the Transvaal, and their families are to be found in several of the different South African Colonies. Sir John Buchanan's eldest son, Douglas M. Buchanan, is a barrister, and has commenced practice in the Cape Supreme Court.

The youngest son of James Buchanan, David Dale Buchanan, after the breaking up of the brothers' school in Cape Town, removed to Natal, in the early days of that settlement. He started the Natal Witness newspaper, a journal which still has a flourishing existence. He also entered the legal profession, and, though generally on the people's side in the contest with the autocratic government of the early days of the Crown Colony, he was called upon to act as Attorney General before the establishment of a parliament in Natal. He was an elected member of the first Legislature and always to the front in all public movements. He died in 1874, but left a distinct impress on the history of that young Colony. He has many descendants in Natal and the Transvaal.[1]

Sir John Ebenezer Buchanan was born on the 8th March, 1844, and was called to the Bar of

---

[1] The above account was kindly communicated by Sir John Buchanan in 1906.

the Inner Temple in 1873. In 1880, he was appointed a Judge of the Supreme Court of the Cape of Good Hope, and in 1901 received the honour of knighthood. He married, in 1878. Mary H., daughter of D. Mudie, of Cape Town, His eldest son, Douglas Mudie Buchanan, M.A., barrister, married, in 1909, Elsie, daughter of J. Bryant Lindley, C.M.G., of Barber House, Claremont.

Sir George Buchanan, M.D., F.R.S.

We regret to announce the death, on Sunday, of Sir George Buchanan, M.D., F.R.S., formerly medical officer to the Local Government Board. He was known, by his intimate friends, to have been in ill-health for some years; and it was this that led him to resign his official position early in 1892. Latterly it became necessary, with a view to the prolongation of his life, that he should submit to an operation; but at this juncture Lord Basing died, and Sir George was asked to take the chairmanship of the Royal Commission on Tuberculosis, which has recently reported. After much hesitation he accepted the post, and he told one of his friends that in this he was mainly actuated by the desire to serve his Sovereign, in one or other capacity, as long as he possibly could. With very considerable labour, he brought the proceedings of the Commission to a close, and directly the report was issued he submitted to the necessary operation. It was eminently successful, and convalescence was fully established. But on Sunday morning he was seized with a sudden faintness and pain in the heart, and he died in a few minutes. He will always be remembered as a leader in the great progress that has been made in this country in that branch of his profession known as preventive medicine or public hygiene, and his contributions to official public health literature are recognized as classical wherever the English language is understood.

Born in 1831 in Myddelton-square, where his father[1] was in practice as a surgeon, Sir George was educated at University College, on whose council he served for many years. He took an active part in matters affording University education for women. He was also member of Senate of the University of London from 1882.

Sir George graduated in 1856, and was one of the first medical officers of health in London, being appointed to St. Giles's in 1856. He originated methods of inquiry in sanitary matters not before attempted, working at the relation of overcrowding and other insanitary conditions of disease, at the prevention of smallpox and cholera, and originating a system of collecting statistical information of the public health of the district. The results of this work were soon appreciated. As a physician to the London Fever Hospital, he further became known as an investigator of scientific problems. In 1861, he was asked by the Privy Council to assist in the elucidation of various sanitary questions. He conducted a systematic inquiry into the working of the Vaccination Acts, an inquiry which had for one of its results the amendment of these Acts by that of 1867. In 1862, he was employed to inquire into the occurrence of typhus fever in some of the northern towns during the cotton famine, and, in 1865, he inspected 25 towns in order to report upon the improved health which had followed from the adoption of better methods of drainage, of filth removal, and of water supply. His report gave a great impulse to similar reforms elsewhere. Incidentally he discovered the extent to which mortality from consumption could be diminished by drainage.

---

[1] George Adam Buchanan.

In 1869, Dr. Buchanan was permanently appointed as a medical inspector under the Privy Council; in 1871, he was transferred to the Local Government Board as assistant medical officer; and in 1879, he succeeded to the headship of his department. The defences against cholera, which have lately been used with so much effect by his successor, Dr. Thorne Thorne, were largely of his suggestion and organization; and, zealously seconded by able subordinates, he has reduced the preventable mortality of England in a very remarkable degree.

In 1892, on his retirement, Dr. Buchanan received the barren honour of knighthood; but the Lords of the Treasury, or their subordinates, refused to consider his almost continuous services from 1861 to 1869 as " official " work, or to reckon the eight years during which they were rendered as time counting towards the increase of the scanty pension which was the sole reward of his services In his own profession he was held in high esteem.

Sir George was twice married: first, to a daughter[1] of the late Mr. George Murphy; secondly, to a daughter[2] of the late Dr. Edward Seaton. He leaves two sons and four daughters, his eldest son[3] being a medical inspector to the Local Government Board. Of his daughters, one was the first lady elected to the Fellowship of the University of London, and another is a B.Sc. of the same University.
—*The Times*, May, 1895.

Mr. Robert Buchanan[4] (1841-1901).

We regret to learn that Mr. Robert Buchanan's long illness ended yesterday in his death at Streatham, in the

---

1 Mary Murphy.
2 Alice Mary Asmar Seaton
3 Dr. George Seaton Buchanan.
4 In 1903, his sister-in-law published an account of his life, Robert Buchanan, Some Account of His Life, His Life's Work and Literary Friendships, by Harriett Jay (Unwins).

house of his sister-in-law and sometime collaborator, Miss Harriet Jay. He was in his 60th year. In the middle of October, last year, Mr. Buchanan was struck down by paralysis without any warning. He had been in indifferent health for some time before, and had been obliged almost to give up work, depending upon the assistance of friends and a small Government pension. His savings had been swept away in a disastrous speculation, which obliged him to go through the Bankruptcy Court and to part with all his copyrights. Just before the stroke of paralysis, however, he had begun to gain strength and to recover his spirits, and had taken up work again. In his helpless state, he had once more to rely upon the aid of friends. He had been a very generous man when he was prosperous himself. He had never refused help to any one in distress, and in his time of need he was generously assisted. His old friend Mr. John Coleman, actor and author, busied himself in starting a fund, and enough money was raised to meet the immediate needs of the case. It was seen from the first that no permanent recovery could be hoped for, and the end has come as a merciful release from a state of the most pitiful helplessness and living death.

Mr. Buchanan was a man of great mental activity, who seemed, at one time, to be in the way to become a permanent intellectual force. Twenty-five years ago, he was regarded by many good judges as the coming poet. But his energies were at once too widespread and too undisciplined for his mind to make a mark upon the age. It was not the fact that he was " ever a fighter " which told against him; it was his method of controversy and the nature of the subjects which took him into the field. Activity of mind he inherited, for his father was, in his own words, a " Socialist missionary," lecturer, and journalist;[1]

---

[1] His father was Robert Buchanan (1813-1866), Socialist and Journalist.

and no doubt he inherited, too, that dissatisfaction with the world as it is which came out especially in his later life, and which made his humour often bitter and his endeavours to alter this "sorry scheme of things" seem over-hasty and petulant. Had he devoted himself with single aim either to poetry or to fiction, or even to criticism, he would probably have gained a lasting name. As it is, the future chronicler of letters will take note of him mainly as a very industrious worker in various fields of literature, who was once connected with an incident that greatly stirred the literary world. This incident was, of course, Buchanan's attack upon Rossetti in the pseudonymous article called "The Fleshly School of Poetry" which appeared in the *Contemporary Review* in 1871. Even to those who do not recollect the article, the nature of the attack is sufficiently indicated by its title. In itself, it was unimportant—merely one of those attacks to which most poets of distinction are subjected in the course of their careers. Mr. Buchanan himself soon saw that he had done Rossetti an injustice, and showed it, among other ways, by dedicating "God and the Man" to "An Old Enemy." But it created some sensation at the time, and in Rossetti's life it became "deplorably prominent," since, according to his brother, it happened just at the worst possible moment and had an effect upon the poet's mind from which he never recovered.

At the time when this incident brought him prominently into the public eye Mr. Buchanan had already attracted notice by his poetry. His first book, issued in 1860, was dedicated to the memory of his unfortunate friend, David Gray, with whom he first came to London. They were at Glasgow University together, and, both bitten by the desire of literary fame, they determined to take their fortunes to the great city where they were sure speedy recognition and fame awaited them. The sequel was sad.

Gray, a delicate lad, gradually wasted away in consumption, and he died before he had time to give full proof of his talent. Mr. Buchanan felt his loss keenly and always spoke of this early friendship with touching, wistful pathos. He himself was of more robust constitution, and he soon found his place in the world of letters. His work improved rapidly, and the reputation that he and Gray had dreamed of came to him in full measure. His first book of poems, "Undertones," appeared in 1860, and his talent was recognized at once. The dedication verses "To David in Heaven" were of a moving pathos and beauty, and the young writer's gift of expression was clear proof of poetic power. "London Poems" (1866) brought him into wider notice. The lyrics which composed it were the outcome of his life—a lonely and, for the most part, a sad life—in a London garret. They hit off phases and episodes, now with humour, now with a pathetic force that touched the chord of tears, always vividly and effectively. "Napoleon Fallen" was ambitious, too ambitious for his powers, but there are fine passages in it. The same may be said about "The City of Dream," which, however, won public praise from Mr. Lecky. Mr. Buchanan's verse came too easily and he was too little self-critical to distil his inspiration into the vessels that would best have held it. Still, he had an individual talent; and, although it was intermittent, there was inspiration in his work. If he had kept to poetry, the promise of his youth might have been fulfilled. But his energies were dissipated in too many directions at once. He became a novelist and a playwright as well as a poet and critic. His fiction was vigorous and often boldly original. "God and the Man" is the best remembered of his novels, but there were several others well above the average. He was no more constant, however, to novel-writing than he had been to poetry. He found a profitable outlet for his energies in the drama, and for a number of years he provided the stage with a fairly constant succession of plays of all kinds. His greatest success was with an adaptation of "Tom Jones" which was played at the Vaudeville Theatre under the name of *Sophia* for nearly two years. Encouraged by this, he extracted plays also from "Joseph Andrews" and "Clarissa Harlowe" and managed again to hit the popular taste. Among his other successful efforts in this line was a familiar melodrama called *Alone in London*, which still holds the stage.

Of late, Mr. Buchanan had turned again to verse, but, though there was still plenty of vigour, there were lacking the poetic qualities that promised well in his earlier work. He had been for several years his own publisher, but he undertook this additional labour too late to profit much by it.—*The Times*, July 11, 1901.

Some Buchanans in the United States of America.

Some Buchanans in the United States of America.

FAMILY OF JAMES BUCHANAN, XVTH PRESIDENT OF THE UNITED STATES OF AMERICA.

Thomas Buchanan, of Ramelton, in the county of Donegal, was the fourth son of George Buchanan, of Blairlusk. He had a son, the father of,

John Buchanan, of Ramelton, who married Jane, daughter of Samuel Russell, and had two sons, (1) James, of whom hereafter, and (2) John, who died in Ireland.

James Buchanan, born about 1761, emigrated to the United States in 1783; married, in 1788, Elizabeth Speer, and died in 1821, leaving issue:—(1) James Buchanan, who became fifteenth President of the United States of America; (2) William Speer Buchanan, died s.p.; (3) George W. Buchanan, died s.p.; (4) Revd. Edward Young Buchanan, D.D. (Oxford), of Philadelphia, Pa.; married 1833, Ann Elizabeth, daughter of William B. Foster, of Pittsburg, Pa., and had, with other children, (1) James, (2) Edward Young, (3) William Foster, (4) Maria Lois, married Alexander J. Cassatt, of Philadelphia, and had Edward Buchanan; Katherine Kelso; Robert; and

Elizabeth Alice Conyngham, who was married to Maskell Ewing, of Philadelphia, (5) Jane, married 1813, Elliott T. Lane, and had James Buchanan; Mary, wife of George W. Baker, of Lancaster, Pa., died s.p.; Harriet Jane, married Henry Elliott Johnston, of Baltimore, Md., and had James Buchanan, born 1866, died 1881; and Henry Elliott.

James Buchanan, fifteenth President of the United States of America, was born at Stony Batter, near Mercersburg, in Franklin County, Pennsylvania, on the 23rd April, 1791. He was admitted to the Bar of the State of Pennsylvania in 1812, and became Envoy Extraordinary and Minister Plenipotentiary to Russia from 1831 to 1833, when he was elected a Senator. From 1853 to 1856, he was Ambassador of the United States at the Court of St. James, and President of the United States from 1857 to 1861. He died unmarried at Wheatlands, near Lancaster, Pennsylvania, on the 1st June, 1868.

Buchanans of Cumberland County, and later of Meadville, Pennsylvania.

The ancestor of this family was Robert Buchanan, of co. Tyrone, Ireland, son of Patrick Buchanan, of co. Tyrone, who is said to have been a son of William Buchanan, of Tyrone, son of George Buchanan, of Blairlusk, who sold that estate and emigrated to Ireland in 1672.

Robert Buchanan, of co. Tyrone, had two sons:—(1) General Thomas Buchanan, who removed from co. Tyrone, Ireland, to Cumberland co., Pennsylvania, and was a Commander of the Pennsylvania Line during the war of the Revolution. He married and left four daughters, who were all living in 1857, but without issue.

(2) Captain Alexander Buchanan, was born in Ireland in 1760, and also emigrated to Cumberland co. He was an officer in the Pennsylvania Line during the Revolution, and married, 30th March, 1796, Elizabeth Leonard, born 4th March, 1772. He removed, in 1797, to Meadville, Pennsylvania, where he died on the 8th May, 1810, leaving issue:—

I. Robert Buchanan, of "Green Hill," Clifton, Cincinnati, Ohio, born Westmoreland co., Pennsylvania, on the 15th January, 1797, and settled, in 1811, in Cincinnati, Ohio. He married, 31st October, 1822, Harriet Susan Lee-Wright Browning, born 2nd May, 1802, only daughter of Thomas Browning, of Mason co., Kentucky; and died on the 23rd April, 1879, having had issue:—Charles MacAllister Buchanan, of Clifton, Cincinnati, born 6th January, 1835; married, 9th June, 1857, Emily Cornelia, eldest daughter of A. J. Wheeler, of Clifton, Cincinnati, and had, Robert Buchanan, of Toledo, Ohio.

II. James, died s.p.

III. Mary, married William Compton, and had issue.

IV. Alexander Buchanan, married Caroline Compton, and had issue:—(1) William Buchanan, died in 1894, without issue; (2) Edward Buchanan, White Cloud, Kansas; (3) Mary, married M. E. Shrom, whose daughter, Clara S., is married to Edwin S. Templeton, Attorney-at-Law, Greenville, Pennsylvania; (4) Elizabeth, married ——— Smith; (5) Colonel Robert Buchanan, St. Louis, Missouri; (6) Rebecca, married, in 1869, Corinth J. T. Bensen, Meadville, Pennsylvania, and had issue, Caroline Gertrude Bensen and Mary Buchanan Bensen, Meadville; (7) Sarah, married J. C. Smith, Meadville; (8) David Buchanan, Meadville; (9) Alexander Buchanan, died in 1866, without issue.

V. Thomas Buchanan, died s.p.

VI. Sarah, married to Dr. Edward Ellis, Meadville, and had issue:—Ruth Elizabeth, who married Revd. Morrison Byllesby, Pittsburg, and had issue.

VII. John Buchanan, who married and left one daughter.

Thomas Buchanan, of Wall Street, New York.

Thomas Buchanan, the eldest son of George Buchanan and Jean Lowden, his wife, was born on the 24th December, 1744, at Glasgow, in Scotland, where his father was a wealthy merchant. Thomas Buchanan went to New York when he was about 18 years of age, and shortly after entered into business with Mr. Walter Buchanan, a cousin of his father, at that time engaged in business in New York, the firm being known as Walter and Thomas Buchanan. He became a member of the Buchanan Society in 1765. He married Almy Townsend, daughter of Jacob and Mercy Townsend, of Jericho, Long Island, and died at his residence in Wall Street, on the 10th September, 1815. He left eight children, of whom, Jean, his eldest daughter, died unmarried; Almy married Peter P. Goelet, the grandfather of the late Robert and Ogden Goelet and of Elbridge T. Gerry and Mrs. Frederick Gallatin; Margaret married Robert R. Goelet, whose daughter married Elbert Kip; Martha married Thomas Hicks, son of Whitehead Hicks, Mayor of New York; Elizabeth married Samuel Gilford, father of Thomas Buchanan Gilford, who married Sarah Parkin, and has three sons, Samuel Gilford; Thomas Buchanan Gilford, who married Mrs. David Trumbull Lanman Robinson, daughter of the late Colonel and Mrs. Frances Carpenter

Hooten, of Philadelphia; and John Parkin Gilford, who married Emily Louisa, daughter of the late Joseph Lentilhon; George, his only son, died unmarried; Hannah died unmarried, and Frances, the youngest child, married Thomas C. Pearsall.

THE BUCHANANS OF NEW ORLEANS AND OF JEFFERSONVILLE, INDIANA, AND LOUISVILLE, KENTUCKY.

Captain William Eccles Buchanan, R.A., of Fintona, county Tyrone, Ireland, served through the Peninsular War and was present at the Battle of Waterloo, at which he was severely wounded, and though he lived some years afterwards, died from the effects of his wounds. His uncle, or grandfather, was General William Buchanan, R.A., who was Lieutenant-Colonel Royal Regiment of Artillery in Ireland, in 1795, and held the rank of Colonel in 1802. In the Army List of 1803, his name appears on the list of Colonels and on the list of Officers of the "Late Royal Irish Artillery, who have been allowed to retire on their Full Pay." Captain William Eccles Buchanan was twice married, his first wife was Elizabeth, daughter of the Revd. Dean Paul, and had issue:—

    1. William Eccles Buchanan, born 26th December, 1817, at Fintona, who went to America and settled at New Orleans. He married, on the 18th December, 1841, at

Louisville, Kentucky, Sarah Eliza, daughter of James Warnock Buchanan, M.D., Royal Navy. William Eccles, the younger, died in May, 1859, and left issue:—George L. Buchanan, of Jeffersonville; Spence Abinger Buchanan; Eulalie M. Buchanan, d.s.p.; Eccles C. Buchanan, married, and has a son, Aaron Everly Buchanan, who is married and resides in the City of Mexico; and James Warnock Buchanan, of Jeffersonville.

2. Jane Buchanan.
3. Robert Buchanan, settled in Missouri, married and died there.

Captain William Eccles Buchanan married, secondly, a sister of Andrew Buchanan, of Louisville, and of George Buchanan, of St. Louis, Missouri, and died in the Isle of Man. Andrew Buchanan, of Louisville, had a son, George Coulter Buchanan, living, in 1900, in that place.

James Warnock Buchanan, whose daughter married William Eccles Buchanan, the younger, was the second son of John Buchanan, of Tattykeel and Botera, county Tyrone, Ireland. This John Buchanan, who died about 1799, had three sons:—

1. George Buchanan.
2. James Warnock Buchanan, M.D., Royal Navy, who married Georgina, youngest daughter of Sir Patrick Spence, of Jamaica, and had three children, all born in Jamaica:—

(1). Mary Jane.

(2). Sarah Eliza, who was married to William Eccles Buchanan, of New Orleans.

(3). William Allen Buchanan, late of Asheville, North Carolina, left issue:— Stella Buchanan, married Mr. Barrett and died leaving two sons; William Allen Buchanan, younger, of Asheville; Georgiana Buchanan, married at Venice, Italy, Mr. Duckett, of New York City, and James Wathen Buchanan, of Asheville.

3. John Buchanan, who was first an officer in the British Army, and later, a clergyman in the Church of England. He married and left two daughters, who married and lived in England. He died about 1860, at Aldershot, in England.

The Buchanans of Druid Hill, Baltimore.

Dr. George Buchanan, the third son of Mungo Buchanan, W.S., of Hilltoun and Auchintorlie, was born in 1698 and went to America in 1723, acquiring lands in Maryland, which he called Druid Hill, on the site of what is now the City of Baltimore. In 1727, he was admitted a Member of the Buchanan Society. He married Eleanor, daughter of Nicholas Rogers, and died 23rd April, 1750, having had issue:—

1. Lloyd, born 1729, who married, and had a daughter, Eleanor, married to her cousin, Nicholas Rogers. Their son, Lloyd

Nicholas Rogers, married Eliza, daughter of Thomas Law and had a son, Edmund Law Rogers.

2. Eleanor, married Richard Croxall, and died s.p.

3. Andrew.

4. Archibald, d.s.p.

5. George, died unmarried.

6. Elizabeth, married James Gittings, and had issue.

7. James, died unmarried.

8. Katherine, died unmarried.

9. William, born 1748, died 1824, who was twice married, and had, among other issue, (1) the Hon. James Madison Buchanan, U.S. Minister to Denmark, born 1803, died in 1876; who had issue, William Jefferson, James Madison, John R., Edmund Key and Harney. (2) Charles A. Buchanan, who had one son, James Hollis Buchanan.

II. Andrew Buchanan, second son of Dr. George Buchanan, was born 22nd October, 1734, and died 12th March, 1786. He was General of the Maryland Troops and Presiding Justice of Baltimore. He married Susan Lawson, and had issue:—(1) Dorothy, married Benjamin Lowndes; (2) George; (3) Alexander Pitt, whose descendants are in Tennessee; (4) Andrew, father of Brevet-Major General Robert Christie Buchanan, U.S. Army, who died in 1878, leaving no issue; (5) Elizabeth, married David C. Stewart; (6) Lloyd

Archibald; (7) Susannah, married Thomas Johnston.

III. Dr. George Buchanan, eldest son of General Andrew Buchanan, was born 17th September, 1763. He removed to Philadelphia in 1806, and died 9th July, 1808. He married, in 1789, Laetetia McKean, daughter of Hon. Thomas McKean, Governor of Pennsylvania, formerly Chief Justice of Pennsylvania, Delegate to the Continental Congress of which he was President, and had issue:—(1) George of Auchintorlie, Pennsylvania, born 1796 and died 1879; (2) McKean, of whom afterwards, and (3) Franklin, born 17th September, 1800, in Baltimore; entered the United States Navy in 1815; organized the Naval Academy in 1845; and entered the Confederate Navy with the rank of Captain. He commanded the "Merrimac" in the attack on the Federal Fleet in Hampton Roads, when the "Cumberland" was sunk and the "Congress" on which his brother, McKean Buchanan, was Paymaster, was blown up. He was so severely wounded in this action, that he could not take command of his vessel in the engagement which took place on the next day with the "Monitor." For his gallantry at this time, he was thanked by the Confederate Congress and raised to the rank of Admiral and Senior Officer of the Confederate Navy. Subsequently, he was placed in command of the Naval defences of Mobile, and then appointed to superintend the construction of the ironclad ram, "Tennessee," which he commanded during the action with the Union Fleet in Mobile Bay on the 5th of August, 1864. He was again wounded and taken prisoner, but was exchanged in February following, and died on the 11th May, 1874. He married Nannie Lloyd, daughter of Governor Edward Lloyd, of Wye House, Maryland, and left a large family.

IV. McKean Buchanan, Pay Director, U.S. Navy, born 27th July, 1798; married, in 1834, Frances Selina, daughter of Col. Isaac Roberdeau, Chief Topographical Engineer, U.S. Army, and died 18th March, 1871, leaving a son, Roberdeau, and a daughter, Laetetia McKean, born 24th December, 1842; married 3rd October, 1867, G. F. Fife, Asst. Surgeon, U.S. Navy, by whom she had issue, George Buchanan Fife, born 9th August, 1869.

V. Roberdeau Buchanan, Assistant in the Nautical Almanac Office, U.S. Naval Observatory, at Washington, born 22nd November, 1839, in Philadelphia, is the male representative of Dr. George Buchanan, the first. He took his scientific degree at Harvard University and subsequently received an appointment in the U.S. Patent Office, at Washington. He has published genealogies of the Roberdeau, McKean and Shippen families, and has written "The Mathematical Theory of Eclipses," "The Projection of the Sphere" and the "Introductions to the Differential Calculus by means of Finite Differences."

He married 12th September, 1888, Eliza M. Peters, of Washington, a descendant of Sir Chas. Burdett, Bart.

The Family of Sir Francis James Buchanan and of the Buchanans of Maryland. [1]

The family of the late Sir Francis James Buchanan, R.A., and of Thomas Buchanan, who settled in Maryland, is descended from the Rev. Charles Buchanan, a Scotch clergyman who settled in England. The Rev. Charles Buchanan had, besides a daughter married to Mr. Britton, a son, Charles Buchanan, who lived in London, and died at Camberwell. This Charles Buchanan was twice married, and had by his first wife, a Scotch lady, two sons:—

I. Francis James Buchanan (Sir), who entered the British Army, was knighted, in 1762, for his services at the storming of Havana, and died a Lieutenant-Colonel of Artillery, in 1787. He married, in America, a Miss Farquar, and had a son, who died in his father's lifetime, and a daughter Eliza, married to Major Thomas Reed of Dublin, [2]

---

[1] This family claims to be descended from Buchanan of Lenny.

[2] Mrs. Cecil Frances Alexander was born in Dublin in 1818; her father, Major John Humphreys, of Milltown House, Strabane, came of an old Norfolk family. He joined the Royal Marines in 1798, and fought under Nelson at Copenhagen in 1801. He afterwards went through a campaign in the West Indies, and on his return home invalided was made brigade major of County Tyrone. When the yeomanry were disbanded, he filled, for some time, an important official appointment in Dublin, afterwards becoming agent to the Earl

father of General Sir Thomas Reed, K.C.B., of Ampfield House, Hants. General Reed, who was born in 1796, served in the Peninsular War and was present at the Battle of Waterloo. In 1846, he commanded a Brigade of the Army of the Sutlej, and, in 1856, a Division of the Madras Army. He married, in 1835, Elizabeth Jane, daughter of John Clayton,[1] of Enfield Old Park, Middlesex, and granddaughter of Charles Buchanan, and had a son, Major Francis James Buchanan Reed, 51st Foot, and two daughters. He died in 1883 at Romsey.

II. Thomas Buchanan, who settled in Maryland about 1760, married Mary Cook, daughter of William Cook, of Graden, Prince George County, Maryland, and of his wife, Eliza Tighlman. He had two sons:—

1. Thomas Buchanan, born in Prince George County, Maryland, September 25th, 1778, and died September 28th, 1847.

---

of Wicklow; and, subsequently, to the late Duke of Abercorn, whom he served in that capacity during the remainder of his life. Major Humphreys married a daughter of Captain Reed, of Dublin, and Mrs. Reed, a daughter of General Sir James Buchanan, K.C.B. Mrs. Humphreys' brothers, Colonel John Reed and Sir Thomas Reed, G.C.B., were distinguished soldiers. In October, 1850, Cecil Frances Humphreys married the Rev. William Alexander, then Rector of Termonamongan, now Primate of All Ireland. Mrs. Alexander's fame as a poetess rests chiefly on her sacred songs. Mrs. Alexander died at the Palace, Derry, on the 12th October, 1895. *"Notes on the Literary History of Strabane," Tyrone Constitution, June, 1902.*

[1] On the 8th inst., at Bathwick Church, Lieut.-Colonel T. Reed, of the 62nd Regt., to Elizabeth Jane, eldest daughter; and the Rev. James Bliss, M.A., of Oriel College, Oxford, to Emily Mary, third daughter of John Clayton, Esq., of Enfield Old Park, Middlesex, and of Pulteney Street, Bath. *(The Spectator, 17th January, 1835.)*

He was Judge of the Fourth Judicial District of Maryland, and Associate Justice of the Supreme Court of that State. He married Rebecca Maria Harriet, daughter of James Anderson, banker, of Maryland (who died in 1840), and had issue:—(1) Dr. James Anderson Buchanan, born 1804, married twice, and, by his first marriage, had Thomas Buchanan, born 1829, died in 1854; Harriet, born 1833, married to Cumberland Dugan, of Baltimore; by his second marriage, he had Mary Anderson, born in 1840, died in 1863; Anna, born in 1841, died in 1863; James A. Buchanan, Brigadier-General United States Army, Washington, D.C., born December 11th, 1843, married 1855, Helen Warren Meyers; (2) Thomas, who died about 1845, unmarried; (3) Mrs. Steele; (4) Mrs. Macpherson; (5) Mrs. John R. Dall, and (6) Harriet Rebecca Anderson Buchanan, born in 1803, died in 1872.

2. John Buchanan, born in 1772, died in 1844, who became Chief Justice of the State of Maryland.

3. Mary, (Mrs. Pottinger) of Hagerstown, Maryland, died in 1851, in her 88th year, and had issue, Dr. John Hudson Pottinger.

4. Sophie, married Dr. Duckett, of Maryland.

By his second marriage Charles Buchanan had a son, Charles Buchanan, and a daughter, Arabella, who was married to Mr. Donne, son of Dr. Donne, of Norwich, by whom she had a son, Charles, who went to India and died there without issue, and three daughters, Mrs. Harvey, Mrs. Fields and Mrs. Bliss.

III. Charles Buchanan, of Frodsham co., Chester, who married twice. By his first wife, a French lady, he had three sons and one daughter, but only the second son Charles, left issue. By his second wife, Elizabeth Ashley, of Frodsham, Chester, he had, with other issue:—(1) Thomas Buchanan, who died unmarried; (2) Daniel Buchanan, of Overton, Liverpool, who married Elizabeth Owen, by whom he had Charles Benn, Daniel Cranmer, Thomas Owen, William Henry, George Frederick, Eliza Ann, James Clayton, Emily Cranmer, Margaret Louisa and Mary Ann; (3) Elizabeth; (4) Margaret, died unmarried; (5) Arabella, died unmarried; (6) Jane, who married John Clayton, of Enfield Old Park, Middlesex, and died, leaving issue:—Rev. John Henry Clayton, of Enfield Old Park, born 1809; William Ashley Clayton; Thomas Arthur Clayton; Elizabeth Jane, Arabella, Emily Mary, Mary Ann and Margaret Harriet.

Charles Buchanan died, in January, 1804, at Burton-on-Trent.

The Buchanans of Ulster County and Orange County, New York.[1]

I. Robert Buchanan, born about 1700, in Ireland, emigrated to America, in 1737, and settled in the Wallkill Valley, west of Newburgh-on-Hudson, Province of New York. He was a builder and was in the first military corps organized (1738) in Ulster County. He married Catherine McDonnell, and had at least five sons:—1. James, born 1723, in Ireland, died 1775; 2. Robert, a builder, who, in 1780, had served twenty-two years in Colonial wars and the Revolution, born about 1734 in Ireland, and died about 1818, at Milford, Pike County, Pennsylvania. He married Elizabeth, daughter of Alexander Falls, Sr., of Orange County, New York, and had issue: (1) Alexander, born in 1757, in Newburgh, New York; died in Milford, unmarried. He was a soldier in the Revolution. (2) Jane, born in 1759, in Newburgh, married Joseph Greer, of Orange County, and had, among other issue, Joseph Greer, a judge of the Sussex County Court, New Jersey, and George, a sugar refiner and an extensive freeholder in New York, who was the father of Charles Greer, of "Brookside Farm," Rye, N.Y., and of his sister, the wife of J. Edward Simmons, President of the Chamber of Commerce, New York; (3) James Buchanan, born in 1761,

---

[1] The account of this family is compiled from information supplied by Mr. Chauncey K. Buchanan of Tarrytown, New York.

a soldier in the Revolution, died in Haverstraw; (4) George, who wrote his name Bowhanan, born in 1763, twice married,—first, in 1795, to Susan Eldred; (5) Arthur, born in 1766, near Goshen, N.Y., died, in 1824, at Milford, married Mary (Polly), daughter of Jabez Hamilton. They had a daughter, Olive, married to John B. Rockwell, father of Charles F. Rockwell, of Honesdale, Pa., who was born in 1825. (6) Isabella (Arabella), born in 1768, married in 1789, James Eager; (7) Falls (Lewis Falls) Buchanan, born in 1770, in Little Britain, and died, in 1843, near Haverstraw, N.Y.; (8) Elizabeth, born in 1773; married, in 1788, John Mandeville, of Orange County, and located in Montgomery County, Pa.; (9) William, born in 1776, and located in New York; (10) Margaret, born in 1779, married John McCarty, and died in Milford.

3. Thomas, born 1736, in Ireland.

4. William, born 1739, in Wallkill Valley, and died in 1775.

5. George, born in 1743, in Goshen.

II. James Buchanan, a freeholder in Little Britain, born in 1723, died in 1775, having had issue:—1. James, married, in 1790, Martha, daughter of Thomas Eager, Sr.; 2. Robert; 3. William, went to Long Island; 4. John, a soldier in the Revolution and afterwards a captain by N.Y. State appointment, married Miriam, daughter of Thomas Eager, Sr. About 1800, he moved to the Mohawk Valley, where he died, in 1808, leaving, with other sons and daughters, James and Thomas, the latter a prominent citizen of Utica, N.Y., born in 1791, who married Mary Churchill, and had, among other issue:—Thomas, born in 1821, the father of E. Everett Buchanan, of Elmira, N.Y., Member of Buchanan Society; and Milford De Witt, born in 1835, father of Gordon Buchanan, of Chicago, Member of Buchanan Society; 5. Polly, married Alexander Stewart; 6. Nancy, married Thomas Eager, Jr.; 7. Peggy, married James Bell and settled in New Jersey; 8. Betsy, married John Kelso; 9. Susan, married Edward Miller, from Dublin, Ireland, from whom the late Alexander MacGraw, of Detroit, was descended.

III. Robert Buchanan, the second son of James Buchanan, was born in Little Britain, 1752, builder, a soldier in the Revolution, married Hannah Campbell, daughter of John Campbell, and had:—1. James, married Jane Reed, died 1823, had, with other issue, a daughter, Amelia (1803-1896), married William Fish; 2. John, of Little Britain, married Phoebe Thurston; 3. Samuel, married Jane Beck, died 1813; his widow married William Moffatt and moved to Ohio with her children, Hugh and Ellen Buchanan; 4. William; 5. Jane, married Thomas King, settled in Lake co., Ohio; 6. Charles, married Lois Armstrong, and had, with other issue, a son, Thompson Buchanan; 7. Mary, married William King and settled in Lake co., Ohio; 8. Miriam, married Alexander Scott, father of Rev. Charles Scott, D.D., President of Hope College, Holland, Mich.; 9. Susan, married John N. Boyd.

IV. William Buchanan, of Monroe, Orange co., the fourth son of Robert Buchanan, was born about 1783, in township of Monroe; married, first, Jemima Jones; secondly, Mary Helme, daughter of William Helme, and of his wife, Eleanor Dobbin. The latter was a daughter of Hugh Dobbin, who emigrated to America from Ireland, a son of "Hugh Dobbin, Magerhany, co. Monaghan, gentleman." William Buchanan had two daughters by his first wife: Eliza, married John Chase, went to Providence, R.I.; Hannah, married Eli Wallace, located at Stroudsburg, Pa.; and by his second wife, two sons: Vincent, who died young, and Coe Stewart Buchanan, and a daughter, Eleanor Jane, wife of James Turner Derrickson. He died in 1843.

V. Coe Stewart Buchanan, inventor, paper merchant in New York and manufacturer of paper in Saratoga County; born 3rd June, 1824, in Township of Wantage, Sussex Co., N.Y.; of the firm of Buchanan, Perkins and Goodwin, paper merchants; retired from business in 1870, and died 13th March, 1883, at Tarrytown, New York; married, 6th April, 1848, Jane Taylor, daughter of Moses Taylor and Sarah Onderdonk, of Tarrytown, and had issue:—

1. Chauncey K., of Tarrytown, New York,

Member of Buchanan Society, 1884, born 5th March, 1851, in Williamsburg, N.Y.

2. Moses Taylor Buchanan, born 8th April, 1853, in New York, married his cousin, Mary Elizabeth, daughter of William H. Cooper, and died 17th November, 1901.

   1. Frances, married George Townsend, formerly of Lynn and Boston, Mass., and has, Eleanor Townsend.

   2. Mary Eleanor.

The Hon. William I. Buchanan, Late U. S. Minister to Panama.

William Insco Buchanan was descended from a branch of the family of Buchanan which settled in Virginia in the early history of that State. His great-grandfather was Colonel George Buchanan, who was very prominently identified with the early settlement of the State of Ohio, the family moving to that State in the beginning of the last century. His great-grandmother was Nancy Cassidy, of another well-known Virginia family. They had a son, James Harvey Buchanan, who married Joanna Hall, daughter of William Hall, a Revolutionary soldier from South Carolina.

William Insco Buchanan was the son of George Preston Buchanan and Mary Gibson, born near Covington, Ohio, 10th September, 1853; removed to Sioux City, Iowa, in 1882. In 1890, he was appointed a member of the National

Commission that directed the World's Columbian Exposition of Chicago, and was Director of the Department of Agriculture, Live Stock and Forestry of that great work. In 1894, he was appointed by President Cleveland, Minister to the Argentine Republic, and his services were so satisfactory to the Government that he was continued in the office by President McKinley. In 1894, he was selected by the Argentine and Chilean Governments as Arbitrator in the settlement of a long outstanding boundary dispute between those countries, and won the special gratitude of the Argentine Government by his diplomatic success in the settlement.

In 1900, he became Director-General of the Pan-American Exposition at Buffalo. In 1902, he was appointed a Delegate on the part of the United States to the second Pan-American Conference, held in Mexico. In 1903, he was appointed first United States Minister to the Republic of Panama. In 1906, he was appointed Chairman of the United States Delegation to the Third Pan-American Conference, held at Rio de Janeiro. In 1907, he was appointed a Delegate on the part of the United States to the Second International Peace Conference at The Hague, and in the same year the Representative of the United States in the Central American Peace Conference held at Washington. In 1909, he was appointed by President Roosevelt a Special

Commissioner to Venezuela and arranged the treaty between that country and the United States, which resulted in the termination of the long outstanding disagreements between the two countries. He was a member of the Buchanan Society since 1899.

He married, in 1878, Miss Lulu Williams, daughter of J. Insco Williams, and died suddenly on the 16th October, 1909, in London, while on a diplomatic mission for the United States in connection with the Venezuelan claims, leaving a son, Donald Buchanan, and a daughter, Mrs. Charles H. Williams, of Buffalo.

George Buchanan of Northern New York.

George Buchanan, of Northern New York, the son of Thomas Buchanan and Miss Livingstone, was born at Stirling, Scotland, and educated at Edinburgh. He married, first, Cornelia Parmele, of Cambridge, Washington County, New York, and had issue:—John, who died, in 1880, in Pennsylvania, leaving no issue; Abbie, married Doctor C. S. Longstreet, of New York, and died in 1889. He married, secondly, Miss Allan, of Whitehall, New York, and had issue:—Cornelia, married Mr. Dunn; and Frances L. Buchanan, of New York. He had two sisters, one the mother of Bishop Kingsley, and the other, Mrs. Waite, of Batavia, New York.

Charles J. Buchanan, of Albany.

Charles J. Buchanan, of Albany, New York, born 27th December, 1843, served in the American Civil War in the First Regiment U.S. Sharpshooters (Berdans) and rose to the rank of Lieutenant and Adjutant of the Regiment. He was admitted to the Bar of New York and has practised law at Albany since 1870. He married, in 1875, Caroline Van Valkenburgh. He was admitted a member of the Buchanan Society in 1885.

Appendix.

Appendix.

Note to page 189.

1. The other three sons of George Buchanan, second Laird of Gartincaber, were : (2) George Buchanan, who had a son, Thomas Buchanan, in Cretichael, in Buchanan Parish ; and Andrew Buchanan, who had two sons, George and Patrick, of Ledrish. (3) Thomas Buchanan, of Gartincaber, married Janet Buchanan, and had two sons, William Buchanan, who acquired Ardoch, and George Buchanan, of Gartincaber. George Buchanan, of Gartincaber, born 1662, married 1688 Janet McGregor, and had four sons, John, Thomas, Dugal and Robert. John Buchanan, of Gartincaber, born 1671, married in 1715 Agnes Forrester; admitted member of Buchanan Society in 1727 ; disposed of part of his lands to John Buchanan, in Cretichael about 1731, and the remainder to James Buchanan, of Nether Gartincaber, in 1743. And (4) Andrew Buchanan, who had three sons, two of whom went to Ireland, the other to Drymen. George Buchanan, of Gartincaber, had a daughter married to Andrew Buchanan, of Gartacharne.

Note to page 189.

2. William Buchanan, who bought Blairlusk from his brother George, married in 1681 Isobel McKean, and died in 1727, and had besides daughters (1) George, his successor, and (2) John.

George Buchanan married in 1705 Margot, daughter of James Bauchope, and died about 1747, and was succeeded by his son George, who sold Blairlusk before 1750 to John McAlpine, in Auld Murroch. (Strathendrick, page 352.)

APPENDIX

Note to page 306.

3. Dr. W. B. Munro, Assistant Professor of Government in Harvard University, author of "The Seigniorial System in Canada," and editor of "Documents Relating to the Seigniorial Tenure in Canada," in which the report of the Commissioners is given at length, says : The first Parliament of Canada gave the question of abolishing the seigniorial system its earnest attention by appointing a commission of three to make a thorough investigation of the workings and to propose some practical scheme of compulsory commutation of tenure which would be satisfactory to the seigniors and habitants alike. This task the commissioners (Alexander Buchanan, James Smith, and André R. Taschereau) promptly accomplished, and in 1843 addressed the results to Parliament in an elaborate report containing much interesting and important information relating to the subject with which it dealt. This paper may be commended to readers as affording the most comprehensive and trustworthy outline of the seigniorial system to be found in any official document prior to 1854. It contains some inaccuracies, and in some cases the attitude of the commissioners towards various incidents of the system is not without obvious bias, but on the whole it is an able and illuminating state paper, and must have been a notable contribution to contemporary discussions of the subject."

MR. T. R. BUCHANAN.

Note to page 405.

4. We regret to announce the death of the Right Hon. Thomas Ryburn Buchanan, which occurred yesterday at Bournemouth, at the age of 65. He had been ill for some time past—indeed he had never been in good health since a severe chill which he caught two years ago.

Thomas Ryburn Buchanan, born at Glasgow in 1846, was the younger son of John Buchanan, of Dowanhill ; his elder brother, Mr. John Y. Buchanan, F. R. S., has attained distinction as a man of science. T. R. Buchanan received his schooling at Glasgow and Sherborne ; in 1865 he entered Balliol College, and his undergraduate career was remarkably successful. He took a double first class in Moderations and a first class in "Greats ;" he also gained the Stanhope prize in 1868 with an essay on "The Effects of the Renaissance in England." In 1870 he was elected a Fellow of All Souls ; he retained his Fellowship until his marriage, and served in various college offices. For some years he was in charge of the Codrington Library ; he discharged this duty with zeal, and with great pleasure to himself, for Buchanan was a book lover of the old school, a considerable authority on editions and bindings.

Mr. Buchanan was called to the Bar, but never practised. In politics he was always an advanced Liberal, and at the momentous General Election of 1880 he came forward unsuccessfully as a candidate for Haddingtonshire. About a year later he entered the House of Commons as one of the members for Edinburgh. Before the election of 1885 came round the City was divided ; of the four divisions Mr. Buchanan chose the West, where the Conservative Party hoped to score a victory. The contest turned mainly on the Disestablishment of the Church in Scotland. If Mr. Gladstone had given a decisive lead in that direction, Mr. Buchanan would have followed, and very possibly would have lost the seat. Mr. Gladstone saw Disestablishment coming, but he saw it "at the end of a long vista ;" it was not an issue in the pending election, and his declaration, unsatisfactory as it was to Liberal supporters of the Established Church, was enough to carry the seat for West Edinburgh.

A few months later the party was rent asunder by the Home Rule controversy. Buchanan was a sensitive man, perhaps too sensitive for the rough work of politics, and his position at this crisis was far from comfortable. He found the arguments against Mr. Gladstone's policy unanswerable, but it cost him a painful effort to vote against his leader and his party. Very reluctantly he threw in his lot with the dissentients ; at the "penal dissolution" of 1886 West Edinburgh returned him again, this time as a Liberal Unionist. Like Sir George Trevelyan, he soon found himself unable to bear the continued strain of co-operation with the men whom he had always opposed ; the Crimes Act of 1887 gave him, as he thought, a good reason for returning to his old allegiance. He thought it right to vacate his seat, and after a keen contest he retained it by a narrow majority. The Unionist candidate was also a Fellow of All Souls, Mr. (now Sir Thomas) Raleigh. At the election of 1892 West Edinburgh was captured by Lord Wolmer, now Lord Selborne; Mr. Buchanan found a safe refuge for a time in East Aberdeenshire, but there also he was defeated in 1900. From 1903 until his retirement from Parliament at the General Election of January, 1910, he represented East Perthshire. As a candidate he was always personally liked; his accent and manner suggested Oxford rather than agricultural Scotland, but his constituents recognised his sincerity, and they came to rely on his careful attention to the industrial and other questions in which they were interested.

As a member of Parliament Mr. Buchanan was assiduous and useful, but he did not rank with the most effective debaters of his party. When Sir Henry Campbell-Bannerman was forming his administration in 1905, Mr. Buchanan became Financial Secretary at the War Office ; his chief, Mr. Haldane, spoke for that office in the House of Commons, and left but little scope for the eloquence of his colleagues. In April of 1908, when the Ministry was rearranged, Mr. Buchanan succeeded Mr. Hobhouse as

Under-Secretary of State at the India Office. He had always taken a special interest in questions relating to India, and he welcomed the opportunity of studying the economic and political problems with which British Administrators are endeavouring to cope. Lord Morley's departure to the House of Lords left his Under-Secretary to deal with the questions addressed to Government by those Radical members who claim to speak on behalf of the people of India. This difficult duty was performed by Mr. Buchanan in a very satisfactory manner ; he was always straightforward, and he was firm in declining to answer that kind of "supplementary" question which is really a new question put without notice. Ill-health compelled him to resign the office in 1909.

In 1888 Mr. Buchanan married Emily, daughter of Mr. T. S. Bolitho. Mrs. Buchanan survives her husband.
—*The Times*, April 8, 1911.

INDEX.

	Page
Alexander, Henry	199, 200, 202, 205
André, Major John	223
Ardoch, Buchanans of	261
Arnpryor, Buchanans of	327
Arnprior, Buchanans of (second family)	347
Auchineden, Buchanans of	341
Auchintorlie, Buchanans of	375
Auchmar, Buchanans of	273
Buchanan, William, first of	273
" Patrick, second of	274
" George, third of	274
" Patrick, fourth of	276
" John, fifth of	276
" William, sixth of	163, 277
" Alexander, seventh of	277
" William, eighth of	277
" James, ninth of	277
" Peter of Auchmar	277
" Peter the younger of	278
" Andrew of Auchmar	277
Baillie-Hamilton, John Buchanan, of Arnpryor	352
Baldernock, Buchanans in Campsie and	385
Baldwin, William Augustus and family	242
Baugé, Battle of	169, 170
Blackwell, Robert, and family	237
Blairlusk, Buchanans of	189
Blairvockie, Buchanans of	290, 301
Blairvockie Hill	69
Brady, Sir Francis, K.C.	197, 316
Brady, Sir Maziere	197, 207
Brock, Sir Isaac	4, 6, 7
Buchanan House	59
Buchanan, Account of Origin of Family of	164
" Arms and Crest of	186
" Essay upon the Family and Surname of	163

		Page
Buchanan, Surname of		168
"	Alexander, of Ednasop	3
"	Sir Alexander	169
"	Alexander, Q.C., Life of	1–159
"	Alexander, Q.C., family of	305
"	Alexander Brock	155, 308
"	Alexander Carlisle (first)	196, 214
"	Alexander Carlisle (second)	234
"	Alexander Wilson Gray, of Parkhill	163, 268
"	Andrew, of Auchintorlie	376
"	Andrew, of Ardinconnal	376
"	Andrew, of Buchanan House	366
"	Sir Andrew, Bart., of Dunburgh	378
"	Andrew, of Drumpellier	367
"	Andrew, of Greenfield	369
"	Gen. Andrew	461
"	Archibald, of Auchintorlie	367, 375
"	Archibald, of Auchintorlie and Hillington	376
"	Archibald, of Drumhead	397
"	Lt.-Col. Arthur Louis Hamilton, of Mount Vernon	371
"	Sir Arthur, of Auchlessie	351
"	Beavor	198, 206
"	Bever	316
"	Charles J.	475
"	Chauncey K.	471
"	Claudius, D. D.	433
"	David	435
"	David (second)	436
"	David Carrick-, of Drumpellier and Mount Vernon	369
"	Sir David Carrick Robert Carrick-	370
"	David William Ramsay Carrick-	371
"	Dugald	438
"	Douglas	279
"	-Dunlop, Robert	399
"	-Dunlop, Rev. Robert	400
"	Sir Eric Alexander, Bart., of Dunburgh and Craigend Castle	381

		Page
Buchanan,	Francis Christian	406
"	Admiral Franklin	462
"	Sir Francis James	464
"	Dr. George, of Druid Hall, Baltimore, and family	460
"	Dr. George, of Fintona and family	315
"	Lt.-Col. George James Ferguson-, of Auchintorlie	377
"	Sir George, 17th laird of Buchanan	183
"	Sir George, 18th laird of Buchanan	183
"	Sir George, Ambassador at St. Petersburg	379
"	Sir George, M.D.	444
"	Sir George, Col. of Stirlingshire Regt.	183
"	George, M.A., M.D., LL.D.	403
"	George, of Blairlusk	189
"	George, of Buchanan House	365
"	George, the historian	391, 419, 423
"	George, of Gartincaber	189
"	George, of Keston Tower	191
"	George, of Munster	190
"	George, of Northern New York	474
"	George, of Omagh	3
"	George, Treasurer of Glasgow	366
"	George, son of David Buchanan	437
"	George, the Quatercentenary of	423
"	George Carlo Vidua	150, 306
"	Gen. Gilbert	386
"	Gen. Gilbert John Lane	387
"	Rev. Gilbert	386
"	-Hamilton, Francis, M.D., of Spittal, Bardowie and Lenny	293
"	-Hamilton, John, of Spittal, Bardowie and Lenny	296, 338
"	Harris	278
"	Lt.-Gen. Henry James, C.B.	439
"	Henry, of Lenny	337
"	Hon. Isaac	278
"	Isaac Robert	279
"	James Clarke	233

		Page
Buchanan, Sir James, Bart.		380
"	James Isaac	279
"	James, H.B.M. Consul at New York ..67, 189, 190, 197, 233	
"	James, of Blairvadock	377
"	James, of Dowanhill	405
"	James Gray-, of Scotstown 262, 267	
"	Hon. James Madison, U.S. Minister to Denmark	461
"	James Ross Gray-, of Scotstown	267
"	James, President of the United States 190, 219, 453	
"	Brig.-General James A.	466
"	John, of Auchlessie and Arnpryor	351
"	John, of Ardoch and Balloch	263
"	John, of Blairlusk	190
"	John, of Donaghanie	190
"	John, of Dowanhill	405
"	John, of Gartincaber, ...189, 253	
"	John, of Lisnamallard 181, 214	
"	John, of Omagh	190
"	John, of Powis	353
"	John, of Tyrone	180, 190
"	John, last laird of Buchanan	185
"	Sir John, 18th laird of Buchanan	183
"	Sir John Ebenezer	440
"	John	13
"	John, Chief Justice of Maryland	466
"	Dr. John, 49th Regiment..............1, 305	
"	John Blacker	191
"	Lt.-Col. John Blacker, of Edenfel	193
"	John Hamilton-, of Spittal, Bardowie and Lenny	297
"	John Parkes, of Ardoch	264
"	John Stewart	340
"	John Young, M.A., F.R.S.	405
"	Col. Lewis Mansergh, C.B., of Edenfel	192
"	Maurice, author of the Book of Pluscarden	179
"	Sir Maurice, ninth laird of Buchanan	168

		Page
Buchanan,	Sir Maurice, tenth laird of Buchanan	168
"	McKean, Paymaster U.S. Navy	462
"	Michael Rowand Gray	268
"	Neil, of Hillington	367
"	Peter Toronto	278
"	Capt. Richard Dennistoun	376
"	-Riddell, Major-Gen. Charles James, C.B.	397
"	-Riddell, Sir John Walter	397
"	-Riddell, Sir John	397
"	Robert Andrew Washington	278
"	Brevet-Gen. Robert Christie	461
"	Robert Jarvis	279
"	Robert Carrick-, of Drumpellier	370
"	Robert Dunlop	398
"	Robert the novelist	446
"	Robert Stewart	234
"	Thomas Gray-, of Ardoch and Scotstown	267
"	Thomas John, of Ardoch	264
"	Capt. Thomas Alexander, of Powis	353
"	Thomas, of Powis	352
"	Thomas, of Ramelton	190
"	Rt. Hon. Thomas Ryburn (appendix page 2)	405
"	Judge Thomas	465
"	Sir Walter, eleventh laird of Buchanan	169
"	Sir Walter, twelfth laird of Buchanan	179
"	Lt.-Col. Walter James T.	320
"	Wentworth James	153, 307
"	William, of Auchmar, historian of the Family of Buchanan	163, 277
"	William, of Craigievairn	393
"	William, of Londonderry	52
"	William, of Tyrone	189
"	William, of Yamaska	108, 194, 214
"	William	437
"	Gen. William	458
"	Hon. William I.	472
"	Capt. William Eccles	458
"	William Oliver	246

	Page
Buchanan, William Robert	154, 308
Buchanans of Ardoch	261
" of Arnpryor	327
" of Arnprior (second family)	347
" of Auchineden	341
" of Auchintorlie	375
" of Auchmar	273
" of Blairlusk	189, 253
" of Blairvockie	301
" in Campsie and Baldernock	385
" of Carbeth	253
" Carrick-, of Drumpellier	365
" of Cumberland County	454
" of Drummikill	391
" of Drumhead	397
" of Druid Hill, Baltimore	460
" of Edenfel	192
" of Finnick-Drummond	403
" of Fintona	453
" of Gartacharne	357
" Gray-, of Scotstown	267
Buchanans of Hales Hall	283
Buchanan Phillips	283
" Rev. Alexander Henry	283
" William Theophilus	283
" James	283
" Phillips	284
" Capt. James Maxey	284
" William	284
" Rev. Alexander	285
" Clement	285
" Lt.-Col. H. B.	285
" H. B. M.	285
Buchanans of that Ilk	163
Buchanans of Lenny	335
Buchanans of New Orleans	458
Buchanans of Powis	351
Buchanans of Spittal	289
Buchanans of Ulster County, N.Y.	468

	Page
Buchannans late of Miltoun	413
Buchannan John of Whitby	414
" George of Whitby	414
" Charles of Whitby	414
" Hugh Cholmley	415
" Arthur	415
Buey Okyan, Anselan	165
Campsie and Baldernock, Buchanans in	385
Carbeth, Buchanans of	253
Carlisle, Alexander	197, 199, 200, 213
Carrick-Buchanans of Drumpellier	365
Clarke, family of James	207, 213
Clareinch	167
Copenhagen, Battle of	4
de Lanaudière, Hon. Charles T.	9
Drumhead, Buchanans of	397
Drummikill, Buchanans of	391
Drumpellier, Carrick-Buchanans of	365
Ennerkeithing, Battle of	184
Finnick-Drummond, Buchanans of	403
Fintona, Buchanans of	315, 458
de Gaspé, Mémoires of	9
Gartacharne, Buchanans of	189
Gartincaber, John Buchanan of	189
Genealogical Note	419
Gugy, Hon. Louis	12
Hales Hall, Buchanans of	283
Higginson, Col. Theophilus, C.B., and family	240
Johnson, Francis Godschall	123
Leith-Buchanans of Ross Priory	409
Leith-Buchanan, Sir Alexander Wellesley, Bart.	409
Leith-Buchanan, Sir George, Bart.	409
Lenny, Buchanans of	335
McFarlane, Henry, and family	195, 214
McNab, Archibald, Laird of McNab	348
Maryland, Buchanans of	460
Miltoun, Buchannans late of	413
Moffatt, Col. Kenneth, and family	249
Ogden, Hon. Charles Richard	85

	Page
Perrault, Hon. Joseph Francois	14, 17, 80
Pluscarden, The Book of	169
Powis, Buchanans of	351
Reed, Gen. Sir Thomas, K.C.B.	465
Richardson, Lucy, wife of Dr. John Buchanan	1, 12, 16
Robinson, James, and family	191, 198, 207, 214, 250
Scotstown, Gray-Buchanans of	267
Spittal, Buchanans of	289
Strathendrick, by J. Guthrie Smith	163
Stuart, Andrew	17, 21
Stuart, Hon. James	72
Taylor, Hugh, and family	229
Verneuil, Battle of	169, 174
Westminster Abbey, Monuments in	27
Whitla, George, and family	238
" Surgeon-General George	238
" Capt. James Buchanan	238
" Lieut.-Col. William	238

BIBLIOLIFE

Old Books Deserve a New Life
www.bibliolife.com

Did you know that you can get most of our titles in our trademark **EasyScript**™ print format? **EasyScript**™ provides readers with a larger than average typeface, for a reading experience that's easier on the eyes.

Did you know that we have an ever-growing collection of books in many languages?

Order online:
www.bibliolife.com/store

Or to exclusively browse our **EasyScript**™ collection:
www.bibliogrande.com

At BiblioLife, we aim to make knowledge more accessible by making thousands of titles available to you – quickly and affordably.

Contact us:
BiblioLife
PO Box 21206
Charleston, SC 29413

Made in the USA
Lexington, KY
18 June 2017